GHOST HUNTERS

OF THE SOUTH

GHOST HUNTERS

OF THE SOUTH

Alan Brown

University Press of Mississippi   Jackson

www.upress.state.ms.us

The University Press of Mississippi is a member of the Association of American University Presses.

Copyright © 2006 by University Press of Mississippi
Manufactured in the United States of America

First edition 2006

Library of Congress Cataloging-in-Publication Data

Brown, Alan, 1950 Jan. 12–
    Ghost hunters of the South / Alan Brown.— 1st ed.
        p. cm.
    Includes bibliographical references (p.   ) and index.
    ISBN-13: 978-1-57806-892-0 (cloth : alk. paper)
    ISBN-10: 1-57806-892-4 (cloth : alk. paper)
    ISBN-13: 978-1-57806-893-7 (pbk. : alk. paper)
    ISBN-10: 1-57806-893-2 (pbk. : alk. paper) 1. Parapsychologists—
Southern States—Biography. 2. Haunted places—Southern States.
3. Ghosts—Southern States. I. Title.
    BF1026.B76 2006
    133.10975—dc22   2006001991

British Library Cataloging-in-Publication Data available

To the memory of my father, who instilled in me the
love of reading

CONTENTS

Contents

Contents

PREFACE

In January 2005, the University Press of Mississippi, publisher of my three collections of southern ghost stories, proposed that rather than another similar collection, I pursue a book on Southern ghost hunters. I had included information on paranormal investigators in my last collection of ghost stories, *Stories from the Haunted South*, and my editor at the press was intrigued by the topic. I accepted the project with some reluctance. A book of this nature had never been written before, so I was venturing, in a manner of speaking, into uncharted territory.

I started my research in January by accessing the *Shadowlands* Web site, which provides a listing of ghost investigation groups from the United States and Canada. I then sent an e-mail message to groups from the twelve Southern states, inviting them to participate in the project. Of the seventy-six groups I contacted, forty-four founders/directors expressed their desire to have their group included in the book. All of the interviews were conducted by telephone in February and March 2005.

When I first began working on this project, I knew very little about who these people were, how they conducted their investigations, what kind of equipment they used, or why they spent all this time and trouble trying to prove the existence of something that scientists say cannot be proven. By way of answering these questions for myself and the reader, I devised the following questionnaire:

What is your day job?

How did you first get interested in ghost hunting?

When did your group get started?

What is your overriding philosophy or goal?

How many members do you have? What are your qualifications for membership?

What are the backgrounds of your members?

Do you charge for investigations?

Do you prefer to investigate in the daytime or at night?

Do you prefer historic sites or private residences?

What kinds of equipment do you use?

Does each member buy his or her own equipment?

What is your view of orbs and EVP's?

What percentage of your investigations reveals genuine hauntings?

Are you disappointed when you find an alternate or scientific explanation for the disturbances?

Which of your investigations do you feel are most successful in terms of proving the existence of the paranormal?

Can you recall anything that happened during one of your investigations that was particularly memorable?

Have any of your members been visibly frightened during an investigation?

What kinds of criticism or obstacles have you encountered over the years?

Do you promote your group (e.g., through fliers, logos, T-shirts)?
Are there any places that you would like to investigate?

Maintaining my objectivity was essential to presenting an accurate portrayal of these individuals who spend hours of their free times and hundreds of dollars of their own money on an endeavor that still has not gained universal approval. While I admit to having had reservations about ghost hunting at the outset of this project, by the time I finished, I had lost any preconceptions I might have held of ghost hunters. I found all of these individuals to be gracious, intelligent, and, above all, curious people. I also learned that Southern paranormal investigating groups defy pigeon holing; for the most part, they reflect the individuality of their founders/directors. The image of the Southern ghost hunter, comically expressed by one of the directors as a "bunch of goobers tromping around in graveyards," is totally inaccurate. While talking to these people, I felt inspired by their enthusiasm and dedication. I am proud to say that several of them have become personal friends of mine.

After sorting out my feelings, I have concluded that the writing of this book has not made me a believer in the paranormal. I will admit, though, that some of the evidence produced by these groups, as well as their absolute devotion to their craft, has intensified my belief in a spiritual dimension to life. Probing that dimension produces questions about existence and the meaning of life that have tantalized human beings for centuries. Paranormal investigators are taking a different route in answering them than philosophers, theologians, and writers. Who is to say that the ghost hunters' way is the wrong way?

ACKNOWLEDGMENTS

I am deeply indebted to all of the paranormal investigators for taking the time to talk to me and for trusting me to present their groups in an objective manner. I am especially grateful to Anna Blythe, Pam Gates, Peter Haviland, Roger Johnson, Angela and Alan Lowe, Jeff Reynolds, Gordon Small, Patti Starr, and Tim Tedana for sending me additional information on their groups. I would also like to thank Bobbie Atristain, Andrew Calder, Robert Hunnicut, Angie Madden, Scott McClure, and Chris Rod for putting me in contact with some of the groups in this book.

INTRODUCTION

The history of paranormal investigations can be traced back to the 1850s during the heyday of spiritualism. In 1848, two mediums from upstate New York, Kate and Margaret Fox, began receiving messages from the dead in their home in Hydesville, New York. Within a decade, they began holding séances for some of the country's most prominent celebrities, including Mary Todd Lincoln, Harriet Beecher Stowe, James Fenimore Cooper, and William Cullen Bryant. By the end of the 1850s, hundreds of mediums began holding séances in homes throughout the United States and England. These "home circles" became the nucleus of the spiritualist movement, which held that the soul entered the spirit world immediately after death and that communication with these spirits was proof of the afterlife (Guiley 2000, 362).

Ironically, spiritualism inadvertently gave rise to what was to become modern paranormal investigations. Eager to debunk these alleged mediums, a number of scientists began looking into mediumistic communications in the second half of the nineteenth century. Before long, they had exposed many mediums as frauds, especially those who had claimed to materialize spirits. However, a small number of these scientists who had attended séances became convinced that the spirit world was worth investigating. The best known of these scientists, a chemist named William

Crookes, began studying the activities of mediums in 1869. He was so convinced that one of them, Daniel Douglas Home, was genuine that he wrote a paper in which he attempted to prove the existence of a "psychic force." After Crookes's paper was published in the *Quarterly Journal of Science*, he was discredited by the scientific community (Taylor 2001, 26–27).

Two of Crookes's colleagues, Henry Sidgwick and Frederick Myers, were sympathetic with his plight. Along with Sidgwick's friend, Edward Gurney, the three men formed an association dedicated to the investigation of the paranormal in London. In 1882, the group became the Society for Psychical Research (SPR), with Henry Sidgwick as the first president. Its founding members included such luminaries as Mark Twain, Lewis Carroll, and William Gladstone. In 1885, an American branch of the Society for Psychical Research (ASPR) was founded. By the end of the nineteenth century, the Society for Psychical Research, which concentrated on the exposing of fraudulent mediums, set the standard for ghost research. Both groups exist to this day (Taylor 2001, 27).

One of the early members of the SPR, Harry Price, became the most famous ghost hunter of the first half of the twentieth century. Ostracized by many of his colleagues because of his lack of scientific training after joining the SPR in 1920, Price, nevertheless, became one of the first to employ modern technology in his investigations. His ghost-hunting kit appears quaint compared to the high-tech equipment used by today's ghost-hunting groups:

Felt overshoes
Measuring tape
Tape, electric bells, lead seals, and other items for making motion-detecting tools

Dry batteries and switches
Cameras
Notebooks and drawing pads
Ball and string, chalk
Basic first-aid kit
Mercury for detecting vibrations (Wilson 2005, 15)

Price's most celebrated investigation was his probe into the alleged hauntings at the Borley Rectory, known as "the most haunted house in England," from 1929 until 1947. Borley was drawn to the rectory by stories of the sounds of dragging footsteps and loud rappings and the ghostly apparitions of a headless man and a nun. The large brick house was built in 1863 supposedly on the site of a monastery. According to the legend, in the thirteenth century, a monk had tried to elope with a beautiful novice. After the couple was apprehended, the monk was hanged, and the nun was bricked up alive in the walls of a nearby convent. Price had just started investigating the old house when poltergeist activity ensued. Lights flashed, bells rang, and objects flew through the air. Price was particularly interested in written messages that began appearing on the walls and scraps of paper. In 1937, after the rectory was abandoned, Price rented the house for a year and recruited forty researchers to assist him with documenting the investigation. To instruct assistants on the proper way to conduct an investigation, Price wrote a handbook in which he explained what to do and how to use the equipment (Hauntings 65–66). Before Borley Rectory was finally torn down in 1947, Price published two books detailing his investigation of the old house: *The Most Haunted House in England* (1940) and *The End of Borley Rectory* (1946). Although Price's critics attacked him for grandstanding and fabricating evidence, he is viewed by paranormal investigators worldwide as an icon, a pioneer in the field (Taylor 2001, 48).

Ghost research experienced a revival in the United States in the 1990s and the 2000s. Within the span of a decade, independent ghost-hunting groups have conducted hundreds, if not thousands, of investigations. The popularity of movies such as *Poltergeist* (1982), *Ghostbusters* (1984), *The Sixth Sense* (1999), *The Others* (2001), and *The Ring* (2002) is at least partially responsible for the creation of hundreds of local paranormal research groups toward the end of the decade. The 1990s also saw the production of ghost theme television series, such as the History Channel's *Haunted History*. Not coincidentally, the oldest group included in this book dates back only to 1991. Advances in technology, such as digital cameras, digital voice recorders, electromagnetic field meters, and negative ion detectors, not only made it seem possible to gather convincing evidence of the existence of the paranormal, but they also lent the groups using these instruments a luster of respectability, even though most of this equipment was designed for other purposes. However, most directors agree that the primary reason behind the recent explosion of interest in paranormal investigations is the Internet. For over a decade, paranormal groups have been creating Web sites as a means of promoting themselves and displaying their visual and audio evidence.

In 2005, one television show in particular also increased the popularity of paranormal investigating as an exciting pastime. In the spring and fall, the *Ghosthunters* television show was broadcast on the Sci-Fi Channel. Each week, full-time plumbers Jason Hawes and Grant Wilson led the members of The Atlantic Paranormal Society (T.A.P.S.) on investigations at public and private locations, using state-of-the-art equipment. In the episodes broadcast in the spring, T.A.P.S. concentrated their investigations on sites located in and around their home base in Rhode Island. In the fall episodes, however, T.A.P.S. expanded their investigations to other states, such as Louisiana and North Carolina, with the help of other groups that have become part of the T.A.P.S. "family." Three of the groups featured in this book—South Louisiana Ghosthunters, Haunted North Carolina, and Observations (Mississippi)—became members of T.A.P.S. in 2005; two of them—South Louisiana Ghosthunters and Haunted North Carolina—were featured on the show in the fall. As the show's audience grows, so does the likelihood that more Southern groups will be absorbed by T.A.P.S. It is also possible that the show will inspire other aspiring ghost hunters to form their own groups.

Advances in technology, beginning in the 1960s and 1970s, are also responsible for the popularity of ghost hunting. Ever since John Cutten created the first viable electronic ghost-detection device using vibration, light, sound, and temperature sensors to trigger a camera, paranormal investigators have packed their ghost-hunting kits with an impressive, and often expensive, collection of "cool gadgets," most of which were created for other purposes years before. Although some of the equipment used by T.A.P.S. is far too expensive for most paranormal investigators, a few less-expensive items have become standard:

Notebook and pen or pencil—Names of witnesses, experiences, and environmental conditions should be recorded (Warren 2003, 139).
Flashlight—Flashlights are important primarily for safety reasons, especially in unfamiliar places.
Watch—Watches are used to record the time when activity occurs (140–41).

Compass—A simple, inexpensive device for detecting electromagnetic fields (142–43).

Electromagnetic field (EMF) meter—EMF meters can detect erratic fields of energy with no physical source. The best EMF meters filter out fields created artificially by wiring, appliances, and so forth. EMF fields that fluctuate are said to be paranormal. EMF meters are also used in conjunction with cameras, which can photograph the energy detected by the meters (143).

Still cameras—Digital cameras are cheaper to operate and provide immediate feedback. Also, some digital cameras are sensitive to infrared light. Film cameras produce higher-quality images and can produce a negative (147).

Video cameras—Video cameras can be used to record entire investigations, but they can also capture unseen entities, like still cameras. Video cameras are also sensitive to infrared light (166).

Tape recorders—Tape recorders are widely used on investigations to record electronic voice phenomena. It is said that sounds and voices undetectable to the human ear can be recorded on an electromagnetically sensitive medium, such as audiotape (168).

Infrared meter—Infrared meters register levels of infrared activity. They are useful when taking infrared photographs. Like EMF meters, they can be used to large concentrations of energy so that they can be photographed (169).

Digital thermometers—Digital thermometers use electrical resistance to measure temperature. They can be used to detect cold spots, which are said to be caused by spirits that drain the energy from the area around them (Wilson 2005, 24).

Night vision scopes—Night vision scopes are sensitive to infrared light. They also enable the investigator to see in the dark without creating light pollution (Warren 2003, 174–75).

Motion detectors—These devices can be placed outside a door or inside a room to monitor for energy fields or cold spots. For best results, motion detectors should be backed up with still cameras or video cameras (Wilson 2005, 69).

Walkie-talkies—Two-way radios enable investigators to keep in contact with each other in the event of an accident or a paranormal occurrence (Wilson 2005, 73).

Dowsing rods—These metal rods are the most controversial instruments used in paranormal investigations. Often made from coat hangers, dowsing rods can be used to locate energy fields (Warren 2003, 169).

The following electronic devices can also be valuable additions to the ghost hunter's kit, but most of the groups interviewed for this book did not use them because of the expense:

Geiger counters—Geiger counters can be used to monitor the changes in the background radiation of a location (Wilson 2005, 71).

Ion particle counters—Any anomalies with any density to them should register on the ion particle counter. These devices are rarely used, though, because they are so expensive (Wilson 2005, 72).

Thermal scanners—Also known as noncontact thermometers, these devices can check for cold spots by detecting unexplained temperature variances (Warren 2003, 172).

Oscilloscopes—These devices measure voltage and time, effectively giving the ghost hunter a graph as he or she measures the frequency of interference in EMF meters (Wilson 2005, 72).

One of the thousands of people who have been inspired by the exploits of paranormal researchers to take up the hunt is this writer. For ten years, I have been approaching the field of the paranormal from an academic perspective. My interest in the paranormal has its roots in folklore. In 1992, I published a collection of folk tales, folk beliefs, and life histories collected for the WPA in the 1930s by Ruby Pickens Tartt in Sumter County, Alabama. I was particularly taken with the ghost stories, whose power lay in the sincere tone of the tellers. My next two books—*The Face in the Window and Other Alabama Ghostlore* and *Shadows and Cypress*—were first-person narratives of their own or other people's ghostly experiences. In 2002 and 2004, I published two volumes of Southern ghost stories—*Ghost Stories from the American South* and *Stories from the Haunted South*, respectively—but even these objectively told accounts of the history and lore behind a selection of haunted sites contained eyewitness sightings. My growing fascination with the reality behind ghosts led, quite logically, to the scientific investigation of the paranormal.

In October 2004, I went on my first real paranormal investigation. On October 27, 2004, radio station WOKK invited me and several guests to spend the night at the F. W. Williams House, an old Victorian home in Meridian, Mississippi. Even though I had accompanied WOKK on overnight visits at haunted sites on three previous occasions, this was the first time that I brought along ghost-hunting equipment. Because the plumbing was not operable in the F. W. Williams House, we had to use the restroom at Merrehope, which is next door. While I was there, I decided to scan the rooms with my electromagnetic field meter. The meter detected nothing unusual until radio personality Debbie Alexander and I went up to the Bride's Room at 11:00 P.M. As we moved the EMF meter around the bed, the EMF levels jumped from 1.0 all the way up to 5.4, then to 7.6, then to 10.5. We returned to the same room at midnight and detected very few fluctuations in the electromagnetic field. At 1:00 A.M., we scanned the Bride's Room for a third and final time and detected more spikes in the EMF readings. Both Debbie and I succumbed to the rush that always accompanies the feeling that one is in the presence of the supernatural. Although I was certain at the time that we had gathered irrefutable proof that Merrehope is haunted, my conversations with the directors of different paranormal groups have convinced me that we should have also taken photographs of the bed or used a digital thermal thermometer at the same time. I know now how easy it can be to suspend our logic and believe what we want to believe. The most experienced of these groups have learned how to control this urge.

I am certain that I will bring along my ghost-hunting kit the next time I spend the night at a haunted house with WOKK, but I will probably not become an active paranormal researcher. I lack the drive, the time, the conviction, and the disposable income that this hobby requires. Actually, ghost hunting is more than just a hobby. For the best researchers, investigating the paranormal is a passion, a calling. These dedicated men and women spend hours and thousands of dollars walking through old buildings and cemeteries, not because they want to, but because they have to.

GHOST
HUNTERS
OF THE SOUTH

Alabama

Birmingham Paranormal Society

BIRMINGHAM, ALABAMA

Donovan Murphy, Founder and Director

The Birmingham Paranormal Society is a good example of a relatively new group whose members have years of experience in the field. The director, Donovan Murphy, has been a ghost hunter for ten years. He founded the Birmingham Paranormal Society in 2004. At the time of the interview, his group had six members, most of whom have college degrees. Donovan, a former zookeeper, is now a lab supervisor at the University of Alabama in Birmingham. Two of his coworkers are members of his group.

Unlike most of the groups interviewed for this group, the Birmingham Paranormal Society does not have a Web site. Being the Alabama representative for the Alabama Ghost Society, Donovan has been able to publicize his group without one: "We don't have a Web site yet, but we probably will in a couple of weeks or so. People find out about us through Troy [Taylor's] Web site. They contact the American Ghost Society, and then they e-mail me from there." Donovan's years of experience as a paranormal investigation have helped him determine which e-mails are worth following up on: "I filter out some of the wilder, crazier stuff. Recently, I've gotten an e-mail from somebody who might have some possession problem. She was a woman in Alabama. I told her that I'm not a policeman. I'm not a psychologist. I'm not a religious person. The best thing to do if you're religious [and you have a possession problem] is to seek out your religious adviser."

As a new group, the Birmingham Paranormal Society has not accumulated nearly as much equipment as some of the more established groups have. All of the members buy their own equipment, and to begin with cameras are the easiest and least expensive items. Donovan has more equipment than the other members, but he relies most heavily on his Sperry EMF detector, which is more versatile than his Tri-Field EMF detector: "The Tri-Field is a standard electromagnetic field detector. It doesn't work well if you are walking around. It's better if it's left stationary. A lot of folks hook it into their computer systems. Then they will record over an eight- to ten-hour period. I'd rather be a little more active, a little more on the move. So I take my little Sperry unit and walk around." Donovan is the only director interviewed for this book who uses a Polaroid camera as well as a digital camera and a 35 mm camera: "The Polaroid gives us a steady, solid, super high-resolution version of a still-life picture. As far as results go, you can see what you've photographed. You don't have to find a developer or anything. That was something I found useful in one of Troy Taylor's earlier books—the first or second version of the *Ghosthunter's Guide Book*." According to Donovan, the digital camera is less reliable because the computer will make substitutions for colors when it picks up something anomalous. "[The anomaly] could be bugs or something else. The computer will fill up that spot with whatever color it thinks will fit best. I want to counteract that."

Donovan agrees with the Chicago paranormal investigator Dale Kazamarek that 90 percent of all orbs are completely natural. Therefore, he is inclined to dismiss most of the orbs that are posted on the Internet: "If somebody's taking pictures and they get that on standard cameras or Polaroid, I'd be a little more inclined to consider it valid, but for the most part, when I think of orbs, I think of a glowing ball, not a spot on a photograph. All the spots that people are putting on their Web sites—no, I don't put any stock in those." Donovan is more interested in glowing spheres that appear in folklore, like a glowing ball that is said to have appeared outside of an antebellum home called Saltmarsh Hall in Cahaba, Alabama.

So far, all four of the group's investigations were conducted at private residences. Donovan has set several ground rules that he expects his members to follow when they investigate private residences: "The folks are kind enough to let us check out their place, so be courteous, don't smoke in the house, don't be drinking before we go. Don't drink on site unless it's a small snack. And even then, do it outside. Just basic courtesy." To keep from alarming the homeowners, Donovan tells his members that if something really starts to bother them, they should come up to him, excuse themselves, and go outside: "Don't make a big show of it because if one person gets scared, everyone else will. It will start bouncing to the others. If you feel like coming back in, then come back in."

In the fall of 2004, Donovan investigated several private residences by himself. In one week he visited three homes in Leeds and St. Clair County: "I didn't find any ghosts, but in one place, I found that some cute little animals had taken up residence there. I was disappointed, but the people who owned the house were relieved. They were afraid that they were going to have to bring in an exorcist." After Donovan broke the news to the family that their intruder was a mammal, the husband sighed with relief: "I can live with raccoons. I don't know what I'd do with a ghost."

Donovan's most memorable investigation took place at Merrehope, an antebellum home in Meridian, Mississippi. Built in 1860, Merrehope was one of only three houses left standing after General William Tecumseh Sherman burned Meridian to the ground on February 14, 1864. It is reputed to be haunted by the spirit of Eugenia Garry, the daughter of the builder of the house, and by the ghost of a retired schoolteacher who shot himself in the head in the 1940s when the old home was converted into apartments. On October 30, 2002, Donovan accompanied WOKK radio personalities Debbie Alexander, Scotty Ray Boyd, five teachers from Patrician Academy, and this writer on an all-night stay at the old house. Video cameras were set up in every room in the hope of capturing something on film. From the moment he crossed the threshold, Donovan sensed that the atmosphere in Merrehope was special. Although his EMF detector registered a few spikes, Donovan did not have any real paranormal experiences until midnight when everyone else was watching the main computer monitor in the first-floor dining room: "Somebody said the one of the cameras cut out, so I went upstairs to reset it. I was in Eugenia's room. I turned to look at the curio cabinet, and the cabinet door opened. I froze for a second. That scared the Beejesus out of me. I'll admit it. That's the only time I've ever been scared doing one of these things." Unfortunately, Donovan had his back turned when the curio cabinet door closed by itself. Everyone downstairs in the dining room saw it, though.

Donovan's exciting experience in Merrehope raised the level of his expectations for his group. To his disappointment, all of the places they have investigated in the past year have had natural causes. This is not to say, though, that the group has never been scared: "We went into the basement of one place, and we heard a rattle, and everybody tensed up. All of a sudden, a raccoon came walking by, and everybody jumped." Donovan's group learned what most experienced groups have known for years: that meeting up with the unexpected is always a frightening event.

Donovan does not believe that the Birmingham Paranormal Society will really get off the ground until he sets up his Web site: "Right now I want to get some good data and some great photographs and get them up on my Web site." The first order of business, though, is to shape the group into a cohesive unit: "Even though we have been together for a year, we are still a relatively new group. We are still in the planning stages and getting to know each other. I need to get comfortable with what I'm doing and get our procedure worked out."

The Mobile Order of Paranormal Investigators

CHUNCHULA, ALABAMA

Vada Cejas, Founder and Director

As a child, Vada Cejas saw figures and shapes that seemed to be otherworldly. As an adult, she became reading books about the paranormal: "I became curious to prove that there was something out there, that it wasn't

9

just me." She became part of a local ghost-hunting group in 2002 but split off in 2003 and formed her own group with several other former members. Instead of taking someone else's word that a place is haunted, the members pack up their equipment, do a walk-through, take readings, and question the witnesses who experienced the activity. Then they pick up with the investigation itself. "One gentleman in our group is the 'tech guy' who makes gadgets for the group to investigate with. He's currently working on a machine to help us pick up EVP's," Vada says. "That's what we really focus a lot on. Photos get criticized a lot, so we don't really read a whole lot into photos. So our tech guy is taking apart microphones and adding new devices to it to make it supersensitive." Other members have specific roles as well: "We have another gentleman who's a PR guy. Another girl and I work up potential sites, and this guy checks them out for us. Each of us does research. We help each other out."

The Mobile Order of Paranormal Investigators (M.O.P.I), which has an open membership, currently has ten members. The members include IT technicians, two police officers, two housewives, two nurses, and people in management. The group's Web site is such an effective recruiting tool that people come up to Vada and ask if they can join. Not everyone who is interested in joining the group is accepted, though. In fact, Vada has had to turn some prospective members away: "Some people weren't into research. They just wanted to hang out in a cemetery all night. We're about much more than that." When deciding whether or not to accept a member, the group considers the person's background, the equipment the person already has, and the person's ability to mesh with everyone else.

All of the members purchase their own equipment. "If there's something we really, really need, we pool our money together and buy it," Vada says. "For example, we have bought two weather stations. Everyone has their own recorders, EMF meters, digital cameras, video camcorders. You never have enough of that." Some day, Vada would like to buy a thermal imager, but the cost is prohibitive. "They cost five to six thousand dollars. Firefighters use black-and-white imagers when they go into a house. Color thermal imagers will reveal heat or cold. They're hard to use outdoors." Instead of dreaming about buying a thermal imager some day, the group has set a more realistic goal for itself: to someday buy wireless infrared Web cams with night vision.

M.O.P.I. prefers indoor investigations, but gaining access to historic sites has proven to be extremely difficult. "Oakleigh, an antebellum home in Mobile, hasn't given us permission to investigate there," Vada says. "We tried another old house in Mobile, Braxton-Mitchell, but they turned us down, too." Outdoor sites can be productive, but cold temperatures can affect the equipment, and water droplets on camera lenses can create false orbs.

Cemeteries are the group's outdoor sites of choice because they are open to the public. M.O.P.I. has investigated cemeteries throughout Mobile and Baldwin Counties. Vada recalls one cemetery where the group picked up some dramatic EVP's: "There's one cemetery where the land was donated by the family. We used a video recorder, and we'd ask questions, like 'What's your name?' The lead investigator asked, 'Is anybody here?' And a child's voice answered, 'I'm here. I'm right here.' And then a half-hour later we set up another recorder in a different spot, and we asked questions. When we played it back, we heard children running and a child's voice calling out, 'Ready or not!' Then we heard a male voice saying, 'Ready or not!'" After hearing the male voice, the group decided it was time to pack it up. "We got a little nervous after that," Vada said.

Two of the strangest EVP's the group has ever collected were recorded at a small cemetery in the Mobile area. "We went to another cemetery, and we got a child crying and then someone coming up to my microphone and saying, 'Valconda,'" Vada said. "To this day, we have absolutely no idea what that means. We looked and we looked and looked, and we couldn't find anything for it, but it's definitely a woman's voice whispering 'Valconda.'" Vada always brings along at least five members on an investigation so that she will have several pairs of ears listening to the recordings at the same time.

Vada has found that investigating cemeteries can be problematic for reasons that have nothing to do with the weather: "We're more afraid of the living than the dead. We go into cemeteries, and we're isolated in the middle of nowhere in the woods surrounded by a fence. One member of our group saw a man leaning against a tree in a cemetery. That really freaked us out. Three girls alone in a cemetery's not good. The only time we ever really get scared is when we realize that there's someone out there with us, and they might be doing drugs." To ease the fear of human encounters in cemeteries, Vada relies on the policemen in her group: "The law enforcement guys in our group check out a site before we get there. They've had to break up teen parties in cemeteries. We've had cars drive up while we're doing an investigation." On the Web site, Vada never gives the exact names of the cemeteries her group visits because she does not want other people to think it is all right for anyone to visit these sacred places and do whatever they want there.

Occasionally, M.O.P.I. is invited to investigate indoor locations. Before the group goes out on investigations, Vada sends out a witness questionnaire for the people who requested them. "It's what we call a profile," Vada says. "We ask if they're on medication because we've had people ask us to come to their homes, and we discover that they're alcoholics or delusional, or they're on medication which causes them to hallucinate."

At the family home of one of the members, Vada picked up a family name that only he would know: "They said his name, 'William,' on the tape. We looked through the viewfinder on our night vision, and we saw all these orbs flying all over the place. We had recorders set up all over the house—this house was over one hundred and fifty years old, and it was in Baldwin County. I said, 'Oh, they just like the attention.' And when we played the cassette back, there was this male voice that came on and said, 'No, we don't.'"

Sometimes, EVP's pop up while the members are in the middle of a conversation. A case in point is an investigation M.O.P.I. conducted in Baldwin County at the Courier Building. At one time the local newspaper, the *Fairhope Courier*, was housed there. "We were asked to investigate the building that's located in downtown Fairhope," Vada said. "We knew that there was a suicide that took place in the back of the building. Several people reported the distinct smell of tobacco smoke. We set up a tape recorder, and we got male voices and female voices. We couldn't make out all they were saying. But when someone said, 'O.K. It's time to pack up,' we heard a voice saying, 'Oh, that's good!'" One of the group's skeptics, the "tech guy," smelled the pipe tobacco in the conference room. Another member who was in the room also smelled it. Vada did not smell the pipe tobacco.

Although M.O.P.I. depends heavily on word of mouth for publicity, the local media has gained the members access into places that are usually off-limits to ghost hunters. For example, in October 2004, M.O.P.I. was featured in the October issue of the *Mobile Monthly*. "An editor of the newspaper wanted to do a Halloween story," Vada said, "so they contacted the city sexton, and he got us special permission to go into the Church Street Cemetery at night for four hours, which was excellent. We could have used twelve hours!" While the investigators were in the Church Street Cemetery, they photographed the Boyington Oak, which is supposed to have grown over the grave of convicted murderer Charles Boyington. Surprisingly, no paranormal activity has registered at all on their photographs: "We've taken photo after photo of the Boyington Oak. It's close to the water, so it's humid most of the night, and that doesn't make for good photos. We haven't gotten anything there." The city sexton was so impressed with M.O.P.I.'s professionalism that he has agreed to let the group spend the night at Mobile's other historic cemetery, Magnolia Cemetery.

Vada takes a very philosophical attitude toward those investigations that produce no evidence at all: "Just because nothing happens when we're there, it doesn't mean that there's no activity. Different things affect spirits, so I guess if they don't want to be seen, they blow the joint until we leave." When the spirits refuse to cooperate, the group occasionally asks the homeowners to keep a journal of subsequent activity, just to make sure that the house is not "dead," so to speak. "If the activity starts up again after we're gone, we'll come again another night," Vada says.

Ghost Hunters of the South

MOBILE, ALABAMA

Russ Bennett, Founder and Director

ronically, the only paranormal event the founder and director of Ghost Hunters of the South (G.H.O.T.S.) has ever witnessed occurred when he was ten years old. At the time, his family was living in an air force base in Oklahoma: "My sister and I were playing hide-and-seek. I was hiding in a dark closet. It was really dark. No lights came through the doors. I saw a hand reaching toward me that was darker than the darkness of the room. It scared me, and it made me afraid of the dark. To this day, I still have a phobia of the dark. Not a bad one, but I actually sleep with the lights on in my house or with the door open and the lights on down the hall." From that point on, Russ has been interested in finding out what that was that scared him so badly. Since then, he has read up on the history of the base and has found out that it has been reputed for years to be haunted.

Despite Russ's fear of the dark, he has been a member of two ghost-hunting groups: "I am the leader of G.H.O.T.S., but I'm also part of M.O.P.I., Vada Cejas's group. My views differ from theirs, so I try to avoid stepping on their toes. I have my own Web site and do my own research. So I'm still part of M.O.P.I., but I've got my own little group as well. On occasion, people from M.O.P.I. or friends of mine I've met along the way will join me." Russ dreams of a time when all of the investigating groups in the country will form a united paranormal front with everybody working together and sharing the same procedures and ideas and policies. He is enough of a realist, though, to know that this will probably not happen anytime soon.

Like most ghost hunters, Russ does not put faith in one piece of equipment exclusively: "When I'm on an investigation, I carry my EMF detector, my portable weather station, and my thermal probe. I also carry a regular compass with me. I think if you have a strong electromagnetic field and you have an ambient temperature variation for a few seconds, then you might have come across something that's actually disturbing the area. If you walk around with an EMF meter, and it beeps once in a while, you know that you've got an electromagnetic field somewhere, but you have an electromagnetic field with temperature variation, then you know that you've got something a little different."

Most investigating groups would love to have an ion counter in their ghost-hunting arsenal, but the cost is prohibitive. Russ is in the process of building his own ion counter from parts: "Some theories suggest that ghosts create a disturbance in the ionic field. When there's a high ion count, you can feel the hair standing up on your arms. It's kind of like rubbing a balloon on your arms, and your hair stands on end, and that's the ionization caused by the rubbing of the balloon. With an ion counter, I hope to be able to test that theory." He estimates that he can build one from parts from Radio Shack for three to four hundred dollars.

Even though Mobile has a very haunted past, it is not an ideal home base for paranormal investigators. Russ attributes this situation to a local stigma attached to having ghosts in one's house: "We have not been invited into many private homes. If people mention ghosts, they're afraid they're going to be ridiculed. I've noticed that here at work when people find out I'm a paranormal investigator, they look at me weird. It's not something normal." G.H.O.T.S. has also had difficulty obtaining access to historic homes in Mobile. "Sometimes, you have to take a tour and sneak the equipment in," Russ says. In fact, the only historic site the group has ever investigated is Maggie's Farm in Kusla, which has some Civil War history attached to it. Maggie's Farm is also the only place where he has recorded an EVP: "It's a slight whispering. On the tape, I say, 'I'm going to put my camera down here,' and you can hear the faintest whisper that says, 'Turn around,' or 'Turn it off.' I'm not really sure." Other than that one historic site, the members have had to confine their investigations to cemeteries, when they can get permission to go into them.

Russ, who comes from a strong Christian background, understands why some of the local churches oppose his group's delving into the world of the paranormal: "I believe that when you die, you go to one of two places, and if there are ghosts and there's an existence on this planet other than our physical bodies, then something's askew." Although the church Russ and his wife attend support his work with G.H.O.T.S., some of his fellow Christians have warned him to be careful because they consider what he does to be "demonic."

Because much of Mobile is off-limits to his group, Russ and his members have created a list of places they would like to visit one day if the opportunity ever arises: "I'd love to go to Edinburgh, Scotland, to investigate Grayfriars Cemetery. It is supposed to have a mean old poltergeist who is supposed to inflict pain on people.

I'd also like to go to San Diego and check out the Whaley House. That would be a really cool one to do. It's been called one of the most haunted places in the U.S. I'd love to go to the Myrtles and disprove them. I don't believe it's haunted. I believe it's a gimmick to attract customers." A friend of his who belongs to the Oklahoma City Ghost Club has invited Russ to accompany them on an investigation of a haunted hospital: "During one investigation, he tried to open up the door of the hospital, and it wouldn't budge. At the same time, they were taping, and while they were taping, in the recording that they had, there was a female voice in it, and there were two men up there, and the female voice said, 'You should not say things like that.' It's clear as day." Some day, Russ would like to investigate two of Mobile's historic haunted houses, the Bragg–Mitchell House and Oakleigh. "I'm thinking of doing a 'tour' of Oakleigh some time soon," Russ said with a laugh. He hopes that promoting his group by selling T-shirts and door magnets for cars on the Web site increases the number of requests they receive for investigations.

Russ believes that he and his fellow members are good paranormal investigators because they are skeptical: "I think there's more than likely a scientific reason for something occurring. Granted, I might not know what it is at the time, but I think there's a reasonable explanation for everything that happens." Whereas many investigators consider EVP's to be indisputable proof of the existence of the paranormal, Russ does not, because of the human factor: "I've heard some EVP's that you can tell the investigator did too much editing and created the voice themselves. There's always the possibility that the person could be talking and not realize he's talking at that time, or someone could be talking in the background. You've got to be skeptical about those as well, but I've heard some EVP's that will just know your socks off." He puts even less faith in orbs: "I use a camera without a flash because some theories suggest that orbs are self-lighting. So if I catch a glimpse of light in an area that should have been dark, there's something questionable about that. I like to take pictures, but I keep my flash off. Bugs tend to reflect light quite a bit."

Russ Bennett confesses that what started as a hobby has now become more of a passion now. "My main goal is to find out why people are so scared, why I was scared as a child," Russ says. "I think TV has contributed to my fears, movies like *The Grudge* and *Amityville Horror*. I'll probably be researching for the rest of my life until I become a research subject myself."

Ghost Research Society of North Alabama

JEMISON, ALABAMA

Shane Danzey, Founder and Director

As a boy, Shane Danzey's grandfather introduced him to the world of the paranormal by driving him around town and pointing out all of the haunted sites. His first "close encounter" with the spirit world occurred one night when he recorded himself playing the guitar: "The funny thing about it was that when I played it back, it was a growling kind of noise. Then I heard a voice say, 'Let him!' twice, and it was separate from the growling." At first, Shane thought that some-thing was wrong with his tape recorder, so he taped over the first recording. This time, the vocal sounds were not recorded.

In 1997, after purchasing his first computer, Shane began researching ghosts on the Internet. Not only did he learn a great deal about the paranormal on the Internet, but he also began exploring the Web sites of various ghost-hunting groups across the country. Then in 2003, Shane began listening to the "Lou Gentile Show," a show on the paranormal that is broadcast over the IBC radio network. Shane was particularly impressed by Gentile's interview with John Zaffis. The nephew of Ed and Lorraine Warren, John Zaffis produced a documentary entitled *A Haunting in Connecticut*. He is also the author of *Shadows of the Dark*.

After trying unsuccessfully to join one of the groups in Alabama, Shane started his own group in 2003. Once he had learned to write HTML and set up his own Web site, Shane began recruiting members through the Internet. Aside from directing the Ghost Research Society of North Alabama, Shane is also a co-host of the Alabama Society for Paraspiritual Research (A.S.P.R.) Paranormal Talk Radio Show. The host, Dr. Jimmy Lowery, directs the Alabama Society for Paranormal Research as well. The Ghost Research Society of North Alabama is now affiliated with the A.S.P.R. investigating group.

At the time of the interview, the Ghost Research Society of North Alabama had done only two investigations, both of which were historic places: "With a new group, you want to spoon feed them a little bit," Shane says. "You don't want to go into someone's home with people who are green because you don't know how they're going to react in certain situations." He also tries to "weed out" those prospective members who view investigations as some sort of "thrill ride." Because Shane is so selective, it has taken a long time for him to find the four members who now make up his group.

Most of the substantial evidence Shane's group has collected is EVP's. In February 2005, Shane and Dr. Jimmy Lowery were standing in a doorway between the bedroom and the living room when, suddenly, they both heard a loud banging on the walls. Shane said, "Did you hear that?" Dr. Lowery replied that he did, but his digital recorder did not capture the sound. Shane's digital recorder did record it, but very faintly. "As sensitive as these digital recorders are, you'd think it would have picked up clearly on both of our recorders," Shane said. "That one's still got us scratching our heads."

During an EVP session on an investigation in Georgia, Dr. Lowery told the spirits in the house, "You will not find peace here. You must leave!" Shane says that immediately after Dr. Lowery said this, the word "No" appears on the videotape but not on any of the recorders. "We did not hear anything at the time this occurred," Shane said. "We didn't even know we had it till we got back and started analyzing everything. Some EVP's you have to dig for, but this one jumped right out at us."

An EVP the group picked up during another investigation is particularly interesting because it was verified almost simultaneously through a different means. Shane was recording his conversation with an entity in a house, and he asked the question, "How do you feel?" The response on the digital recorder is clearly the word "Pain." Just moments before the EVP session, the EMF meter went off. Shane tried to find a natural cause for it, but he found none. "This was a room where we had nothing else but a couch and a tool box," Shane said. "There was really nothing electrical that could explain the EMF meter going off." Shane's response to skeptics who have suggested that the recorder picked up a radio transmission somewhere is that the word "Pain" seems to be a direct response to a question asked by the investigator.

The group's most memorable investigation was held at a private residence in Atlanta, Georgia. The investigation began at 9:00 P.M. and ended at 4:00 A.M. Before the group arrived, the investigators suspected that the activity might be demonic in origin because the male and female members complained about being sexually harassed: "The male member of the family did not know that this was occurring to him. It was the female who witnessed all of this. It happened at nighttime in the bed, and usually human spirits don't act like this. She was complaining that this thing was going inside of her." Because of the nature of the attacks, the members theorized that the house was haunted by an incubus and a succubus. "There are tell-tale signs you can look for when a demon is present," Shane says. "There's usually a bad smell like rotten eggs or rotten meat or manure." The investigators did not find any evidence that any demons were in the house. If the investigators had, they would have offered to find someone who could perform an exorcism. "If something turns out to be demonic in nature, we reveal this to the family and let them decide which route they want to take," Shane said. "For instance, if you go into a family that might have a Wiccan belief, we feel that bringing in a Catholic priest or Baptist minister would not help very much because they do not have faith in what the priest or minister is doing," Shane says. He has found very few cases of actual demonic activity during his investigations.

The Ghost Research Society of North Alabama seldom receives any criticism from any religious groups in the area, probably, Shane believes, because the group is generally religious based: "The members of our group have different religious beliefs, so this might be why the local churches don't object to what we do. Also, we don't mess with Ouija boards. These things seem to alarm a lot of people."

Shane predicts that he will be conducting investigations until he is no longer able to: "I enjoy it. You get to help people out. It's interesting because no two cases are alike. They all seem to be different." Because Shane believes that he will never discover all of the answers to his questions regarding the afterlife, he hopes that some day, all of the paranormal investigating groups in the country will work together. "Everybody would be on the same page if we worked together and shared our findings. Sometimes, it seems like groups are afraid that someone will steal their findings. What we should do, though, is use our research to help others."

Arkansas

Ghost Hunters Inc.

LITTLE ROCK, ARKANSAS

Lynette Chapin, Founder and Director

Lynette Chapin says that she and her husband have always been interested in ghosts since they were children: "My mom laughs about it and says no matter how much she tried to beat it out of me, I still held on to my interest in ghosts. She said I was just her weird little kid. I told my mom I could be doing something really bad." She credits television with inspiring her to start up a paranormal investigating group: "Back in 2000, my husband and I were watching the Discovery Channel or Sci-fi. It was a ghost-hunting program, and it was telling how you could go out with just 35 mm cameras and you could catch stuff on film. So we took our 35 mm camera out to the local cemetery. We tried it, and we got some results, so we were kind of hooked." Ghost Hunters Inc. actually got underway in 2001. Lynette was familiar with the process of recruiting members because he had been a member of another Arkansas group a couple of years before. The group's mission is to prove or disprove that the paranormal and ghosts really do exist.

Ghost Hunters Inc. now has six members in its group. The group's Web site—Ghosthuntersinc.com—has a link for recruiting new members. "People e-mail us that they want to join the group," Lynette says. "Then we meet with them and go over everything about the group, and they decided whether or not to join. One of them was one of my girlfriends, who decided she wanted to become one of us. She is a widow and a full-time student." Their members also include a telemarketer, a nurse, and a doctor. Lynette is a student getting a degree in graphic design. Her husband is a computer programmer.

Although members are required to buy their own equipment, Lynette and her husband have started buying extra equipment in case somebody doesn't have a camera or a recorder. "We have a lot of people who go along on an investigation to see how they will like it, and they don't bring anything with them," Lynette says. "I like to have an extra camera on hand so they can kind of get into the experience a little better. For the most part, though, members buy their own equipment."

The group uses the Web site to help finance their investigations and to promote themselves. "We have a store linked to our Web site," Lynette says. "We sell T-shirts, and on the front of the T-shirt, it says, 'Ghost Hunters' in big red letters, and on the back, it says, 'Ghost Hunters.com.' We get a lot of comments on that. My husband wears a baseball cap that says 'Ghost Hunters Inc.' on it. We put fliers up in the place we go to, so the town knows us pretty well." Wearing the T-shirts in public has proven to be a good way for the group to gain access to private residences: "People stop me at the grocery store. A woman might stop me and tell me all kinds of stories if I'm wearing my T-shirts. People give me their name and phone number and e-mail addresses."

Lynette says that she finds the places they investigate on the Internet. She begins by researching haunted locations on the Internet. Then she tries to find the telephone number of a contact person: "I'll call and get in contact with that person and let him know who I am and tell him a little bit about our group. I tell them what my intentions are and see if they are receptive to it and see if they have heard anything about that location being haunted, and most times, they get into a conversation with me, and they have experienced something, or they've heard a lot of things. They're just as interested in us coming out as we are." As a rule, they conduct investigations all year long, but once it gets cold, they tend to avoid outdoor investigations because even the breath of an investigator can take a spiritual form on the camera. "That's where it gets tricky because you've got to ask your members to hold their breath while they take a picture," Lynette says, "and even then, you can't guarantee that what you have photographed isn't your breath."

Most of the historical places Lynette has approached about conducting an investigation have welcomed her and her group: "Many of the staff members have experienced things and have heard a lot of stories and they want to get involved and want to be part of the investigation." A good example is the Mayberry Springs Inn, which Ghost Hunters Inc. investigated in 2004. The group was enticed into investigating the old inn because of rumors that old Mr. Mayberry had chopped up his wife and thrown the pieces in the fire. According to the caretaker, a number of people were robbed and murdered there in the nineteenth century when the building was used as a roadhouse.

Locals also say that an old Indian woman once lived in the house. Lynette set the tape recorder on the fireplace mantle and walked outside to talk to her husband and the caretaker. However, the tape revealed that someone else was there as well: "The inn is set back in the woods, so nobody else would have been there, and you can hear footsteps walk up to the mantle, and you can hear a click of mantle like a lighter, and you can hear a woman speaking in a strange language. You can hear her speaking, but you can't understand what they are saying. We don't know if it was that Indian woman or not. I would love to find out what tribe she was from and then see if there was somebody who could translate it. I tried playing it in reverse, and it doesn't make any sense."

Another historic site that Lynette has investigated is the Mazant Guest House, a bed and breakfast we stayed in at New Orleans. "A murder had happened in Room 4, and oddly enough, when a man and woman stay in that room, there have been three or four cases where they've ended up arguing in that room and broken up," Lynette says. She took a number of pictures while she was there, but, unfortunately, did not get anything on film.

Lynette says the group has plans to investigate the Toltec Mounds and Museum in Little Rock: "Apparently, the guards who work in the museum hear a little girl playing around. They hear her laughing, and she moves stuff. They're going to let us come in one night after hours and have the run of all the mounds and the museum."

Unfortunately, some historic sites are off-limits to Ghost Hunters Inc. because of the cost. Lynette would like to investigate Judge Parker's Court in Fort Smith, Arkansas. Known regionally as "the Hanging Judge," Judge Isaac Parker sentenced 160 people to hang in the 1870s and 1880s, more than any other judge in American history. However, the group would have to get a license from the city in order to film there: "We'd have to pay four hundred dollars. We really, really want to investigate that location, but is it really justifiable spending all that money? We would have to pay double time to the employees to stay there, and we also have to pay for the license. They really want us to come there, but it's a lot of money to spend three hours in one location." However, most of the historic places in the area do not charge for investigations. "They're so interested in what we are doing that they don't charge us," Lynette says.

Of all the historic sites around Little Rock, Ghost Hunters Inc. has found cemeteries to be ideal places for investigations. On Christmas Day, 2004, the group went out to Emmanuel and Calvary Cemeteries in Arkansas and photographed a misty shape and several orbs. Lafayette Cemetery in New Orleans proved to be a very active site. "I didn't want to go there at night because most of the cemeteries in New Orleans are in bad areas of town," Lynette says, "but I did get some good photographs during the day. I got some pictures of orbs on some of the crypts that were open. It was a sunny day out, and it could have been lens flare, but it didn't look like lens flare."

Another local cemetery, which is designated on the Web site as "Unknown cemetery," is on Highway 64 near Pottersville. The highway itself attracts people interested in the paranormal because of an urban legend about a "Vanishing Hitchhiker" on that stretch of asphalt. This classic legend about the man who picks up a girl by the side of the road and drops her off at a cemetery, where she disappears, was known by the turn of the century but acquired the automobile motif by the 1930s. The members were in the part of the cemetery where his Vanishing Hitchhiker's family is supposed to be buried: "We were checking the tombstones," Lynette says. "I took a photograph, and I thought something was on it, and when I got home, I adjusted the contrast and brightness, and I got a picture of a woman in a long dress with a shawl and a bonnet."

Lynette thinks she might have captured part of an apparition in an old cemetery in Oklahoma: "I was taking pictures of an area that was fenced in. I was shooting from three or four different angles. On one spot, it almost looks like someone in a dress off to the side. I can't really tell what it is, though."

In 2003 one of the new members of Ghost Hunters suffered a case of "first-investigation jitters" at a small cemetery in a rural area in Arkansas known as Booger Hollow: "The cemetery is set back in the swamp. We went out there at 11:30 or midnight one night. We went down an old road that was lined with big cypresses with moss hanging from them. Suddenly, the gate loomed in front of us, and he didn't want to get out of the car. We'd driven several hours to get to the place, so I told him he had to get out of the car. I didn't want to make that trip for nothing." Lynette was glad they stayed because they photographed some orb activity and a strange mistlike form. "You can see the mist building from the left. Then by the third or fourth picture, it's this big shape," Lynette says.

Despite the fact that the group has collected some very convincing evidence at cemeteries, Lynette actually prefers to investigate indoors so that she does not have to contend with the weather. However, indoor investigations can also be challenging. "We have on our Web site an investigation about Solgolhachia, Arkansas," Lynette says. "We had a family contact us there. Their house is on the Trail of Tears. They have had a lot of activity there, and they were concerned about some of the things their kids were seeing. They invited us to come for an investigation. But when we got there, it was Halloween, and the kids were there, so it was kind of hard to conduct an investigation. The only thing I saw—I was standing in the hall, and there were folding doors that covered the washer and dryer, and the doors flew open, but there could be a logical explanation for this. The floor could have been uneven. I could have stepped on a board that caused them to pop open." Like all good investigators, Lynette eliminates all logical explanations first before assigning responsibility for the activity to a ghost.

Although Lynette cannot say how much longer she will continue researching the paranormal, she has no plans to stop anytime soon because investigating is in her blood. She and her husband are so fascinated by the paranormal that they celebrated Valentine's Day 2005 at one of Arkansas's most celebrated haunted sites, the Crescent Hotel in Eureka Springs for Valentine's Day: "If you're staying for the weekend, the ghost tour is included. It's part of the package. I guess you could say my husband and I are weird."

Spirit Seekers

ROLAND, ARKANSAS

Alan and Angela Lowe, Founders and Directors

One might say that Angela Lowe's connection to the paranormal is "in her genes": "The women in my family have been sensitive to the spirit world as far back as my great-grandmother, who practiced 'white' witchcraft.

My grandmother was extremely psychic, as is my mother and her sisters. One of my sisters and I have seen spirits all of our lives. Until I was an adult, I did not realize that it was unusual."

One of Angela's first paranormal experiences occurred she was ten years old. Shortly after her grandmother died, she and her sister began holding séances to contact her. During one of these sessions, they were sitting on the floor with a candle between them when the flame simply disappeared. After a couple of seconds, the flame reappeared above the candle, floated straight up to the ceiling, and began floating around the room near the ceiling. "We were transfixed for a short while, just watching the flame," Angela says. "Finally, one of us screamed, and we ran out. We were both convinced that we had contacted something evil. From that day on, we would often see the flame floating in the room. We were afraid to go in there alone. We moved when I was fourteen and were happy to leave." That was the last séance Angela participated in until she was an adult.

Angela says that her daughter Violet's psychic powers are even stronger than hers: "When she was very young, she would tell me about the lady who looked like me who would stand by her bed and watch over her at night. Later, she identified a picture of my grandmother as that lady." When Violet was six years old, she had a ghostly "friend" named Sarah who enjoyed playing pranks, such as hiding hair brushes or throwing the contents of her closet around the room. Whenever Violet's family moved, Sarah went with them. Sarah remained in the last house they moved into after Violet went away to college.

Angela's husband, Alan, whom Angela married when Violet was ten years old, saw Sarah shortly after they were married. Angela was talking to Violet in her room about her behavior when

Alan saw a little girl run out of the room and down the hall away from him. Alan assumed the little girl was Violet. "He was concerned that she was so obviously upset and came into Violet's room to talk to me," Angela said. "He found Violet and me still in the room."

Angela credits her husband's gradual "conversion" as motivating her to start a new group after having spent a year in a local ghost-hunting group whose members were more interested in socializing than in strictly following scientific procedures. "Raised as a Christian, he desperately wanted to believe in the eternal soul, but being a very left-brained person, he had a difficult time accepting the concept on faith alone," Angela says. Alan believes that ghost hunting has fortified his parents' teachings: "They taught me that when we die, our soul or spirit goes on living. They taught me that the body is only a temporary home for our soul. The one thing they could not do is show me or prove to me what they taught." Finding evidence of the existence of life after death confirmed for Alan the truths that he could not accept on faith alone. However, the first time he made personal contact with the spirits, he thought he was going crazy: "We've got two spirits in our house. One went down the steps the other night. I waved at him and said, 'How are you doing?' I feel like I'm special. I get to see and hear these people." Alan thinks that he is developing the ability to sense the presence of spirits, possibly as a result of living in a house with a wife who is a sensitive and a daughter who is a psychic.

Angela's daughter Violet also led Angela to believe that her family could form the nucleus of a new group. It was not long before Violet confirmed Angela's suspicions that Violet would prove to be an asset on a ghost hunt: "The more time we spend concentrating on the spirit world, listening, allowing them to contact us, the more control she seems to have over her abilities. By learning to have more control, Violet is better able to 'turn it off' at times and better understand her ability." Alan made use of his daughter's psychic powers in February 2005 when the two of them were in Gurdon, Arkansas, where the state's most famous ghost lights, the Gurdon Lights, have been seen. According to the legend, the lights are made by the lantern of a murdered railroad foreman, whose ghost still walks along the railroad tracks. Alan and Violet were walking along when, suddenly, Violet stopped and said she felt something following them. "So I turned around and took a picture, and it's one of the best pictures I've ever gotten," Alan says. "It looks like a person stepping off the railroad tracks. He's got a leg up in the air. I've got it framed and hanging from my wall. Whether it's orbs or ectoplasm or mist—it looks like a big, glowing form of a man."

Spirit Seekers did not really get underway until the Lowes set up their Web site in 2004. "We do not seek out members; they find us. Anyone who is seriously interested in discovering, contacting, and documenting the spirit world is welcome," Angela says. Skeptics are also encouraged to join because they make sure the group has researched every possible option for any phenomena. Prospective members are interviewed and required to participate in one investigation before the decision is made whether or not to accept them in the group. Spirit Seekers now has thirty members and prospective members on their mailing list. The mission of the group is to investigate and document the spirit world through EVP, digital, film, and video photography.

The group's most memorable investigation was conducted at an antebellum house in Lamar, Arkansas. According to a local legend, the old house was used as a hospital during the Civil War. The owners of the house reported a variety of strange occurrences, such as a mist forming in the kitchen, lights burning out prematurely, and spectral voices talking in the children's bedrooms. When the investigators arrived, they found that the family was much more frightened than they had expected them to be. They were so afraid of being alone in the house that no one went to the restroom without being accompanied. Because the lights tended to go out frequently, the family hung battery-operated "torch lights" down the halls.

Spirit Seekers had no sooner begun their research than they were overcome by a feeling of depression, which was not dispelled until the next morning. Angela and Violet focused on the children's bedroom upstairs. The women had been told that none of the children would sleep up there because of the voices they heard during the night. While Angela and Violet were sitting in the darkness, Violet asked the spirits to make contact with them. All at once, a little boy appeared in the doorway. The specter took a couple of steps into the room, looked at the women, walked backward through the doorway, and then walked a few more tentative steps into the room. A video camera that was running at the time captured the image of a light gathering in the hallway, floating toward the camera, and illuminating the entire screen. Afterward, the group told the family that a little boy whose name was "Jackson" had fallen out of a window in the bedroom: "The boy was not hazardous to the family, but felt at home there. The family then informed us that their youngest son was named 'Jaxson' [sic]. That gave us some doubt about our information, thinking the name may have been referring to their son instead of the boy who died." However, several months later, the family contacted Angela to let her know that they had researched the history of the house and that a little boy named Jackson had indeed fallen out of the upstairs window and died as a result of his injuries.

Spirit Seekers also sensed an evil presence while filming in another bedroom as the children slept. One little girl woke up repeatedly and looked around as if someone had been touching her. Convinced that the child was being tormented by a malevolent entity, the group performed a cleansing. Once this was complete, a feeling of peace prevailed in the house. Several weeks following the investigation, the family reported that the feeling of peace was still in the house but that ghostly activity had taken place in the area surrounding the house.

Not all of Spirit Seekers' investigations are as terrifying as the investigation at the Lamar House. In 2004, the group was investigating a house that had displayed spirit activity on a previous visit. Angela says that on the night of the follow-up visit, the house was completely dark: "We had just closed the door, and we were locked in this big, empty, dark, haunted house when out of the darkness, someone said, 'I hope there aren't any mice in here.'" Considering where they were, everyone thought that this was a very funny comment.

Like most groups, Spirit Seekers is always looking forward to the next investigation, which often promises to be better than all the others. At the time of this interview, Alan Lowe was attempting to obtain permission from the state of Arkansas to investigate a variety of historic buildings. One wonders how Alan can retain his enthusiasm for ghost hunting after having several "close encounters" with beings from beyond: "I've had fingers run down my back. I've been talked to. I've had something whisper in my ear. One night at midnight, I was in the living room sitting on the couch. All of a sudden, there was an argument right in front of me. It was a man and a woman talking as plain as day. It made the hair stand up on my head." As long as he considers these intrusions on his personal space as opportunities to prove the existence of the paranormal, Alan Lowe is likely to continue investigating for a long time.

Florida

Daytona Beach Paranormal
Research Group

DAYTONA BEACH, FLORIDA

Doris Smith, Founder and Director

Doris Smith claims to have become interested in ghost hunting quite by accident while she was on a ghost tour in St. Augustine: "I took some very unusual photographs that particular night, and when I found out that it wasn't a problem with developing, that it was actually something with the negative, I began researching what it was. I discovered that there was this whole subculture of people who do this. I was hooked. That was it."

Doris founded the Daytona Beach Paranormal Research Group in 1997. The group became an official nonprofit corporation in 2000. "Our mission is to help people who are experiencing paranormal activity in their place of residence or business, to educate the public, and to work with our sister organization, the International Association of Cemetery Preservation," Doris says. The group uses the funds received from the ghost tour they operate in Dayton to support its cemetery preservation efforts.

The Daytona Beach Paranormal Research Group currently has twenty-eight active members, but only fifteen members go into the field with Doris. "I don't recruit members," Doris says.

"I let people approach me. You have to be careful because it seems like everybody wants their fifteen minutes of fame, and not everybody can be like the guys in the *Ghosthunters* TV show. These are not the types of people I want. Our goal is not to be on TV. Our goal is to educate and help people." Doris has kept the size of her group relatively small by requiring applicants to sign a contract agreeing to work one afternoon per month with the cemetery research group. Although she prefers to recruit people who have specific skills, the only quality that she really requires is a willingness to learn the field. Consequently, the Daytona Beach Paranormal Research Group has a very eclectic membership: "I have a retired sheriff who works for us. She notices details the other members don't. I've also got a waitress, a man who repairs kidney dialysis machines, a man with Homeland Security, an electrician, a full-time student, a home remodeler, and a guy who works for Boston Whaler making boats. This is great because it adds to the diversity of the group."

Doris also uses two sensitives in her group: "One gentleman has been with us for four years. He is phenomenal. He actually sees ghosts, which is kind of frightening. We've helped work with him to shut that [ability] down when he's not working on a case. It was getting crazy at home." The group's other sensitive is a woman who is adept at contacting spirits: "When she's out doing her thing, she's always running her tape recorder, and she usually gets better than her share of EVP's," Doris says. Even though the sensitives have come in very handy during investigations, Doris does not view them as just another piece of equipment: "I ask them for guidance, especially when we've been in a home several times and we can't nail down a specific area of activity. Of course, they have no prior knowledge of the case when we bring them in, and we don't use that as evidence in our case files because you can't prove what they're impressions are." However, if one of the sensitives says something like "There's something right above me!" and one of the members captures an unusual image on film, Doris includes both pieces of evidence in her case file.

Doris derives more enjoyment from the investigations she has conducted at historic buildings and cemeteries because she and her members can be more laid-back: "We don't have to be as 'on' at historic locations as we do at private homes," Doris says. "When you're working in a private residence, you are part family counselor and part psychologist. We have to be as professional as we can be because these people do not really know what is happening to them, and they're scared. They have to live with this activity seven days a week. In a historic building, though, the staff is there only from nine to five. It's more fun for us to work these places because we can loosen up a bit."

The Daytona Beach Paranormal Research Group has a higher percentage of successful investigations than many groups do. "Forty percent of our cases have proven activity," Doris says. "It might be because the Native American population here was so huge five thousand years ago, and there were so many battles fought here. The last battles between the whites and the Seminoles were fought where we have done a lot of cases. I don't know if that's the reason, or it's because we have just gotten lucky." Doris admits, though, that she is proud of her group's high success rate.

Two locations stand out in Doris's mind as being particularly haunted. One of these sites is a private residence called the Neely House. "The house was actually put together from three older buildings," Doris said, "and the large spare room was the sanctuary of a church." Doris brought her group to the Neely

House because the owner had been hearing people walking through the house and knocking on the walls: "We went out there one night and set up the cameras. We put one outside pointed toward the dogs out back because the dogs react to something in the middle of the night. Of course, it could have been an armadillo, and if it was, we would catch it on camera. Lo and behold, here comes this full-body apparition stepping into the frame of the video camera. It pats the dog on the top of the head and looks up into the camera for a half second and turns around and walks back out of the field of vision." The camera that captured this startling image was set up by the owner, who accidentally laid it on its side. "Fortunately, technology being the way it is, we were able to take that piece of footage and turn it rightside up so that we can see it clearly, and it's absolutely a great piece of footage," Doris said.

When the Dayton Beach Paranormal Research Group investigated the Huguenot Cemetery, it certainly lived up to its reputation as the most haunted cemetery in St. Augustine. Doris's group was invited by an area preservation group and the local historical society to help document some of their hauntings. "These old stories really promote St. Augustine as a haunted city," Doris said. A couple of other groups turned down the invitation out of fear that the high energy levels would damage their equipment. Doris believes that the evidence her group collected was worth the potential risk to her group's equipment: "I got two full-body apparitions on 35 mm film that night, and we know nothing about either of those people. One is reputed to be Judge Stickney, who was originally buried in Huguenot Cemetery, and then he was moved to Washington, D.C., after someone had desecrated his grave and stolen his gold teeth.

Then he was moved back secretly to St. Augustine and buried in Huguenot Cemetery, but no one knew where. And they say that he's been seen in this one section. Sometimes, he's been seen walking, and sometimes he's been seen sitting. We caught him both standing and seated in the same area where other people have reported seeing him. And then there was Albert Robinson, a Franciscan Monk. It's incredible. You can see the monk robe and the funky little Franciscan monk haircut."

Because the fear factor is very difficult to control in very intense investigation, Doris jokingly tells her new members to bring a spare change of underwear. During an investigation of a business in June 2005, one of Doris's newest members looked fear squarely in the face—and flinched: "She had been with us not quite a year, and she wanted to go up into the attic by herself. I didn't think this was a very good idea, but against my better judgment, I let her go, but I made her take a two-way radio just in case. She was sitting there and talking to the spirits like we do, and sure enough, the handle started jiggling on the attic door, and then it started moving back and forth and swung open. It scared that girl so bad. She said, 'I'm never going into that attic again! I'm never going into that attic again!' I said, 'Oh yes, you are!' The next time we went out on a case, I put her butt right back up in the attic." Although most of Doris's members maintain a professional attitude in front of clients, she has had to let some people go because the fear factor kicked in a little too much: "I had one girl—we were outside at a location, and a leaf fell on her head. She screamed, 'Ahhhh!' I said, 'What?' She said, 'A leaf just fell on my head! The ghosts are trying to tell me something!' I said, 'They're trying to tell you, It's autumn!' Needless to say, she's not working for me anymore."

Even though the Daytona Beach Paranormal Research Group dismisses most of the orbs they have collected as being nothing more than dust particles, pollen, spores, moisture, and raindrops, the members do believe that a small percentage of orbs are once-living human or animal spirits. "I just did a lecture on this at Cassadaga," said Doris. "The theory we go by is that the small percentage of orbs that show movement, show three dimensions, and emit light were once living human or animal spirits. You get a lot of evidence from tourists or hobbyists that is unreliable. Before I go out on a case, I spray my camera lens with canned air, and I wipe it off with a lens cloth. Then I blow it off again. I do this to every piece that has a lens. I don't see tourists or hobbyists do this. We need to set a professional example for everyone else."

Doris's interest in the paranormal ties in very well with her two day jobs: "I run the tours, and I own a desktop publishing company. We produce chapbooks on ghost hunting and the paranormal and cemetery preservation, so that helps pay the bills." Doris has also written a book entitled *Dread and the Dead Fill the Dunnam House*, which she has sent to the publisher: "It's one of the scariest places we've ever worked," Doris said. "It's a private residence. In eight months, what started as a Friday-night cocktail joke for the family turned into an extremely dangerous haunting where we believe that a nonhuman, negative presence was in the home, and we actually videotaped their baby getting attacked in her crib. It was very frightening. I actually got my ribs broken on that case. It was insane!"

Despite the fact that the group's Web site has given the Daytona Beach Paranormal Research Group a somewhat high profile, Doris is thankful that her group belongs to a nationwide community of paranormal investigators: "We are kind of choosy about whom we affiliate with. We are members of the American Ghost Society and T.A.P.S. We are recommended by the International Ghost Hunter Society. I can't thank people like Troy Taylor and Jason Hawes enough because we are isolated here in Florida."

Florida Paranormal Research

ROCKLEDGE, FLORIDA

Tim Tedana, Founder and Director

Tim Tedana's interest in ghosts was the natural result of growing up in a haunted house: "When I was seven or eight years old, I shared a room with a sibling, and we were sitting there talking like kids do, and all of a sudden, we heard the back door to the house open up and slam. Our parents were at church at the time, and the doors were all locked. Then we heard feet stomping, like somebody had on combat boots. It walked through the kitchen into the living room. We could hear it coming all the way up to our room. It made a real loud 'Kchchch!' too, like somebody was strangling. It sounded like somebody kicked the door open. Then the noise stopped. At that point, we covered ourselves up with blankets." When their parents came home an hour later, they could tell that something strange had happened because mud was smeared all over the kitchen door and the door to the boys' room. After this weird incident, Tim embarked on a quest for answers, beginning with the clergy. He was ultimately disappointed because none of the ministers he talked to had any solid answers.

Tim's fascination with the paranormal waned until he enrolled in a music appreciation class in college: "At that point, I was a music major. In one class they played Gregorian chants, and they wanted to know what was going on in history at that time. And that got me delving into the way religions are created. It made me look at my own religious beliefs and why they couldn't help me. It just took off from there." He has been studying the paranormal off and on since he was nineteen years old.

Tim decided to start his own paranormal group because all of the groups he had observed did nothing but take photographs in cemeteries. He envisioned a group that would focus on helping people by employing scientific and metaphysical approaches: "My ex-wife, Monica, was a channeling medium. We knew we could help these people. The average group didn't want anything to do with us because they looked down on the psychic-medium realm. We even offered to be an associate group with a larger group in Florida, but they didn't want anything to do with us because of our angle. We wanted to add that little extra tool (psychics and mediums) to the toolbox, but they didn't want anything to do with it. We finally said, 'We have seen those other ghost groups, and we can do better.' And that's what we've set out to do." When Florida Paranormal Research first started up, it was the only group in Florida that used two teams.

Florida Paranormal Research, which was founded in 2001, is now a network of groups with branches in Miami, Jacksonville, Spring Hill, Pensacola, Tampa, and Orlando. Although Tim is technically the director, he does not really "direct" the activities of the groups: "Once they know what they're doing, I pretty much let them function on their own. All I'll do is coordinate the teams based on their beliefs. I don't want any clashes. We have a wide variety of beliefs, from Christians to pagans. I don't mix up the beliefs. A lot depends on the house we're going to. If the family's Methodist, we try to bring in a team with those beliefs." He believes that it would be counter-productive to team Wiccans with Southern Baptists, for example.

Even though the Florida Paranormal Research teams have investigated museums and one police station, the group visits private residences almost exclusively. Usually, homeowners seeking help send Tim an e-mail message. After Tim receives contact information, the point person in the group closest to the home interviews the homeowner. This person decides if the case is valid or not: "If it looks like a valid case, we'll send in the science team first. Their whole job is to find out if there's something there that's nonexplainable. They're people who aren't psychics. They're Southern Baptists or Christians. They're looking at it from a logical viewpoint. Are the walls rattling because an air vent's loose?"

If the homeowners appear to be credible witnesses, the science team leaves, and the second team arrives. "They are mostly psychics and mediums," Tim says. "They walk in with no information. That's the only way I'll use them. We get a lot of psychics who communicate with us from the entire state. Most of them are usually known only in their region. We're known statewide. A lot of them ask for specifics about the house. If they're genuine, they can walk in cold and figure it out." Tim always advises the clients not to talk to the metaphysical team during the investigation: "If a client says something's going on in a corner of the house, and the science group detects anomalies there, and the psychics pick up something in the corner, too, and go into it even deeper, that's really good validation for me." The purpose of the second team is not to get EVP's or EMF readings. "That's the job of the first team," Tim says. "The main goal of the second team is to clear the house for the family."

Two weeks after an investigation, the group checks back with the family to see if the house is clear, relying primarily on psychics. Sometimes, the group is unsuccessful: "There was a house in Florida that we weren't able to clear. I've opened this case to any other psychics in the state who want to try it. The psychic we'd brought in did a really thorough job, but she wasn't able to clear it. Sometimes, the spirits won't communicate with one psychic, but they will with a second one." Tim went on to say that spirits can read a psychic as well as a psychic can read spirits, a fact that might explain why some psychics do not meld with a particular spirit in a particular house.

Clearing houses is not easy, Tim explains, because 99 percent of the spirits they deal with are disembodied human beings: "They're scared themselves, but they've got free choice. You can't force them to go if they don't want to. Our psychics and mediums try to counsel these spirits. They're like us." A large number of the spirits Tim's group encounters "do not want to cross over to the 'other side' because they have done something in life that they feel will make them unworthy to God," Tim says. "They feel if they go 'to the light,' they will be punished for eternity." The hardest part, Tim believes, is to convince these spirits that they're not going to burn in hell.

Tim's most satisfying investigation was the first one the members did as an organization: "That one was done at a private residence in Rock Ledge, Florida. We were just starting out. There were only five of us. This was really neat because our medium, my ex-wife Monica, stared at a corner of the room while she was talking to me, and she said, 'It's right in the corner. I'm talking to it.'" Tim took a picture in the direction his wife indicated and captured some orbs on his digital camera. Then she started communicating with the spirit. This was the group's first real success.

Florida Paranormal Research's most negative investigation was conducted in a private residence in Spring Hill, Florida, which is a considerable distance from the group's home base. Because the science team did not find any significant evidence in the house, the second team decided not to make the trip. However, Tim changed his mind when he received a telephone call from the homeowners and discovered how terrified they really were. They were so frightened, in fact, that they were staying in a hotel. After talking it over, the second team consisting of Tim, Lisa, and Monica decided to travel down to Spring Hill. The second team scanned the house and did not pick up anything important. "We figured we'd driven across the state for nothing," Tim said. "About the second hour, the family told us the entity had been communicating with them through the computer. That was something I'd never heard of before. Of course, when we tried it, nothing happened. About an hour later, I was back in the bathroom where the family had sensed things, but I didn't get anything. Lisa was in the living room with the computer, and she said, 'Tim, come here!' So I ran in there. 'You know those curtain rods above the blinds? They're heavy plastic. They were swinging like a pendulum.' When we went in there, we'd turned off the fans and the air conditioner, so the curtain rods shouldn't have been doing this. While we were watching the curtain rods, the lights went out. The house had lost power." The second team was convinced that some sort of dark entity might have been present. "They're not really demons. They're just what they are. They've never been to the light. They have no desire to go to the light. They're at the opposite side of the spectrum. We've actually interviewed a dark entity before, and their whole views are different." Because the team was not prepared to deal with negative forces, they were not able to clear the house.

Sometimes, a successful clearing of a house does not always bode well for the group. "There is a backlash now and then, and we really don't know what causes it. It seems like every time we do a successful clearing, we get bad luck, two weeks later sometimes. We've had electronics in our house blow up and stuff like that, and we're still not sure why." Of course, if researchers already had all the answers, then there would be no need for research.

Florida Paranormal Research is frequently criticized by religious groups. Tim says that many churches do not approve of what his group is doing because what they are discovering contradicts conventional religious doctrine: "Technically, according to the major religions in this country, spirits shouldn't be walking around because they'll be asleep until Judgment Day, when we'll be awakened and judged. But that doesn't take into account all the spirits we've run into. Did God forget about them?" Because the group is willing to "look outside the box," nothing is taboo. Tim's group is especially controversial because of its use of Ouija boards: "We hear people say, 'You shouldn't use Ouija boards because they will bring in evil spirits.' Well, as researchers, we want to see if that's true. We've gotten interesting results from Ouija boards, and I'm still alive."

Tim has even been called the "anti-Christ" because, supposedly, he is turning people away from God. Actually, Tim says, his groups do not conform to the teachings of the church because any form of restriction would impair his observations: "Religious groups don't like us because our views are different. My beliefs are probably closest to those of the Spiritualist religion, but I don't see any need to join them because when you do that, you have to tow the party line. Why would anyone want to do that?"

Interestingly enough, Tim does not try to counterbalance the negative publicity the group receives with positive publicity: "We're not really out to be popular. I turn down a lot of interviews for TV and newspapers because this group does not exist to become popular. I get criticized from some of my group members for feeling this way. We exist to learn. I've found that the more popular you become, the more negative potential you get, too, and that can be stifling as well." His group is best described as a group of normal people with special abilities who are dedicated to using these abilities to help people.

Halifax Hauntings: Investigations and Research

HOLLY HILL, FLORIDA

Scott Ferencz, Founder and Director

Scott Ferencz claims to have been into ghost hunting all his life: "I had my first experience when I was a little kid. I saw my great-grandfather in the hallway of my old apartment building. I was eleven. I was coming up to go eat dinner at five P.M., and as I was going up the stairs, he was standing there looking at me, and he stood there for about thirty seconds. I was a little scared, and I wasn't quite sure—my mind wasn't quite processing what I was seeing, so I called for my mother to open the door to make sure nothing was there. I went inside and I told her, and she said she had seen him a couple of days before that. She said it was O.K. because he was just coming around checking on everybody. After that incident, I've always been interested in ghosts." Scott's great-grandfather had died about a month previous to Scott's sighting.

Scott's fascination with ghosts developed even further after he began working as a correctional officer at Tomoca Correctional Institution: "Two other officers and I saw a ghost of an inmate who'd committed suicide in the prison where I used to work. It was on the anniversary of the day he had committed suicide. Of course, we were ridiculed because it slipped out that we had seen a ghost, but it didn't matter because we know what we saw."

Scott became a paranormal investigator in 2002 after an injury forced him to retire. "I couldn't figure out what to do with my life," Scott said. "I asked God if he would give me a little help now that my career was over. It was funny. Every channel I changed to on TV, there was something about ghosts and ghost hunting. So I took that as a sign and started reading and surfing the net. I was always a history buff, so I did research in museums and the library, and I formed my own ghost-hunting group." Scott feels fortunate to be able to investigate hauntings full time.

According to Scott, law enforcement personnel are well-suited to ghost hunting for reasons other than their experience in conducting investigations: "Law enforcement personnel get a lot of weird calls. In one section of Daytona Beach, a lot of our police officers will get calls to the old Victorian houses that are empty. Someone will call and say they saw someone walking inside, and they'll check to make sure it wasn't a homeless person. In another house, there was a woman in white floating around, and there are numerous reports that police filed on it, which is rare. It was so scary, they thought they really needed to say something." Dealing with death as part of the job also opens up the minds of police officers to extreme possibilities: "You're open up to more perspectives on life than you normally would be because you see death, even in prisons. They are killed by other inmates, or inmates commit suicide. You also see it on the streets, and you wonder, 'How did this happen? How did this person get saved?' There's no logical explanation why this person survived this accident or this shooting. They couldn't have survived unless there was some sort of supernatural or divine intervention, so that opens our minds up to a lot more possibilities than just life and death." Scott believes this acceptance of the uncanny explains why so many police departments are using psychics to help them solve cases like the ones in Daytona Beach.

Halifax Hauntings has eight active members and forty-three on-line members. The members come from a variety of backgrounds, including housewives, medical assistants, a customer service representative at Wal-Mart, a nurse, and a paint delivery person. The common bond that makes them a coherent whole is the inherent skepticism: "Yes, we do believe in ghosts," Scott says. "Yes, we do believe in angels, but you have to be skeptical going into a situation. If you tell me your house is haunted, I'm not going to believe you right away. I'm going out there and check it out. And if you are telling me you're hearing noises from a certain part of the house, I will do everything I can to re-create that noise. If there are water pipes clanging or rodents in the walls, I will do everything I can to disprove the haunting. That's my job, to try to re-create all the evidence, and if I'm still left with evidence, then we have more research to do."

Although the members are encouraged to bring their own cameras, Scott supplies most of the expensive, high-tech equipment, some of which was donated by businesses and individuals. "Sometimes we get donations from individuals and business when we do an investigation, and we use that to buy equipment," Scott says. He uses both 35 mm and digital cameras on investigations. Although digital cameras are cheaper because there are no developing casts, he puts more faith in photographs taken with the 35 mm cameras: "You have to take into consideration that with digital cameras, there are lots of digital settings, and people don't know how to use them. There are lots of settings on 35 mm cameras too, but most of them are the basic types of settings, the point-shoot sort of thing. The negative is the hard evidence. It's very hard to screw with a negative. Kodak can verify a negative much easier than they can a digital photo."

Photographs taken by Halifax Hauntings have yielded some intriguing images. From Scott's point of view, photographs of orbs can be very misleading because of the possibility that they have been caused by dust, insects, airborne particles, or reflections; "I'm interested in those orbs where there's a 99 percent chance that there was nothing interfering with your camera shoot. I'd rather see odd-shaped orbs over circular orbs any time. We're out to prove the existence of ghosts, and orbs are not going to do it." The group would much prefer to capture full-body apparitions on film. "We haven't captured any full-body apparitions," Scott says, "but we have captured half-bodied apparitions and torsos, some heads, a leg of a little girl—caught it on film and video— mists in the shape of a person. But my goal is to capture a full-body apparition on a 35 mm camera with a fool-proof negative." The members of Halifax Hauntings are trying to distinguish themselves from those thrill-seeking ghost hunters who settle for orb pictures because they look "cool" on a Web site.

The investigators become much more excited over EVP's. "To me, EVP's are awesome," Scott says. "They're just amazing. I've got maybe EVP's of actual voices where there was nobody in the room at all except for me. I've gotten answers and analyzed it on my computer where the voices are beyond the type a human can make."

One of the most outstanding EVP's the group has ever collected was recorded through an answering machine. Most answering machines cut off after thirty seconds, but this particular telephone message went on for three-and-a-half minutes. "We couldn't really understand what was being said until we had a language expert look at it. It turned out to be some kind of ancient language. There's one we got that's kind of demonic. It took us eight months to figure out what the voice was saying. It came through an answering machine. We analyzed it on the computer, and it was definitely not human." Because the voices was talking about death and Satan, the members suspect that the words were spoken by some sort of demonic entity.

The difficulty of conducting an investigation, Scott believes, is amplified by the fact that most spirits are uncooperative: "Ghosts know we're coming. They know what we're trying to do. When they see all the cameras and all the equipment being set up, they know that the show is on. And sometimes, they don't want to play." On more than one occasion, the members have left a private residence with no evidence at all. Then the next day, they received a phone call from a homeowner saying, "Ten minutes after you guys left, something happened." Not finding evidence during a twelve-hour investigation does not mean that the location is not haunted. "It just means that at the time, we didn't catch anything," Scott says. "This is why only 25 percent of our investigations reveal genuine hauntings." Instead of encountering no activity at all, Scott would prefer to find a rational explanation for the activity because it puts the home-owners' minds at rest and, in some cases, might prevent them from moving out simply because their pipes are banging.

For Halifax Hauntings, the witching hour is between mid-night and 4:00 A.M., the period when many groups claim to have encountered the most paranormal activity. Scott's group has even more success during a full moon or new moon: "You've got three days prior and three days after a full or new moon when the activity really picks up." Scott also prefers investigating at night because in the daytime, the sound of family members walking around the house or glare filtering in through windows can become problematic. "At three A.M., there won't be too much activity inside because everybody's sleeping. It's more of a controlled environment," Scott said.

The majority of the places Halifax Hauntings investigates are historical because it is easier for the members to do research on the place. The members are particularly interested in finding if anyone has died at the site. "Usually in a historic place, you have a lot of remnant energy. And when you have all that energy [in a single place], you are bound to find something," Scott says.

The group's favorite historical site is the Live Oak Inn in Daytona Beach. In the past, the group has done ghost tours at the Live Oak Inn. All totaled, the group has done seven investigations there. The group was attracted to the Live Oak Inn by its sad legacy of misery and death. There are at least seven recorded deaths in the old inn. According to legend, a white male slave who was held captive there for five years eventually died in his room from starvation.

On the group's last investigation, members encountered the spirit of one of the people who actually died at the inn. "This little girl popped out of nowhere," Scott says. "She was driving us crazy, turning off equipment, unplugging stuff, setting off alarm clocks. The alarm clock would go off at midnight, and it was set for four A.M. We caught her walking down the hallway on one of the infrared cameras." The members did some research after the investigation and found out that in 1896, a little girl who was playing in front of the house was run over by a horse and carriage. She was brought inside the house, where she died. "When we found out her name," Scott said, "we went back to do a secondary investigation, and when we said her name, the whole house started going crazy. The lights would flicker on and off, the temperature went up and down, the equipment went berserk. It was totally amazing." Scott believes that learning the identity of a spirit gives a person a great deal of power: "Basically, what they're trying to do in specific hauntings is get your attention. They want your help. They want to know what's going on. They don't know they're dead. And when you know their name, they feel a connection to you, and they're going to try to get your attention any way they possibly can." For the group, this theory explains why the spirit of the little girl was so active.

Apparently, a much less playful entity was also awakened by the group. Before the first investigation, Scott's research revealed that at least twelve guests who have stayed there were physically attacked. People have been touched. They've had their hair pulled. When Hallifax Hauntings began investigating the house, Scott found out how credible the guests' accounts really were: "I was attacked three times while investigating the Live Oak Inn. One time, I was pushed down the stairs. I felt hands grabbing my shoulders and pulling me back and throwing me down the stairs. The other time, something tried to choke me. I couldn't breathe. It felt like I was having an asthma attack. They feed off of electromagnetic energy, and your exhale is full of electromagnetic energy. They'll try to take the breath out of you to use your energy, and you can't breathe. Some people say that's not being physically attacked. Well, anything that is happening to your person, to me, is being attacked."

On another investigation at the Live Oak Inn, everyone but Scott had a terrifying encounter with one of the more playful presences. While he was preoccupied in another room, all of his members ran frantically out of the building. When Scott found them outside trembling, he asked them what had happened: "They said a double A battery started spinning on its own on the floor. It started picking up velocity and going faster and faster and faster. It was going so fast that it was making a whizzing sound. When they told it to stop, it automatically stopped and didn't move anymore. And they took off." Scott returned to the room his members had left so hurriedly and found a brand-new battery on the floor. He picked it up and was surprised to find that it was totally dead: "The entity had totally drained it. We have to go through a lot of batteries. They drain a lot of batteries like crazy—video camera batteries, alkaline batteries, regular batteries. I have two bags just full of batteries for that reason. That's how they get their energy. When we start an investigation, we put in brand-new batteries. Everyone has a little pouch on them just for batteries."

The evidence the investigators have collected during their seven investigations of the Live Oak Inn more than compensates for the trauma they have endured there: "We've got so many photos of amazing things there. We actually have a skeleton hand coming out of the floor, and it's captured on 35 mm film. That's one thing out of at least one hundred that we have from the investigations we did there. We have at least five EVP's from there. The temperature fluctuations are amazing. It's colder upstairs than downstairs, which is strange because heat rises. We've checked the air conditioners, the vents, the ceilings, the roof. A contractor who's part of the team went through the house looking for a structural defect, and he couldn't find anything. There are a lot of unanswered questions at the Live Oak Inn."

In the past, Halifax Hauntings has raised money for the purchase of equipment by holding ghost walks. "We kind of laid off ghost walks because we didn't want people to think that was all we did," Scott said. Their tours differed from the more conventional variety in that the tour groups were allowed to visit locations where the investigators had their equipment set up. People could peer into the monitors or look at the photographs and actually see the evidence that was collected the night before. "Sometimes, they'd see orbs flying by," Scott said. "A few times, they saw half an apparition. It was a great and wonderful thing. Since we stopped, I've gotten about two hundred calls just from out of state of people wanting to go on ghost tours because it was highly promoted, but we wanted to go back to our roots of real investigations." Scott predicts that someday the group will start up the tours once again. Until that time, the members will continue to explore the science of ghost hunting.

Scott admits that his group has been criticized by some Christian groups in the community, but not by all of them. The majority of the members of Halifax Hauntings are Catholic, a fact that could explain why the Catholic Church has not made any negative comments about the group. Members of the local Baptist church, however, have been very vocal in the criticism of the group. "They said we're into witchcraft and all that stuff," Scott said. "We told them we don't use Ouija boards. We don't have séances. We don't do any of that stuff. We are paranormal investigators. We're not witches. We don't dress in black or boil frog's eyes in a black cauldron. We invite anyone who wants to criticize to come with us on an investigation." Actually, a number of people did show up for one of the group's investigations, and the local newspaper reported that they were impressed with the group's professionalism.

Like most investigators, Scott would like to investigate the Myrtles Plantation in St. Francisville, Louisiana, or the Whaley House in San Diego, California. Because of his experiences as a corrections officer, he is also interested in visiting Attica Prison some day: "Prisons are a very negative environment, but thanks to the riots, I think there'd be some interesting things there." Fear of ridicule prevents many prison guards from talking about their experiences, but Scott believes they might open up to him because he is one of them and because he, too, has seen and heard things within prison walls that he can't explain.

Even though Scott has fifty-five reference books in his home library, as well as several years of investigations under his belt, he does not pretend to know everything about his field: "I'm not calling myself an expert on the paranormal because there is no such thing. You can't be an expert on the unknown. So anybody who says they're an expert on the paranormal, that's an oxymoron." His personal mission is to prove not only that there is life after death, but also that paranormal studies is an actual science and not just a hobby.

North Florida Paranormal Research, Inc.

MIDDLEBURG, FLORIDA

Jeff Reynolds

Jeff Reynolds, who has been actively pursuing the paranormal since 1990, received his training at Cassadaga, a spiritualist community founded in 1894 by George P. Colby, a trance medium from Pike, New York. The group has been incorporated since 2001. "I'm not an active member of the Spiritualist Church at Cassadaga, but I used to be," Jeff says. "To drive two hours to go to the Cassadaga church and then come home is not very smart. The spirits can come see me. They know where I live."

Jeff believes Cassadaga is a wonderful place to visit as a spiritual retreat: "If you go there to visit the spirits, you will come back with many riches. If you go down there to visit the people, I'm not so sure because it has become commercialized. The people down there I call close friends are great folks, but there are a lot of other people down there who aren't. There are shopkeepers and hotels down there. Everyone's out to make a buck."

North Florida Paranormal Research, Inc., now has seven members. Jeff believes that by catering to the interests of prospective members, they are more likely to join and stay in the group: "One woman in our group likes to record EVP's, so she walks around these places talking to spirits. Her husband handles cameras." In a perfect world, Jeff would take the advice of a doctor friend of his, who told him, "Jeff, in order to do a true investigation, somebody should go there three hundred and sixty-five days out of a year and log every activity every day." In the real world, though, Jeff's members have day jobs that put bread on the table and a roof over their heads: "I'm a paramedic firefighter. My wife's a vet tech. The other people in our group are employed as well. We do our best."

The group covers the costs of investigations in several ways. When homeowners ask the members to investigate their residence, they are charged eighty-five dollars an hour. The group also sells T-shirts, conducts workshops, and conducts three or four Jacksonville Haunted History Tours a year. The fact that money is coming in does not mean, however, that the group is flush with cash: "We wanted to do an investigation at the Castillo de San Marcos in St. Augustine, but we were told we would have to pay two rangers eighty dollars an hour to be there with us. We don't have the funding for that."

Jeff's views toward the paranormal have been influenced by the time he spent in Cassadaga. He makes a clear distinction between spirits and ghosts: "A spirit is always here. Ghosts are not. Ghosts tend to be more the bothered spirits. They're trying to get attention some way. They're trying to get a message across, or they're trying to redeem themselves. They've got something on their minds. Spirits are just not that way. The spirit is just like us except without the physical body. They are more prevalent than ghosts or entities. Most of the time, I can distinguish between the two."

Jeff also believes that our loved ones are never very far away from us when they pass over: "I think for them to be close and see us—to see our children do wonderful things—that's fantastic. So I think the thought of not actually losing someone is marvelous. So if I detect the spirit of a person, it's not a scary thing, no more than meeting a person for the first time. Most spirits will not cause you a problem. Most of them will be there if you need something or want to talk." He interprets the presence of paranormal activity in a specific location as the attempt of a spirit to communicate with the living or to find something out.

Jeff's view toward orbs is also different from that held by many investigators. While he agrees that not all orbs are ghosts, he has found the presence of orbs in every physical occurrence he has been involved with: "If I see that orbs are beginning to show up when there's no obvious cause—the rooms aren't dirty or there's no air-conditioning vent blowing in front of the camera—or if I can deduce what's causing the orbs, I'll say, 'Hey! Move the camera!' But if I can't find out why, then everybody needs to keep their ears to the ground and keep their eyes open because things can happen. It only takes a split second, and that's why most of the stuff isn't captured on film."

The members of North Florida Paranormal Research feel fortunate to have witnessed some physical activity in places they have certified as being haunted. A good example is the Spanish Military Hospital, which was built on the site of the First Period Spanish Hospital. One day, Jeff received a phone call from Diane, the owner, who invited his group to come in. She told him that a door opens and closes there all by itself and buckets fly across the floor. The next morning Jeff went down there to meet some people who had had a very eerie experience. A lady told Jeff that she and her husband had gone on one of the tours a few days before. Afterward, the couple returned to their hotel and went to bed. The next morning, her husband looked over and asked, "Who's been writing on your back?" She said nobody had. Her husband scrubbed her back but was unable to remove the writing. Finally, he backed her up toward a mirror and took a video camera and photographed the image in the mirror. The couple was shocked to see that the mirror had inverted the writing on her back. "It said, 'Yes,'" Jeff reports. "Well, the lady was walking around the building saying, 'Are there really ghosts in this building?' She was a bit spiritual anyway, and she was looking for some answers, and her answer was, 'Yes.'" Jeff describes the writing as thin black–bluish lines, similar to those found in tattoos.

The next morning, the group arrived at the Spanish Hospital, ready to record or photograph whatever was there. "We took our equipment down there—our cameras, our meters," Jeff said. "We took a lot of pictures or our first preliminary hunt to see if we could come up with anything. We came up with an anomaly I couldn't identify, so we had to go back the next day and re-shoot the same area to see if I could figure out if this stuff was man-made or spirits." While examining the evidence, Jeff found out that the questionable [phenomena] really were man-made: "One was an old pane of glass that has the swirls. The glass isn't really clear. It kind of looked like a face. We try to tell our members not to take pictures of mirrors or glass because it could cause a reflection." Someone had taken a picture and claimed to have captured the image of a face in the glass, so Jeff went downstairs to check it out: "Outside the window, there's a privacy fence. So between the distortion in the glass and the wood grain in the fence, it did look like a face. There was a splatter on the wall that made for a really pretty display of orbs. I said, 'This is not ghost related either.'"

Frustrated by his member's display of unmerited enthusiasm, Jeff set his camera on the counter and declared, "There are no ghosts here!" At that same moment, something happened that proved him wrong. "A garden staff—a shepherd's staff that the staff hangs a candle lantern on outside of the building where they're doing the tours—flew out of a corner and landed at my feet. I'd have to call that my first real encounter. We looked at this and looked at that and got to talking to the people who saw it happen." Jeff was not a witness because his back was turned, but the lady who owns the place and a couple of tour guides did see it happen. Jeff asked them what had happened, and they said, "Jeff, it just stood up from the wall—it was lying against the wall—it stood up straight and catapulted over a couple of boxes and a candle lantern that were sitting in front of it. It didn't slide down the wall. It wasn't knocked down the wall. It stays there all the time. That's where we keep it." Shortly afterward, a member took a picture at the site with some orbs in it, so Jeff is convinced that this was definitely a haunting.

Another historic site that Jeff's group claims to be haunted is the St. Francis Inn. The maids told Jeff that the ghost of a woman had been seen in a room designated as "Lilly's Room."

Unfortunately, Lilly's Room was taken, so the group moved into Room 2A, which is also called "Elizabeth's Suite." After investigating for a few hours, Jeff and one of the other members were getting ready to go out to dinner when a book sitting on a mantle over the fireplace fell on the floor. Jeff says that he heard the book fall from the other room. The other member said that she was standing in front of the fireplace when the book fell to the floor. Jeff walked over to the fireplace and saw the empty slot where the book had been placed. They scratched heads in amazement and went to dinner.

After they returned, one of the members discovered that a series of thirty-two "I's" had been punched into the cell phone. "We tried to re-create that," Jeff said, "but we couldn't get it to punch in that way. It would punch in six or eight or ten. Then it would give an 'Error' message. When we picked up the phone the next morning from the table where it was charging, there were thirty-two '8's' punched in."

At 2:00 A.M., something happened to Jeff that convinced him that the ghost was indeed a female: "The other members had been collecting some interesting evidence in the room for over an hour. I was sitting in a chair when I felt long fingernails touching a 'private' area on my body. I didn't get any EVP's or EMF readings. What I got was the hell out of there!" Jeff was so unsettled by the experience that after the investigation, he went down to Cassadaga and talked to some spiritualist friends of his: "They got my head screwed back straight out there. They said that wasn't a demon. That was just a lady plying her craft."

Jeff's wife, Debra, had an even closer encounter with an entity on an investigation. "This was a case of what I call 'emotional transference,'" Jeff said. "She was walking down a hallway, and she just started crying for no reason in the middle of a group of people. She doesn't normally do this. The same thing had happened to my daughter two years earlier. She was in the same hallway in the same place." Jeff believes that a spirit was sharing its emotions with both of the women.

In 2003, North Florida Paranormal Research investigated one of the most famous haunted houses in the United States—the Myrtles Plantation—with the Discovery Channel. Jeff believes that there is definitely something there, even though they did not wind up with anything conclusive. "You can't do an investigation in three to four hours when someone is following you around with TV cameras," Jeff says. "In my opinion, you haven't thoroughly investigated a place until you've spent at least a year going in there." The strangest piece of evidence the group collected was a couple of EMF spikes while the members were playing cards: "It was as if an electromagnetic field came in to play cards. This isn't enough proof for me, though. I'd love to go back to the Myrtles."

Not every haunted place that the group has certified as being haunted is old. "A common misunderstanding is that a place has to be old to be haunted," Jeff says. "A spirit can be anywhere it feels like it needs to be. If my grandmother thought I needed her for her strength, she would be here. If I don't need her, she's probably somewhere else. Spirits live a life very similar to ours. They've got day-to-day activities just like we do. I believe the Other Side is not that different from what we do here." Jeff cites as an example a private residence the group investigated several years ago. The husband and wife who lived there had built the house from the ground up. "They had things getting in bed with them," Jeff says. "They were getting molested. We went out there one weekend, and I couldn't get more than a couple of orbs. I can't say that nothing was happening just because it wasn't happening to us." Jeff videotaped the gentleman lying in bed saying, "It's on me now." He was a retired schoolteacher in his late fifties. "They were not kooks," Jeff says. "This was very real to them. If it was happening only to him, I could say it was an isolated psychological problem, but it was happening to her, too." The couple eventually sold their house and moved.

Even though North Florida Paranormal Research is definitely benefiting from the field's surge in popularity, he believes that the public's fascination with the subject has also made his job as an investigator more difficult: "When we began down here in St. Augustine, no one had ghosts. All they had was a walking tour. That was in 2001. Now four years later, everyone's got a ghost. I stayed at a couple of bed and breakfasts several years ago, and they didn't have ghosts. Now all of a sudden, they've got ghosts. That makes me a little skeptical." Still, though, this more receptive climate has encouraged some people to speak up. "The more popular this ghost stuff is becoming, we're finding more and more people who have talked to their deceased relatives," Jeff says. "They're more open with it now."

Unfortunately, the group is having difficulty keeping up with the increasing demand for investigations because of rising costs. On more than one occasion, Jeff has told his wife he is spending way too much time and money on investigations: "I could be doing things that are more important to our lives, our family, than running around hunting ghosts. And just about the time I'm ready to 'hang up the camera,' so to speak, something happens that makes me change my mind, and I'll have to go out and find out what's going on." Still, though, Jeff has made a few cutbacks in recent years, such as his Internet radio show: "It was called

'*Ghost Tracker Radio*,' and it was a good show. We had a lot of neat guests on from all over the U.S. We had ghost hunters and researchers and authors. Hans Holzer was on a couple of times." Because the show had no sponsors, the cost of running it became prohibitive: "After a year, I told my partner that I couldn't do it any more. The long-distance phone calls and the electrical bills and the equipment upkeep were killing me. I left the door open. We can come back anytime we want to." The main problem, he says, was that everybody seemed to like the show, but nobody wanted to pay for it. Nevertheless, Jeff does not envision himself getting out of the ghost-hunting business entirely because he has not found out everything he wants to know. "People are always interested in what lies ahead of them. The stuff I've found out in my fifteen years of researching this stuff has made me feel a whole lot better. Still, though, I've found out enough that I could quit anytime and be happy with what I'd found out," Jeff says.

South Florida Ghost Team

MIAMI, FLORIDA

Shaun Jones, Founder and Director
Richard Valdes, Manager

Shaun Jones founded the South Florida Ghost Team in January 2003. The group started out as a gathering of friends who shared an interest in the paranormal and then gradually developed into something much more structured.

The members come from a variety of backgrounds. For example, Shaun Jones is an electrician; Dan Cronin is a health-care adviser; and Tom Palazzo is a firefighter. One of the group's first goals was to dispel the image many people have of paranormal researchers. "We don't go on ghost hunts," insists the cofounder of the group, Dan Cronin. "We go on investigations."

Typically, an investigation begins with a telephone from a homeowner or a business owner regarding some sort of supernatural activity. After researching the history of the location, the group interviews the homeowners or business owners to gather specific information about the nature of the disturbances. The team members pack their bags only if the claims seem credible. Shaun says that when her team embarks on an investigation, their initial goal is to find a logical explanation. "We're looking to disprove what we see," she said.

The South Florida Ghost Team usually spends no more than one or two nights at a single location, recording sounds and taking photographs. Their equipment includes such standard instruments as EMF meters, digital cameras, digital voice recorders, and video cameras. The group also brings along a few unconventional items, such as dowsing rods. The group usually begins by shutting off all the fans and air-conditioning units in the home or business to avoid the possibility that dust particles will show up as orbs in photographs. The members also recite a prayer at the beginning and the end of the investigation.

One of Shaun Jones's most memorable investigations was conducted in May 2003 at the historic Stranahan House in Fort Lauderdale. The Stranahan House was built in 1919 by the trading-post operator Frank Stranahan, who moved to Fort Lauderdale in 1900. Frank married Ivy Cromartie, a schoolteacher, and set up housekeeping in the new town of fifty-two people. After the stock-market crash of 1929, Frank Stranahan's bank failed; he committed suicide by drowning himself in a nearby river. Ivy died in her sleep in the house in 1971. Her father, Augustus Cromartie, died in the same bedroom, which has been converted into a gift shop. Following a tip from one of her team members that the house was haunted, Shaun decided to secure permission from the executive director Barbara Keith to spend the night at the old house. She soon learned from employees at the Stranahan House that rocking chairs tend to rock on their own, doors open and close by themselves, and burglar alarms go off inexplicably.

The overnight investigation began when team member Dan Cronin detected the strong scent of lilac perfume in an upstairs room. Sensing that the spirits were about, he asked them if they had anything to say to another team member, Denise Muhammad, who was holding a voice recorder. When nothing happened, Denise asked the spirits to give them a sign that they were present. Once again, no one heard a thing. Suddenly, team member Stacy Snyder noticed that the dowsing rod she was holding was moving back and forth. Not long afterward, the lilac smell returned. At the same time, Shaun Jones sensed Ivy's presence. "She just brushed right by me," Shaun said. When the group moved downstairs, team member Greg Gawlikowski's EMF detector began beeping, so Shaun asked the spirits some questions of her own: "If it's Ivy Stranahan, tap three times on the glass. If you're Frank's brother, can you tap four times on the glass?" She received no response to her questions, but the group's digital cameras did capture photographs of several glowing orbs.

Richard Valdes, the manager of the group, first became interested in otherworldly phenomena at the age of ten when he began watching television programs dealing with the paranormal. He did not have his first real paranormal experience, however, until he was fifteen: "It involved an out-of-body experience where I experienced my aunt having an epileptic seizure, but I happened to be in her body around the same time it happened. I dreamed I was shorter and I was walking out of my aunt's bedroom, and I all of a sudden blacked out around the doorway. Before I knew it, my mom was knocking on my door, telling me we had to go to my aunt's home because she was having an epileptic seizure. Before I knew it, I ended up waking up five minutes later before my mother had even taken off." After waking up, Richard ran the four blocks to his aunt's house and found her in the same place where he had left her in his dream. Richard, who now works full time as security for a local nightclub, joined Shaun's group in October 2004.

When Richard goes out on an investigation, his primary goal is to capture EVP's, which are credible because many of them are actual responses to questions being asked of whatever entity the investigators are communicating with at the time. Orbs, on the other hand, are much less convincing as evidence of the paranormal. "You have to know how to differentiate between lint, dust, moisture in the air, and genuine orbs," Richard said.

"You have to have a certain light pattern. Dust will go down, not up. When we investigate, we shut off all the fans and air conditioning in a client's home so we can eliminate the possibility of dust being picked up. If it's something that looks like an orb, you have to look at the flight pattern. Usually an orb will go from bottom up, or it will come to the camera and fly away.

It has like a life of its own." He believes that genuine orbs could be manifestations of a spirit, or they could be residual energy left behind by a spirit.

Richard has, in fact, captured something much more impressive than glowing balls on film. In 2003, the South Florida Ghost Team investigated the Arcade Theater at Fort Jackson. The theater was built in 1904. At the time, Shaun Jones and another member were up in the balcony where their equipment had been set up. Richard was walking around the theater seats, asking questions in an attempt to get some EVP's. He did not record any EVP's, but he did take an incredible photograph in the balcony area. "It's a relatively big area. The employees had informed us that there was a spot in the right-hand corner in that one balcony that they called the scary spot. They felt that they were being watched. I didn't take a photograph of that one spot. I photographed the whole spot. When I was looking through the pictures, I worked very closely with one of our sensitives. She told me to start panning in closer to the right-hand side. The closer I got, the more it seemed like something was materializing, and it looked like the face of a young boy. You can see the face, and you can almost see the shoulders forming around the face." Afterward, Richard went through obituaries dating back to 1902 and discovered that the son of the projectionist liked to sit in that one spot, waiting for his father to get off work so that they could walk home together. "The boy was very young when he died," Richard said. "I'm not sure how he passed away. I was excited. It's like catching a big marlin. I've always said that paranormal research is like going fishing. Sometimes you catch something; sometimes you don't. But when you do catch something, you can't contain it. You see that all your work was for something."

77

The most memorable investigation Shaun has ever been on is the Doral investigation. The team consisted of Richard, the case profiler, and two sensitives—Lin, the assistant manager, and Shaun. As soon as they walked in the front door, they began eliminating all possible causes. "Noises could easily be explained away as a tree hitting the roof right down to electrical wiring in the walls that could produce hallucinations," Richard says. "This is why we always run a sweep with sensitives and a sweep with the EMF detectors to see where all the power sources are." The team was called to the house because a young girl was being disturbed in her sleep. She reported that something nudged her in the middle of her sleep and that something growled at her during the night. The group decided to test the girl's story by setting up an experiment. "We sent Cynthia—our case profiler—next to her in the bed," Richard said. "The rest of us were in the maid's room. We set up an infrared night cam in the room with them. She wanted to see if the entity would interact with her. What ended up happening was she started feeling really anxious and didn't want to be in the room anymore. She felt this anxiety come over her. Just as she said, 'I'm going to get up and get out of here now,' all we heard was, 'I'm going to get . . .' and that was it. The power went out in her room and the maid's room, which was right across from hers." Amazingly, the only rooms in the four-bedroom house that experienced the power outage were the girl's bedroom and the maid's room.

To make sure that someone wasn't playing around with the fuse box, the team went to the garage to check it out. What they found really opened their eyes: "It was really hard getting to the power box. We had to remove several heavy pieces of plywood, and there was also a mattress there," Richard said. "We had to remove all those things, and that eliminated the possibility that someone had gone there and shut the power off. When we finally looked, none of the switches were set off." The team deduced that the entity eliminated the power in the girl's room and the maid's room because it did not want the team to record.

With a great deal of effort, the team finally persuaded Cynthia to return to the bedroom, along with a sensitive. Suddenly, the bed began shaking on its own. The sensitive believed that she could feel the bed shaking on its own if she sat on the floor next to it. Every time she felt or heard something, the EMF detector they had left in the room went off simultaneously. The team also caught all of these incidents on videotape. "We got a lot of activity, but unfortunately, we haven't been able to come back," Richard said. "Since then the young lady who was renting out the room in the house moved out and hasn't wanted to come back. That's the one that stands out the most."

Largely as a result of the positive feedback the group has received from its investigations, the South Florida Ghost Team is expanding. "We're trying to set up teams in different parts of Florida," Richard said. "We had a Tampa branch set up, but things didn't really work out, so now we're in the process of setting up another team, and hopefully, in the future, we'll be able to set up other teams in other parts of the state of Florida so we can better help our clients." Shaun Jones adds that even though the group is actively looking for new recruits, they won't take just anyone: "We're looking for somebody who takes this seriously and is open-minded."

Georgia

Blairsville Paranormal Research Team

BLAIRSVILLE, GEORGIA

Joel Goyne and Sean Rice, Directors

The Blairsville Paranormal Research Team is one of the newest—and youngest—paranormal investigating groups in the entire South. It was founded by three high school students—Sean Rice, Joel Goyne, and Matt Prentice. Sean Rice says that he and Matt Prentice became inspired to start their own group after he and Matt started surfing the Internet and found the "Shadowlands" Web site, which lists haunted sites in every state, including Georgia: "Some of the sites around Georgia were pretty close to us, so we started going to them. It was interesting to see if we could find anything. We started our team in September 2004." At the time of the interview, three of the members were in the eleventh grade, one was in the twelfth grade, and the remaining three members were in college. Joel Goyne believes that exploring the Web sites of other paranormal groups helped make them better investigators: "We are really skeptical when it comes to this [field] because we saw stuff on the Internet that can't be real. We didn't want to be a group like that, spreading false information." The group's first order of business was to accumulate the equipment recommended by the Web sites they examined. They now have two EMF detectors, two voice recorders, a night-vision camera, a few digital cameras, and a 35 mm camera.

The directors of the Blairsville Paranormal Research Team claim they learned everything they needed to know about ghost hunting from the "Shadowlands" Web site: "Their Ghost Hunting 101 course tells you what you need and what to do," Joel says. "They also tell about some of their own investigations." The group also learned the importance of praying before all their investigations from the "Shadowlands" Web site: "They said there's no proof that this helps, but it takes five or six seconds to do it, so what's the harm? We pray when we start out. It's not a formal prayer; it's just, 'God, protect us.'" Joel added that even though harmful spirits interfere with investigations only about 5 percent of the time, he and the other members still believe that praying before all investigations is a good idea.

The Blairsville Paranormal Research Team's first investigations were a couple of haunted locations in Fannin County, right across the border from Union County. The Tillybend Church Cemetery was the site of their first investigation: "We investigated outside at the cemetery. What's weird about it is that 70 percent of the people buried there are children one year old or younger. There's a legend that a witch around here caused the kids to die. We didn't collect too much there. We got three pictures of a golden streak above our heads."

The second place they visited was the Chastain House, an abandoned plantation house which has been declared a national historic site. The Chastain House has turned out to be the most productive site—evidence-wise—in the entire county. Sean says that the group decided to investigate the old house on the recommendation of one of the members, who had gone there on his own a few months earlier: "He and a close friend were walking up the stairs, and they saw a light flashing on the inside, and they stopped and ran back to their truck." The members assume that the ghost haunting the house is the spirit of a little girl named Sarah, whose identity they discovered on a tombstone in the cemetery. The group was also attracted to the house by a local legend regarding the death of the child: "Other people say if you walk around back and look in the kitchen window, you see a replay of a past memory of a lady killing a child."

So far, the group has visited the Chastain House three times. The first time the members visited the house, they were impressed with its historic look: "The house is fascinating. The last time it was lived in was the 1950s. The downstairs looks like a normal house with white walls, but when you go upstairs, it's totally different. It looks like a log cabin upstairs." Sean admits that all of the members were scared as they walked into the house because they did not know what to expect: "Matt Prentice went in there first. He set up the camera. After that, he went back into the house to get the camera, and we watched the footage, and right as he walked up the stairs, the camera turned off. We don't know why. We also found a red puddle on the floor. We got a few pictures of it, then we ran out of there."

The second time the group investigated the Chastain House, they gathered even more evidence: "We set up our camera with night vision," Sean said. "We got some orbs, but we're not too sure about some. They are too perfectly circular to be orbs. But others have a white fog behind them. Some have the fog, and some don't. It's hard to distinguish which are orbs and which are not." Joel, who did not accompany the group on their first investigation of the Chastain House, says that he was filled with a feeling of dread from the moment he stepped foot into the structure: "It was just the possibility that something might be there with you. When it first happens, it's just a creepy feeling."

The group's third visit to the Chastain House was by far the most successful. Joel Goyne said that after the equipment was distributed, each member went into a different room. "We sat in the dark by ourselves, and I was assigned to the room of Sarah Chastain. I had my eyes closed, and my head was looking down. That's the time we got an EVP when I was in Sarah's room. Every time we've gotten EVP's—we've only gotten two—it's been in Sarah's room. It's like a beep or some type of thud on the microphone, and then you hear a muttering or a whispering sound. Whether it says 'Sarah,' we're not exactly sure. To us, it sounds like 'Sarah' because we're thinking of her." After the investigation, Joel let his parents hear the tape: "They don't think it says 'Sarah,' but they admit that there's a muttering or a whispering sound there. For my parents to believe anything that we show them is an accomplishment in itself." Sean's impression of the EVP was that it was a beep, then a deep vocal or breathing sound, then another beep.

Even though Sean is glad that the group collected some EVP's on that investigation, he prefers to photograph orbs. "EVP's are too hard to decipher," Sean said.

So far the group has limited their investigations to the Tillybend Church Cemetery and the Chastain House: "We've been to the Chastain House maybe five times and to Tillybend maybe four times," Sean said. Of the seven investigations that the group has conducted so far, Sean estimates that 30 percent have revealed haunting activity.

Neither Sean nor Joel would have been able to pursue their hobby if their parents had not been so understanding. Even though Joel's parents are concerned about how the police would react if they found him and his friends in these old buildings at night, they still allow him to go: "I grew up in a Christian home, and they don't want me messing with evil spirits and that sort of thing, but that's not what we're out there to do. I think they know me and my friends well enough that they know we wouldn't do anything like that. Still, they are afraid that something might happen beyond our control." Joel believes that bringing back evidence in the form of film and sound recordings has convinced his parents that he and his group are not doing anything bad out there. Sean's parents seem to share his enthusiasm for ghost hunting: "My parents don't think it's bad. They think it's neat, too."

According to Joel, the Blairsville Paranormal Research Team has no plans to investigate any private residence until they have had more experience: "We really don't have the authority to go into someone's house and tell them it's haunted. We don't have professional training. We do this as a hobby. We don't want to pretend like we know what we're doing. If we did investigate somebody's house, we could share with them what we find, but I'd tell them that it's not definite because we're not professionals." Joel is certain that going on more investigations and finding more evidence will make them more confident.

Because the group does not feel qualified to investigate private residences, Joel says the members' main goal for now is to hone their skills and to answer as many metaphysical questions as they can: "I'm out there to prove that something is being haunted or being inhabited by some force or something. That's my main goal. I think all of us in the group have the same aspirations." Joel admits, though, that the thrill of being in the presence of the paranormal also has its allure: "Yes, there is a rush when you think there's something there. Just the whole idea of spirits being around us is something I've never been able to comprehend. It's the interest and the curiosity."

Foundation for Paranormal Research

LOGANVILLE, GEORGIA

Rick Heflin, Founder

O ne of Rick Heflin's sharpest memories of growing up in south Mississippi was the alleged abduction of two fishermen, Charles Hickson and Calvin Parker, who claimed to have been abducted from a wooden pier on October 11, 1973. His burgeoning interest in the paranormal culminated in the founding of his group in 2001.

The Foundation for Paranormal Research now has twenty members, including doctors, lawyers, and housewives. Rick is in charge of receiving in a warehouse. "The people I work with think it's great," Rick says. The membership also includes a member of the clergy, whom the group could use as an exorcist if the need arose.

Like many directors, Rick trains his members in cemeteries: "Most cemeteries are public places, so we have no trouble getting in them at night. We have a couple of cemeteries that we use as training grounds. We have one in particular that was the site of a Civil War battle. There was also a plane crash there in the 1960s. We use that to train our investigators. We get a lot of evidence every time." The members prefer to investigate cemeteries at night because they seem to get more results.

The group conducts two different types of investigations: private and public. "Private is like a private home," Rick says. "The homeowners limit the number of investigators we can bring. At some public sites, like battlefields, we can bring lots of investigators. We do mostly private investigations." Most of the members bring along digital cameras on investigations. "From a financial point of view, it is cheaper to download photographs on a computer than to have hundreds of photographs developed in a lab," Rick says. "I prefer 35 mm because then you have a negative that can be examined. When we go on an investigation, we might take two to three hundred pictures, and that gets really expensive after a while."

Rick estimates that only 10 percent of the group's investigations produce genuine hauntings. He credits this low estimate to the members' skepticism. The members always begin an investigation by looking for the physical cause of the manifestation. "We aren't looking for something paranormal," Rick says. "We want to know the truth. We want to know what's really going on. If we find a rational or scientific explanation, we aren't disappointed because we found the truth." Rick cites as an example a case where a knocking sound is caused by faulty plumbing. For some reason, when most people are told that their disturbance has a rational explanation, they become angry and disappointed. "It's human nature to want to believe in something larger than ourselves," Rick says. "Most people want to have a ghost in their house."

Rick sets down ground rules for members before going to a private residence. For example, he cautions his members against telling the homeowners anything during an investigation. "Afterwards, we return to the homeowners with a final report," Rick says. "The worst thing a field investigator can say is, 'Oh, my god! Your place is haunted!' What we try to do is gather scientific evidence. Then after the investigation, we meet and come to a conclusion. Seventy-five percent of the time, the conclusion is, 'You've got squirrels in your attic.'" A good example is a home the team investigated in Walton County. The mother and daughter were convinced that their barn was haunted because they heard these scratching and thumping sounds and thumping. "We were standing there talking," Rick said, "and all of a sudden, there was a bump in the back of the barn. The mother said, 'Oh, my god! Did you hear that?' It just escalated from zero to one hundred percent panic in thirty seconds. They were feeding off each other. The first question we asked was, 'Are there rats or vermin in your barn?' They said, 'None.' After these two ran screaming from the barn, we sat down, turned on our night-vision scopes, and sat there for fifteen minutes until we saw these great, huge rats walking along the rafters on the top of the barn. They were as big as Chihuahuas!" When the group told the women that their "ghosts" were actually rats, they became angry. Rick says that the women had ignored the other possible causes of the noises, such as a horse brushing against the door or a cow flicking its tail against the wall.

Although Rick expects his investigators to follow the rules, he is careful never to lose his temper during an investigation: "I never yell at my members. These people are volunteers. They are paying their expenses out of their pocket. They're absolutely not employees and can't be treated that way because if they are, they'll walk off. There are six other paranormal groups in the city of Atlanta they can go to."

For many groups, EVP's are considered to be much more significant than orbs. This is certainly not the case with the Foundation for Paranormal Research. "We don't put more stock in EVP's than in orbs because we don't know what either is," Rick says. "We don't know what an orb or EVP is or where it's coming from. We sit around for hours arguing with each other about orbs and EVP's, and that's part of the fun. We have a consultant to our board of directors who is a physicist. He is absolutely convinced that as far as orbs are concerned, we have discovered a new form of life." Using a photograph that Rick took at a cemetery showing a moving orb, the physicist used the distance from a known object and figured out how fast this object was moving. "It was moving about fourteen hundred feet per second," Rick said. "Now nothing in nature can move that fast, and [the physicist] is positively convinced that we had discovered a new form of life. It's the questions that drive us. That's why we spend our time creeping around cemeteries in the middle of the night."

The group's visit to the Springer Opera House in Columbus, Georgia, is the most memorable of our investigations. The Springer Opera House is supposed to be haunted by the ghost of Edwin Booth, who played the role of Hamlet in 1876. Rick was impressed by the fact that, unlike some historic sites, the Springer Opera House has not tried to capitalize on its reputation: "There have been several books written about it, but not by management. They don't feel that it's detrimental to their business." In 2003, the group was invited to do a twenty-four-hour televised investigation at the Springer Opera House. "WTVM in Columbus had a crew with us," Rick said. "The crew followed us around and did updates at five o'clock, six o'clock, and ten o'clock and six A.M. Our only condition was that we be allowed to run the show. The TV cameras were not obtrusive. They probably filmed twenty hours. They edited out all the boring stuff." We really did a good job that night. We got EVP's, we got orbs, we got a picture of a seat in the audience in the Springer that was glowing like it was on fire." Afterward, the group received a large number of e-mails from residents of Columbus thanking them for doing such a good job at the Springer. Unlike some of the local media, which has depicted Rick's group as a bunch of "goobers" or "weirdos," WTVM portrayed the group as a collection of serious-minded professionals. Rick's only complaint was that the television crew interviewed all of the members of his group, but his interview was the only one that aired. "This was the first time I'd ever done that," Rick said. "I really wasn't very comfortable being on television."

Most investigators admit to having been frightened at least once while investigating. Rick's most terrifying moment occurred during a visit to a cemetery at Walton County, Georgia, with a large group. The members had used the cemetery as a training area in the past. On this particular investigation, they had photographed some orbs, but nothing really special. All of a sudden, the monotony was dispelled by a strange sound. "One time, it was on one side of the cemetery," Rick said. "The next time, it was on the other. We kept discussing it with each other. Was it an animal? Was it a bird? What in the hell was this noise? We never could decide. Later on, we took a wildlife biologist out there, and she couldn't identify it, either." Late that night, most of the group had left, leaving only Rick, another male, and a female. "We were just about ready to leave," Rick said. "We were standing there, and I was looking off at the parking lot, and right at the edge of the trees, I saw these two red eyes. This was pitch-black dark. I looked at the guy and said, 'Patrick, what do you see down there?' He said he saw red eyes. I turned to the girl, Sherry, and she said, 'I see a silhouette.' I said, 'Silhouette of what?' So I walked about halfway across this open area and stopped, and these eyes started moving toward me, these bright, shining, red points. That's when I pulled my firearm. I leveled off, and I said, 'If you come any closer, I'll let you have it.' I was O.K. with that until the eyes blinked, and it kind of creeped me out. Then all of a sudden, the sound we had been hearing all night occurred right there in front of me fifteen degrees, thirty degrees, forty-five degrees. All of a sudden, I realized that this thing was running through thick brush and woods at better than running pace and not making a sound." As Rick headed for the parking lot holding his firearm over his head, Patrick asked Rick what had happened. Rick explained that something was trying to get behind them. Patrick then asked a very pointed question: "If that is something paranormal, what are you going to do with that gun?" Rick looked back at him and said, "You know what? We need to go!" All three investigators jumped in their cars and didn't stop until they were in a church parking lot ten miles away.

Rick explained that he normally goes armed to outdoor investigations because five years ago in Dallas, Texas, a group was attacked by some teenagers during an investigation. All of their equipment was stolen. Some of the cemeteries in Atlanta are in gang territory, and the members have been advised by the police not to go to these places at night alone unarmed. "I have a permit to carry a concealed weapon and all our members who go armed have permits. We're all legal," Rick said.

Like some other groups located in the Bible Belt, the Foundation for Paranormal Research has come into direct opposition with religious groups in the community. "There was one investigation we were set up to do in a specific town here in Georgia," Rick says. "We were invited by the mayor to do the investigation. We were all set and ready to go, and the mayor called us back and said, 'You know what? One of our local Baptist churches found out about the investigation, and they are going to picket, and it is going to be really unpleasant, so please don't come.'" So we canceled the investigation because one of the local churches thought we were intruding.

Rick Heflin believes that the importance his members place on collecting scientific evidence distinguishes his group from all the others in Atlanta: "We have physicists, electrical engineers, and exorcists that we consult with on a regular basis. What we are trying to do is put together repeatable results. That's really, really difficult because unless you can find a haunted laboratory somewhere, you can't repeat these results in a laboratory." Because the investigators are very slow and deliberate in the way they collect evidence, Rick believes that the average person would find one of his group's investigations to be very boring: "It's about the love of the unknown and being out there, looking for the truth. It's not about excitement and flashing lights and moving chairs and all that. It's an expensive hobby." When asked by a reporter from Boston why he wastes his money chasing ghosts, Rick asked, "Have you priced a bag of golf clubs lately or a new Bass Tracker? Yes, it's an expensive hobby, but all hobbies are expensive."

The Georgia Ghost Society

MACON, GEORGIA

Robert M. Hunnicutt, Founder and Director

Robert M. Hunnicutt's interest in the paranormal began in 1975. At the time, he had just graduated high school in Tuscon, Arizona, and had gotten a part in a bicentennial play as an extra: "One of the theaters that we were having rehearsals at in Tuscon naturally had an old history about it. It was the Pima Community Theater. There was supposed to be the ghost of an old wardrobe employee there. One evening around ten o'clock or so after dress rehearsal, I went into the wardrobe room and turned in my costume to the lady sitting there, and when I turned around, she was gone. Everyone had a big thrill telling me that she was a ghost. I was just seventeen, so I was scared to death. At the same time, it was such a thrill and adrenaline rush that I couldn't wait to get my hands on as much information as possible. Within a three-year period, Robert read every book in the library and the local bookstore on ghosts.

Robert established the Georgia Ghost Society in 2002. It is an offshoot of another group called the Georgia Paranormal Research Team. The group currently has six charter members and four associate members. Robert says, "They're full members, but they don't always participate in investigations. They'll work in a backup capacity if we need an extra pair of hands or if we need someone to learn how to use a particular type of equipment." He recruits members by posting ads on ghost-related message boards and Web sites. The associate director, Drew Hefter, is in charge of the interview process. Kimber McDermott, the group's research director, checks out historical information on the sites. Joanne Miller is a psychic who has also worked with several police agencies throughout the United States. Julie Dye is the group's main interviewer. When Robert Hunnicutt is not working for Bell South advertising and publishing, he serves as the director of the group. He cross-trains his members so that one member can substitute for someone else if that person cannot participate in the investigation.

Aside from directing the Georgia Ghost Society, Robert also works extensively with Andrew Calder, director of the Georgia Paranormal Research Team: "I am the assistant director of the Georgia Paranormal Research Team. Andrew Calder is an Anglican priest. He's the real deal. He specializes in intervention and assistance. I have volunteered on numerous occasions to go with him, but we try to keep our areas separate, and I guess he does that to look after my well-being. He has described some of the activities that have gone on during some of those rituals. I would not say that all of Andrew Calder's rituals are exorcisms. I'm sure he has performed those. I'm sure his rituals are Christian in nature, but I have never heard him come right out and call them exorcisms. He has taught me so much in the last six to eight years." Robert claims that he would probably have never started his own group if it had not been for Andrew Calder.

Some members of the Georgia Ghost Society suspect that some of the entities they have encountered might be a sort of malevolent force. Robert has found church leaders to be much more receptive of the existence of devils than they used to be: "I come from a Catholic background, and I can remember when reforms changed our view of hell. The reformers said that hell was not a physical place. They used hell as a metaphor. Now they are going back to the original thinking that there is evil, there is a Satan, and there is a hell. For so long, the Catholic Church was trying to change their image. Now, hopefully, they are worried less about their image and more about what they are trying to accomplish." Robert credits the Catholicism's reinstatement of exorcism to the conservative factions within the church.

Robert has purchased 80 percent of the group's equipment: "I'm glad to do that because that way, I have control of it and can make sure it's taken care of and maintained properly." The majority of the group's video equipment is analog and digital recorders and Sony Nite Shot camcorders. The group also has Panasonic closed-circuit video cameras, all of which are infrared capable with infrared projectors so they can be shot in total darkness. Although the group uses digital cameras, Andrew prefers 35 mm35 mm cameras: "Digital photography, in my opinion, is still in its infancy. And even though they now have ten-mega-pixel cameras, there is still too much danger of the evidence being doctored or misrepresented, so I use them more or less as a tool when I go in to just get a layout of the property or a home, but 80 percent of the photographs are going to be film." Because none of the group's equipment was designed to hunt ghosts or to prove that ghosts exist, the investigators prefer to have verification through more than one source of equipment.

Robert knows from experience that buying the latest high-tech equipment is no guarantee that a group will begin collecting astounding evidence: "If you're dealing with something of a sentient level, if it doesn't want you to know it's there, it's not going to broadcast itself for everyone to see and hear. So a lot of times, a group will go to a location one time for a few hours and base their outcome on that. This is wrong. Sometimes, you will have to go back six or a dozen times to see what's really going on. You've got to take into account the client's schedule or the team's schedule, but I prefer to spend at least a day there. If possible, we would do it repeatedly." Robert believes that his credibility as an investigator is enhanced if he gets the same results over and over again.

Robert estimates that 80 percent of their investigations are conducted at private residences: "A lot of our clients are people who are experiencing activity in their homes in one way or another. I'm not going to turn my back on them. I did not want to drive myself into one particular role, so we have more or less continued on with that. We've handled everything from little Ma- and Pa-type ghosts that were very benign up to the really bad and malevolent cases." The group never charges homeowners for an investigation, but Robert has asked for expenses if the members have to travel out-of-state: "We have accepted donations, but we never solicit them." The group tries to schedule their investigation around the time when most of the activity occurs. He has found that most paranormal activity in private residences occurs at 8:00 or 9:00 P.M. From 75 and 80 percent of the group's investigations at private residences have revealed genuine hauntings.

The very first case that Robert ever worked on-site was a family who had twin daughters. The children were so afraid that one of the little girls was cutting paper crucifixes and plastering them all over the house. "I'm a father myself," Robert said, "and I naturally assumed this would work because the child was so frightened, and I didn't like the fact that there wasn't something the family could do right away to remedy it. That's probably the main reason I got into those types of hauntings."

On one of the investigations the group did at a private residence in 2004, the Georgia Ghost Society encountered a violent entity: "A family described a situation where they were being physically touched, the wife in particular, almost to the point of its being of a sexual type nature. On the investigation while I was taking some photographs, I was grabbed in the groin. I've done this long enough so that when something happens, I try not to react in front of the family. I more or less stood up and left the room to get my composure." Even though Robert has been investigating for fifteen years, he admits that he still gets frightened occasionally, especially when he makes personal contact with the spirits he is researching.

In 2003, Robert worked a small case in South Carolina with a young family who had a child who was interacting with a ghost, although the parents were not aware of this until the Georgia Ghost Society arrived. They were afraid that their little girl would fall off the deck or balcony while playing with her invisible friend and drown in the pond below. "It turned out that it was the spirit of the gentleman who had lived there previously and had died," Robert said. "He had come from a big family and was used to big family get-togethers. Once the parents found out what they were dealing with, they were able to lead a normal life." Even though this particular case would never be turned into a novel or a movie of the week, it gave the members the satisfaction of knowing that this family would be able to continue with their lives in a normal way because of information the society was able to give.

The most haunted place Robert has investigated is a private residence outside of Atlanta in 2000. The house was so actively haunted that the teenage children moved out. No one in the family would sleep upstairs. During the night, the investigators heard knocking on the walls. They also captured the most convincing video evidence Robert has ever witnessed: "When we were using the video, we had someone at each camera either viewing our monitor or looking at the view screen, and you could actually see basketball-size globules literally fly past the camera. Then when we viewed the video the next day, you could actually see someone looking down from the upstairs banister. At that time, there was no one upstairs." The group also captured a full-body apparition on film. What is more important to Robert, though, is giving the family peace of mind: "Once you have seen a family who are too afraid to sleep in their own house, you begin to realize that this is more than just video and photography and a little audio. Someone's life that has been ripped apart by something they don't really understand. When I first started, it was more or less curiosity. I wanted to see if paranormal events really happened. But when you start seeing people who are genuinely frightened in their homes, that's pretty sobering because the home is supposed to be a place of refuge and safety."

Not everyone is pleased when the Georgia Ghost Society finds no evidence of haunting activity. Some of these people are trying to capitalize on their "ghosts." Robert has been investigating long enough that the tone of a person's voice over the phone sometimes raises a red flag. When this happens, he checks with his friends in other groups in Georgia to see if they have been approached by this person. One such individual was a man who was hoping to have his house featured in a book or a movie.

"He'd contacted every newspaper—large and small—in Atlanta," Robert said. "The man said, 'I wonder if I can get a book deal out of this.' You still have to go in without any preconceived notions that that's his goal. I'm not going to think bad of anyone who thinks they might be able to make a living, but if their only goal is to drum something up, then I don't have any interest in helping them." The majority of the phenomena the group found in this guy's house were atmospheric and environmental. After Robert told the man that electromagnetic energy produced by nearby power lines was probably responsible for the activity in his home, he still contacted other groups to see if they would investigate his house.

The Georgia Ghost Society also investigates historic sites: "If a historical location invites us to come in and do an investigation, we are glad to share any photographs with them, and we give them a certificate stating that an investigation was conducted at such and such a date. As far as coming out and verifying that a location was haunted, no one can do that." However, the group has not investigated very many historic sites, primarily because of the stigma attached to having a haunted reputation: "The problem is that Macon is in the Bible Belt, and some historic sites will not publicize that they are haunted," Robert says. "The strange thing is that they have a big cherry blossom festival here, and several years ago, they started having ghost tours. The tour guides will go down the street by these particular locations and tell the stories that are associated with them, but none of these locations will let you come in. I have tried for years to build a rapport with some of these historical sites down on Georgia Avenue. A couple of them have let me come in once or twice but would not let me publicize any of the findings from fear of people wanting to come in and hear about the ghosts and not the history associated with the homes." Because so many of Macon's historically haunted houses are off-limits to investigators, they go to battlefields around Macon and Kennesaw, Georgia, to train their new members. Unfortunately, visitors are not allowed to stay in the parks after dark.

The most haunted historic site the group has ever visited was not in Georgia at all. "We were invited by a local news station to investigate an old hotel in Memphis. It was beautiful. It had carved wood columns inside. It was immaculate. They had a room where people who stayed there during the night requested another room because of the activity. A prostitute had either been murdered or [had] committed suicide in the room." The investigators set up their equipment across the hall in another room. Robert was sitting in the haunted room by himself when he was overcome with an eerie feeling: "It's one of the few times I have ever felt uncomfortable. It was the first time I realized that I'm in this room by myself. The lights are turned off, and the only thing I've got close to anyone being here is a camera with somebody watching me twenty feet away." Despite Robert's momentary reservations about being in a haunted room all alone, he still rates this investigation as one of his most enjoyable. The only real problem was the constant stream of people walking down the hallway. Nevertheless, the investigators went away with photographs of mist and moving orbs.

Attracting media attention to Georgia's haunted places has always been Robert's dream: "One of the employees of the local TV stations a few years ago talked about doing what the other states have done, either a continuing piece or a periodic piece. I'd love to do a program about Georgia ghosts or hauntings. This state has such a rich history. It goes back to the Revolutionary

War—Savannah, Kennesaw, Andersonville. This state has so much ghostlore associated with it." Unfortunately, television programs like the Sci-Fi Channel's *Ghosthunters* have not always portrayed paranormal investigators in a favorable light: "A lot of television programs that have been on the past couple of years or so have really damaged the credibility of the field. People naturally assume that every team or group will behave in the same way. When we go in, we have a set dress code. We have standards of behavior. We try to behave and perform just as if we were a professional group going in."

Most of the places Robert would like to visit are in Georgia, such as the Springer Opera House in Columbus. He would also like to visit two sites in Macon that have not received much attention: "There's a local place that's a florist's shop now, but when I was a child, it was a pharmacy. The story goes that the pharmacist accidentally mixed the wrong prescription, and now the building is haunted by his spirit. There's another place here in Macon that used to be a restaurant. I believe it's an office building now. It was built in 1860. A young lady threw herself out of an upstairs window because her lover or husband was killed during the Civil War. The story goes that where she had fallen, there was a stain, and no matter how much they had washed it, it always bled through. The bad thing was that once I got in the field and tried to check it out, it was pretty much unavailable."

Robert Hunnicutt and his fellow investigators readily admit that their goal is to collect as much evidence as they can when they visit a private residence. Robert never forgets, though, that the same phenomena that he views as evidence is something that the people living in the home have to deal with every day. Keeping this fact in mind, Robert tells his new members that their most important mission is to bring relief or, at the very least, answers to their clients. Therefore, investigating the paranormal is more than just a hobby or a pleasant diversion for Robert Hunnicutt: "This is something that is very dear to my heart and something that I take very seriously. I'd have to say in all honesty, though, that if there were any way I could do this and earn a living and provide for my family, I would switch in a moment."

Georgia Paranormal Research Team

DUBLIN, GEORGIA

Andrew Calder, Founder and Director

Andrew Calder has been interested in the paranormal since childhood, but he did not really develop this interest until he became an adult: "I first got started into paranormal investigations with a friend of mine out in Texas whom I had known for a number of years, but little did I know, she had been suffering from some paranormal phenomenon for a number of years. Through my contact with her and trying to find help for her, I came into contact with a lot of people in the field and was eventually asked to start a chapter." Andrew founded his present group in 1998. He likes to keep his group small—between three to six people—because of the headaches involved in dealing with a large group.

The members of Georgia Paranormal Research Team come from fields such as law enforcement, sales and marketing, human resources, telecommunications, and engineering. Andrew's job is in sales and marketing. He is also an ordained minister. Recruiting members has never been a problem: "They contact me and ask how they can become a paranormal investigator. About 98 percent of the people who reach me come into contact with me through our Web site and our Internet presence."

Georgia Paranormal Research Team does not have to actively search for places to investigate, either. "We don't have to promote our group. Sometimes, we have more cases than we can handle," Andrew says. The group does not work very many historical haunts because they receive enough calls from private residences to keep them busy." For this reason, Andrew does not refer to his group as a collection of ghost hunters: "People who call themselves ghost hunters go out seeking it in historical sites or cemeteries. We have more than enough to do without going out and finding something." The demand for their services is so high that his members conduct investigations 365 days a year.

Financing investigations is a problem that Andrew has never totally solved: "A lot of people think if you call yourself a research team, you're federally funded. That's not the case. You're going to find out that every group is paying for their own equipment out of their own pockets or somebody else's pockets." The cost of the equipment the members have purchased, ranging from still and video cameras to Geiger counters and EMF detectors, amounts to thousands of dollars. He is amused by e-mails he receives from people asking how they can get a job as a paranormal investigator: "I tell them they can't. Go starve to death! Some of the people who do it full time have got someone else who supports them, like a husband or wife." Because of his day jobs, Andrew has to do his investigating after hours.

The Georgia Paranormal Research Team uses both 35 mm 35 mm and digital cameras because if an investigator gets similar results with both types of cameras, he or she can say more affirmatively that it is a positive reading. Andrew has found that using different models or brands can also lend more credibility to the photographs. Although digital cameras offer instantaneous results without film processing, they are prone to what Andrew calls "false phenomena": "For example, I took a picture of my partner standing still. The digital camera's aperture or shutter is slower than a 35 mm's. I had him step sideways whenever I clicked the camera. There's a picture of him, and there's a ghost image standing next to him because of the shutter speed. With digitals with less than 5.0 megs, you will get false images if you don't hold the camera completely still. If you snap a digital camera with one hand, just the motion of pushing the button can cause light streaks or light rods that's coming from a light source. With 35 mm 35 mm, you don't get that. The best digital has five or six million pixels. The best 35 mm 35 mm has fifty million pixels. That's why I say use both."

The Georgia Paranormal Research Team specializes in malevolent or "negative" haunting cases. Andrew's group tends to act as the "middle man" to help people in these situations: "Unfortunately, it's not like a magician comes over and waves a white wand over people. You've got to incorporate clergy, pastors, and priests to help eradicate this stuff, especially when people are involved in the occult. It depends on where the people are at and what clergy are available. Sometimes you've got to go through a lot to get any clergy involved because a lot of them don't believe in malevolence or the demonic, which I see as hypocritical. Sometimes, I can easily do it because I might have networks of people I know in that area that I can refer to. But then again, it can be extremely difficult to get help for some families. That's one of the main reasons I became an ordained priest myself. I work with all denominations." The Georgia Paranormal Research Team receives more criticism than many other groups because they deal with malevolent forces.

Because the group deals mostly with malevolent hauntings, the members usually do not try to communicate with spirits: "Any type of communication where you're asking them to show or reveal themselves is opening up a doorway giving them permission to be there. A lot of people do things like divination, pendulums, dowsing, these types [of] things. If any of these things aren't used correctly, they can be a potential hazard out there." He cites as an example the movie *White Noise* (2005), in which the investigator tries to communicate with his dead wife but ends up contacting a demonic entity.

Andrew predicts that as a result of the film's popularity, EVP's will become the Ouija board of the 2000s, even though they are not 100 percent reliable: "A lot of people on TV say, 'This is what it says,' but if you didn't have the caption down at the bottom of the screen, you wouldn't know what the heck it was saying. If you had twenty people listen to an EVP without a caption, you'd get twenty different kinds of interpretations." Although the Georgia Paranormal Research Team has recorded a number of knocking, popping, and rattling sounds, the members have not captured very many EVP's. "Some people seem to be more adept at capturing audio, and some are better at capturing pictures of things," Andrew says. "We've never really proven whether that pertains to any psychic ability on the part of the investigators, but some seem to be more adept at using certain types of equipment than others."

A high percentage of the group's investigations—from 40 to 50 percent—reveal genuine hauntings. Some of the entities the group has encountered seem to be determined to torment the investigators. During one of the group's investigation at a private residence, Andrew was walking through the dark with an infrared camera, just making a sweep, walking along, when something came up behind him making a "Huhhhhhhh" sound. Initially, he thought somebody was playing a trick on him, so he continued along, and all of a sudden, it happened again out of the blue. This time, the heavy breathing raised the hairs on the back of his neck. A short time later one of the investigators came upstairs, and Andrew asked him, "Are you breathing heavy or something?" and he said, "No, I hear it, too." Having validation from his colleague proved to Andrew that his imagination was not "working overtime."

Other investigators have also been terrified by strange sounds from undetermined sources. At one private residence, a female investigator and her husband were upstairs monitoring the bedroom and the hallway. They were sitting in the dark. All at once, the woman ran down the stairs, white-faced, rambling on about hearing something talking in the walls. On a different investigation, one of the male members was taking pictures outside of a two-story home. Andrew was in an upstairs bedroom setting up a video camera in a window overlooking the front yard. After setting up the camera, Andrew went downstairs, where he met the other investigator, who said he was photographing the outside of the house when he heard something knocking on the window— "BAM!! BAM!" Andrew said, "He thought it was me until he saw me come down the foot of the stairs looking out the front door. He said that really kind of freaked him. It gave him the willies."

For Andrew Calder, investigating is more of a mission than a hobby: "I have devoted years to trying to help people. A lot of them are suffering from some pretty horrific types of phenomena." He disparages those groups whose only goal is to collect orbs or EVP's that they can post as trophies on Web sites. Andrew views evidence as a way of giving his clients peace of mind: "I am not disappointed when I find an alternate or scientific explanation for the phenomenon. It's just part of the evidence-collecting process. If we tell our clients the knocking of their house is coming from the heating pipes, it kind of takes the fear factor away from them as well. Our main goal is to help people."

Ghost Hounds Paranormal Network

ATLANTA, GEORGIA

Patrick Burns, Founder and Director

Patrick Burns passed through most of his adolescence believing that ghosts did not exist: "Of course, back then, Mom and Dad always told me there's no such thing as ghosts. They're just the subject of scary stories. Then I took note one day in a bookstore that there were books on haunted houses and ghosts in the nonfiction section, and I thought that was a very curious place to find phenomena that supposedly didn't exist." Patrick found the supposedly true ghost stories to be especially fascinating because, like the old saying goes, "Truth is stranger than fiction."

Until Patrick was thirteen years old, he did not really want to see a ghost: "I thought I'd leave that to someone else." Then one day, his mother told him a story about the house in Illinois where he had lived in for the first five years of his life: "We lived in the house right next door to my grandmother's home. My grandmother passed away about the time I was three or four years old. I really don't remember her very well. My dad's father succumbed to cancer about two years later. After they had both passed on, my parents sold their house, and we moved about forty-five minutes away out to the Chicago suburbs. She told me that one day, the couple who lived down the street from us about two doors down—their names were Mr. and Mrs. Darlington—wound up buying my parents' house from us when we moved, and they sold their house and just moved three doors down to my grandparents' house. My mother said Mrs. Darlington called her one morning and said, 'I really don't know how to explain this to you, but I was standing in the kitchen fixing breakfast. I turned around and looked through the door leading outside, and your mother was standing there watching me. And I saw her for a number of seconds, and she just sort of faded away.' She described what she was wearing as a purple housecoat, and that's what floored my mother because my grandmother did in fact own a purple housecoat. That was her favorite thing to wear around the house, but she never would have worn it outside, and my grandmother and Mrs. Darlington were not really the best of friends. There was no bad blood. I think my grandmother never cared for her as a person, so Mrs. Darlington would have never seen my grandmother wearing that. It's just something that she wore around the house herself, and that's what really floored my mom. I don't know if anything else happened in that house. Unfortunately, Mrs. Darlington died about ten years ago. I would be intrigued one day to knock on the door of the people who own the house now to see if anything unusual has been going on there now as an interesting follow-up." At the time, Patrick was reading every book on the paranormal he could find. Finding out that his own grandmother was seen as a ghost made a topic that he had relegated to the world of books much more relevant to his own life.

Over the next few years, Patrick began noticing things in the world that weren't supposed to be. When he was eighteen or nineteen years old, he started having experiences. He insists, however, that he is not one of these people who say, "I'm sensitive. I see ghosts all the time. There's one standing right next to you." In fact, he is more likely to be skeptical when conducting an investigation: "When I see or hear something strange, I am likely to wonder if my mind is playing tricks on me. If you plant a seed in the subconscious, it will take and run with it. If you are open, your subconscious can play tricks on you. I am certainly not one to dismiss that as a possibility. I tend to believe my equipment when I am doing an investigation more than my own eyes. The equipment is very objective. It's not going into a location expecting to find ghosts."

When Patrick was in his twenties, his interest in metaphysical subjects was deepened by the death of a loved one: "When my brother died, this was the first real family member of mine who has passed on. Both of my grandparents died before I was born. So it was a shock to me and a shock obviously to my entire family. I really became interested in metaphysical subjects and ghosts after Billy passed. I wanted to find some reassurance that Billy was in some place else and in a good place. I wasn't ready to see him or experience him." Following Billy's death, Patrick began reading up on out-of-body experiences. Some of the books he read included exercises for putting a person in a self-hypnotic state to enter the state of outer body experiences (OVP): "That would be cool. That would be the closest way to experience the spiritual realm without being dead yourself." Patrick practiced these exercises for a while but eventually gave up because he was not making any progress: "There was a part of me in the back of my mind that says, 'What if I can't make it back?' " He resigned himself to thinking that if he ever has an out-of-body experience, it will happen on its own.

In 1989, all of Patrick's reading and exercises finally paid off while he was living with his roommate, Louis. He had stayed up late playing his guitar and fallen asleep on the sofa. When he awoke, he could hear voices coming from the kitchen area of the apartment. Assuming that his roommate and a friend were sitting around drinking beer and talking, he tried unsuccessfully to fall asleep: "I couldn't for the life of me tell you what they were talking about. It was something completely trivial. It could have been sports. It could have been fishing. Just a couple of guys sitting there talking with each other. After this went on for some time, I recognized the voices. One of my voices was my brother Billy. The other voice was my uncle Bill, who had just passed away from cancer a couple of months before. I got very nervous and very scared. I closed my eyes as tight as I could. The only way I could describe it is that the conversation finally stopped, and I could feel that their attention was suddenly drawn toward me. They were aware that I was aware of their presence. All I could say is that I kept my eyes as tightly shut as I could at that point because I could tell that my brother Billy was right there. I closed my eyes, wishing it would end, wishing they would go away. Suddenly, I felt I was rolling down the hill end over end, like a child. I didn't know which way was up. And then suddenly, it stopped, and there was this very calm feeling. I opened my eyes, and I found myself floating in the middle of the room. I didn't see my brother Billy at this time."

Patrick sat there for a while and realized that he could either jump back into his body right now, or he could wake up from a dream. He decided to wait a while and put the theories he had been reading about to the test. Patrick closed his eyes to see if his astral body would eventually drift back to earth: "The next thing I knew, I felt myself lightly touch down almost like a soap bubble on the carpeted floor. O.K. That seemed to hold true. Another theory was that the astral body can pass through solid objects, but you feel the actual texture of whatever you're passing through as you are going through it. So I pressed down with my head a little bit, and sure enough, I could feel the carpeting at first, and I could feel the individual fibers. I could feel the carpeting go through my head, and I felt a little more resistance. I thought, 'O.K. There's the carpeting and the padding and the floor.' And I kept pushing, and my head felt a little more resistance going through the wood, but with a little bit of effort, I started passing through the ply-wood. I thought, 'O.K. That was creepy.' And I basically felt myself floating in the middle of the room again. I rotated to the left and looked down the hallway and did not rotate to my right because that's where the sofa was and where my body would have been lying, and I wasn't prepared to look at myself in a situation like that. It would have been a little too freaky for me. I made a mental snapshot to remember how everything looked—the floor was a mess, sheet music was everywhere—and then I decided it was time to go back to my body, if I could. I thought myself back in my body and—SHOOM—just like a rubber band snapping, I was back in my body lying on the sofa. I spent the first two minutes thinking, 'Was that a dream? No. That wasn't a dream.' I realized that the real test was to walk back over where I was and look down at the floor. And sure enough, everything was laid out on the floor exactly as I had remembered it. It was like two pieces of a jigsaw puzzle snapping back together." Patrick was twenty-one years old at the time, and he is 95 percent sure that he had an actual out-of-body experience.

Patrick founded Ghost Hounds in August 2001 following the demise of the group he had belonged to previously. "We're not a group as much as a paranormal network for people in other groups or independent research to share ideas," Patrick says. "I personally have half a dozen members in the metro-Atlantic area who go out on investigations on a regular basis. I'm very, very selective about whom I work with because we have had unfortunate things happen in the past." He was determined that Ghost Hounds would not become politicized like other groups that have a board of directors: "I didn't become a paranormal investigator to become a politician. When I formed Ghost Hounds, I decided to take a back-seat approach and do my own thing and publish my results. People seem to like the fact that the group is unstructured. The formula has worked out exceptionally well." Ghost Hounds has experienced phenomenal growth between 2004 and 2005. In fact, the number of subscribers to the Web site has grown from one hundred in 2001 to over five hundred in 2005. He tries to discourage people who are too enthusiastic from joining Ghost Hounds: "Some of the people who are attracted to this field get very disappointed when you say, 'This orb you've photographed is a reflection of dust particles' or 'These light streaks are being caused by unusually long exposure time in your digital camera.' I realize what you saw and what you think you experienced, but keep your mind open to another possibility."

When Ghost Hounds investigates a private residence, Patrick normally limits the group to himself and one or two other people who are extremely trustworthy: "I'm looking at it from a liability standpoint. I don't want somebody to come around and say, 'You broke this' or 'My wallet is missing.' You can get someone to sign a waiver or release form, but that doesn't prevent them from taking you to court." To protect himself and his members from potential litigation, Patrick held off on doing a lot of private residences until he had some type of legal mechanism in place. In the past, Patrick was not concerned about the legal consequences of investigating private residences because the group did not receive many requests from homeowners. "Now they're coming in twenty per week," Patrick says. "I don't want necessarily to dismiss these cases, but I also don't want to go into the shark lair, either."

Before conducting an investigation, Patrick makes it clear to the homeowners that the mission of the group is not to prove or disprove the possibility that their home is haunted: "We never go into a location and give it a stamp of approval—'This place is haunted.' The word 'haunting' assumes that we have conclusively proven the existence of ghosts. Being the skeptic that I am, I tell people that we'll go in and collect evidence, but at the end of the day, the verdict is always inconclusive for us." Instead of telling homeowners that their house is haunted, Patrick prefers to say, "You've got something strange going on here that I can't explain. I then tell them to draw their own conclusions."

If his group does not encounter any activity on an investigation, he tells the homeowners that phenomena do not perform on command. Therefore, the group might have to come out to the house several times before finding something.

On many occasions, clients have vented their disappointment when the group determines that the activity in their house is not ghost-related. Patrick is not disappointed when he finds a logical explanation, but he is aware of the limitations of science: "I am skeptical of the rational or scientific proposals that are put forth because a lot of them are highly speculative as well." He cites as an example phenomena that have been attributed to underground springs and rock formations: "Scientists really don't have any way of proving that or demonstrating that. And a part of me also says, 'O.K. Maybe that environment does exist,' but how do we know that the environment is the catalyst and not the cause? Perhaps these spiritual entities are attracted to an environment where those conditions are present."

The group's favorite sites are historic buildings. When a homeowner requests an investigation, Patrick is always suspicious of the person's motives. He takes more seriously those sites that have a long history of activity: "Those places are more interesting because you have a chain of events. A number of people have experienced these types of things and reported them. Generally, you go into these places, and most of the time, you find that there are other people who have experienced things here. It's not just somebody pulling our leg." Someday, Patrick would like to produce a documentary series on historically haunted places in the South. He is also looking at it from the standpoint of producing a documentary series called *Haunted* because, as Patrick puts it, "*Active* does not have the same 'ring' to it."

The most haunted historic site Patrick has ever investigated is a restaurant in Atlanta called Anthony's. It is an old antebellum plantation house built in 1795 in Washington, Georgia. The man who bought it wanted to open a restaurant in Atlanta in an antebellum plantation house, but as a result of General William Tecumseh Sherman's march to the sea in 1864, there were none left in Atlanta, so he meticulously moved the house brick by brick, board by board, over a period of five years. He took thousands of photographs of the house to make sure that the house was assembled at its new location exactly the way it had been originally. Even the boards in the attic and the wooden pegs holding the boards together were numbered and put back into their original positions. Since the restaurant has been in operation, it has become as well known for its ghosts as it has for its fine cuisine.

In October 2003, Ghost Hounds conducted an all-night investigation at Anthony's. CNN sent reporters and a cameraman to cover the event. After nightfall, Patrick was upstairs interviewing several witnesses: "I was sitting at the top of the staircase. I had my laptop set up there with my data logging software running. I had about three other witnesses. One member of the team was with me and two employees of the restaurant. They call the ghost 'Annabell.' It's the ghost of a small girl whose mother had sewn bells on her petticoat so she'd know where she was in the house when she was playing. This is why they call her 'Annabell.' So I started asking out loud, 'Annabell. Are you here? Can you give us a sign?' Just after I asked, 'Can you give us a sign?' the track lights turned on by themselves. I sort of looked around and said, 'O.K. You guys see this, too?' They said, 'Oh, yeah.'" Unfortunately, the cameraman was downstairs and did not capture the incident on film.

Another incident occurred while the group was at Anthony's after the restaurant was closed and the CNN cameraman had left. Patrick went downstairs, and one of the investigators said, "Patrick, there's something going on in the women's bathroom. You close the door, and the toilet paper roll in one of the stalls spins around, like a cat would do, playing with it. You've got to check it out." The first person to witness this phenomenon was Christine, one of Patrick's investigators, while she was going to the bathroom. "She came running out of the women's room with her pants around her ankles," Patrick said. "She came high-tailing out of there and said, 'You guys got to go check this out.' So the other members confirmed that it was doing it. They said, 'Patrick, you gotta go in there!'"

When Patrick went into the restroom, he found that his members had the video camera running. He sat down in a chair across from the stall, and within four or five seconds, he heard, "Dududududududud!" Patrick and two other investigators took off running in the direction of the stall: "About three or four feet of toilet paper was unraveled onto the floor. What we did at that point, we opened the door to the stall and put a video camera in there pointing into the stall so we could observe it as it happened. Of course, it stopped." The group did not get any more activity after that incident.

Patrick is surprised that he has never received any hate mail from the community. He believes that establishing a comfort zone enables him to discuss this topic with anyone. Frequently, in the middle of the conversation, people tell Patrick about experiences they or someone they know have had. The only criticism he has ever received from the "Religious Right" came from his boss: "It's very difficult to keep ghost hunting completely hush-hush when you're on TV several times a year. A couple of years ago, I showed up at work one morning, and my boss was smiling. He said, 'I saw you on TV this weekend.' I said, "That's something I do. It's one of my little hobbies.' And he said, 'Tell me something about it a little later on.' I'm a computer technician by trade, and I said I'd be in the back room working on a pc. An hour or two later he came back there and sat down next to me and said, 'Tell me a little bit about this.' I told him I'd been interested in this sort of thing all my life, but it's just a hobby. I said it goes beyond mainstream religion. I told him I'd like to find my own evidence of an afterlife beyond what is written in the Bible. At that point, he said, 'Well, you know, I couldn't call myself a Christian if I didn't say I'm concerned. The analogy I'd use is somebody who uses drugs. He starts out with marijuana and then moves on to more dangerous drugs.' I thought to myself, 'Oh, god! I'm the spiritual equivalent of a crack addict!' I did my best not to burst out laughing at that point." Patrick's boss never mentioned ghosts again, probably because the last thing he wanted was an uneasy environment at work.

Someday, Patrick would like to re-locate to Savannah, which a majority of the people polled on his Web site consider to be a "ghost hunter's Mecca." In 2005, he and his wife traveled to Savannah to examine a possible location for a coffeeshop and a paranormal bookstore. While they were talking to the realtor, it came out that Patrick and his wife were ghost hunters. The realtor paused a second and said, "I've got some property you guys need to check out. I'm the property manager for the Red Cross building, which is here in the historic district. It's vacant, and it's for sale. The people who are trying to sell it told me it's haunted. The old morgue is still in the basement. There's a tunnel leading from across the street. I guess they had a tuberculosis outbreak in the 1930s, and this is where they brought the dead bodies for the morgue. We'll leave the place at night, turn off all the lights, go back the next day, and every single light in the building is turned on because that happens pretty regularly." Patrick plans to assemble a team some time in 2005 and tape an all-night investigation.

Even though Patrick Burns has been involved in the paranormal most of his life, he still becomes frightened occasionally: "I call myself 'The Shaky Hand Ghost Hunter.' It's really amazing to certain people who wonder why I go off in search of the thing that scares me. I think the fear mechanism is overridden by my curiosity and my desire to know that there's an afterlife, to find evidence of an existence following death. When my physical body expires, I want to know that some part of me in some capacity continues on."

Northwest Georgia Paranormal Investigation Team

LAFAYETTE, GEORGIA

Mike Watkins

Unlike most investigators, Mike Watkins does not really know how he became interested in the paranormal: "My family experienced a lot of paranormal events, and I guess I just became curious. I work in law enforcement, too, which tends to make me more curious than most people. I'm trained in how to proceed in an investigation." Mike formed the Northwest Georgia Paranormal Investigation Team in May 2004. The group has six members, two of whom are provisional. All new members go through a trial period to see if they will follow the group's established protocols and to make sure that they are not looking for thrills. Mike also wants to make sure that the new members will be careful with the group's equipment, all of which was purchased by the members themselves. He admits to preferring Christians with a good faith-based background: "I believe that you have to have a faith system because what we encounter can be troublesome, it can be very frightening, and it can—I'm reluctant to use this word—it can haunt you. A lot of nights, I have trouble sleeping because of where we've been. So I think you need that faith system to be able to reconcile what you've experienced to yourself and ask God what it means."

Even though the Northwest Georgia Paranormal Investigation Team is a fairly new group, the members have done a dozen residential investigations and approximately one hundred investigations at graveyards and old, abandoned properties. "At one point, we were going out two nights a week and hitting about five to six sites a night," Mike says. The group has been concentrating on outdoor investigations because it is easier to get access to them. Mike believes that once a group becomes more and more established, people will have enough confidence in the members to invite them into their homes: "But you need to have some good experiences to tell them about to lend credibility to what you're doing because many people don't like discussing what's going on in the privacy of their homes."

Mike admits that finding a rational explanation for a disturbance in a home is a "double-edged sword." On the one hand,
he takes a sense of pride in his ability to trace a buzzing sound
in a house to a transformer. On the other hand, disproving a
haunting can hurt a client's feelings. "I do feel bad in a way of
disproving somebody because many of these people are proud
that their house is haunted," Mike says. "Some people consider
it a token of esteem that weird things are happening in their
house, and it hurts them when you say, 'The reason your keys
are moving around to different rooms is because you've got
Alzheimer's.' But I have a responsibility to the truth."

Mike has found word of mouth to be the most effective
method of publicizing the group. Sometimes, his friends in law
enforcement also direct people his way: "It's even gotten to the
point that one time, an officer received a call from a woman about
something strange going on in her house. The policeman said,
'There's nothing I can do for you, Ma'am, but call this officer
here whenever he's off duty, and he can probably help you.'" Of
course, the group also attracts attention from local television stations and newspapers during Halloween.

In Mike's opinion, his members receive more criticism than
most groups do because the Northwest Georgia Paranormal
Investigation Team is a Christian group: "To clear up any misconceptions people might have about the group, I speak at
churches and work with pastors. A lot of Christians are beginning to believe more and more that there is more going on than
meets the eye." He believes that because the younger generation
is more receptive to the possibility of paranormal phenomena,
churches will also change their attitude toward paranormal
investigations. Mike also feels that people are tired of keeping

things to themselves: "A lot of people when they call me, the first thing they say to me is, 'You're going to think I'm crazy, but . . .' And I tell them, 'I don't think you're crazy, but let's see if we can't explain it.'" Because Mike majored in theology and minored in psychology in college, he believes he is uniquely qualified to help people who believe they are having problems of a supernatural nature.

So far, only a very few of the group's cases have revealed genuine hauntings. Of the fifteen hundred photographs the group has taken, only six or seven contain images that might be otherworldly. Mike admits that he has visited many more places, though, that made him feel uneasy: "I've been some places that give me strange feelings, but I can't go on feelings. If I thought, 'This place is creepy, so it must be haunted,' then half the places we visit would be haunted."

One of the most haunted places the Northwest Georgia Paranormal Investigation Team has visited is the Chickamauga battlefield. In September 1863, Braxton Bragg's Army of Tennessee, reinforced with most of James Longstreet's corps of Lee's army, delivered a stunning blow to William S. Rosecrans's Army of the Cumberland. The combined casualties for the two-day engagement amounted to 37,129 soldiers. Not surprisingly, Mike's group has been to the battlefield at least a dozen times, and the members have never gone away without significant evidence, such as EMF readings: "It never fails to offer up some evidence. There's no electricity running through the battlefield You can be walking along the road, and all of a sudden, you'll have electromagnetic energy spikes. There are no power lines around to cause that." The members have also had temperature fluctuations that have gone from sixty degrees to thirty degrees and back to sixty degrees in a matter of two or three seconds. Of course, you can hear twigs snapping around you.

Even more unsettling is the feeling of being watched at Chickamauga. "It's just a gut feeling that somebody's staring at you," Mike says. "One night, six of us went out there. We got done with the investigations, and it just turned out that all of us felt the same thing, but nobody was willing to talk about it until somebody finally said, 'That was weird. I felt like somebody was watching me.' Then everyone else admitted it." On the group's third trip to Chickamauga, one of Mike's team members had a particularly creepy feeling at 1:00 A.M.: "It was one of her first times out. She was really frightened. Every little noise bothered her. I don't know if it was her or the circumstances or if there was something there."

Mike's group has taken some amazing photographs at Chickamauga: "We captured a foggy apparition on the battlefield, and we've captured several orbs. There's a little one-lane bridge that goes across an old federal road through there. There was a major skirmish there, and something like forty-five hundred people died. We have a picture that has so many orbs that you can't count them. You can tell that there's depth and width and height to these things, and there's so many of them, and there wasn't that much dust in the air. I've never seen three-dimensional dust."

He realizes that some of the noises his members have heard at Chickamauga, like the snapping of twigs, could have a natural explanation. For example, on one visit to the battlefield, the group was on a one-lane bridge that crosses the river when the members were alarmed by a splashing sound. "It frightened me and the other members," Mike said. "We got home and looked at the photos we hastily took, and it turned out it was geese." Obviously, a good sense of humor can prove to be an asset on an investigation.

Most of the group's investigations at Chickamauga were not conducted in the daytime because of the large number of people who tour the battlefield before sundown. "At night, people are a little more leery of being out in the woods like that," Mike says, "and you can really establish better quarantine protocol over an area to make sure that no one is interfering with the investigation." Even though some sightings have occurred during the day, Mike prefers to investigate at night.

Despite the fact that thousands of lives were lost at Chickamauga, the Northwest Georgia Paranormal Investigation Team's most memorable investigations occurred elsewhere. One of these remarkable sites was an old carpet mill that had been shut down for several years. "It was a cool summer night," Mike said. "We were going around using our EMF meter and digital thermal thermometer. It was about sixty degrees outside, but inside this old building, it was well over 120 degrees. I didn't realize it at the time, but heat differences like that are a sign of demonic activity. Our meter had been going crazy all night. When we got inside, it stopped. It just went dead. But we got one of the best pictures that we've ever captured. It showed an orb just above the roof line with a face in it looking down at it. It's one of the most incredible pictures that any of us have ever seen. It's proof that orbs are more than just dust. It's on our Web site."

The group's second most memorable investigation was conducted at a cemetery in an adjoining county where some odd things had been reported. While Mike was taking some pictures, the two investigators who were with him started laughing because his lens cap was on. "I took three more pictures in quick succession and was reviewing them on my digital camera, and I could see this fog on the first picture that comes from behind the camera like it's coming over my shoulder. In the second picture, it takes a turn downward. And in the third picture, it's forming. As I was looking at this, my jaw dropped, and I said, 'You-all need to look at this. This is incredible.' " At that moment, the members heard a blood-curdling growl. "The growl didn't sound like a dog or a cat. It sounded like it was coming from fifteen feet in front of us. There was nothing there when we first came to the cemetery. We slung our flashlights over there, and I actually drew my sidearm. I always carry a weapon due to humans, not ghosts. I drew my weapon and said, 'We need to get out of here!' As we were going out, we hit the lights on the vehicle, and there was absolutely nothing in that section of the graveyard, no animals, no nothing, but something growled at us." Mike says this particular investigation would not have been nearly as memorable if there had not been three witnesses. He regrets that he did not catch the strange sound on tape: "I only carried out my digital camera that night. We went back a week later with full regalia and didn't catch anything. I don't think it likes being caught. I don't know what the deal was. All I know is that it scared me to death."

Mike has also had a terrifying postinvestigation experience. The members went to an abandoned cemetery at the top of a mountain. He had always been afraid of the old cemetery because a number of "bad" people were buried there in the 1800s. During the investigation, the members captured what looked like a face on a tombstone. That night, Mike had trouble sleeping. Finally, Mike called his uncle and cofounder of the group, Henry Stuart, and said, "Look, there's something strange going on here." He said, "No, no, it's your imagination." Then at 4:00 A.M., Mike heard something that sounded like an airplane had hit the side of his house: "The whole house shook. There was no seismic activity around. An airplane certainly did not crash into my house. But the whole house shook." Suddenly, Mike remembered his grandmother telling him that sleeping with an open Bible can ward off evil, so he went into every room and opened a Bible. While he was opening one of the Bibles, he was praying out loud to the Lord to protect him from the evil in the house, and something slapped him on the rear end. "Of course, there was no witness to it, but it scared me to death. So I prayed even more and put anointing oil above all the door posts and all the windowsills, and I've never been bothered with it since."

Anointing oil is olive oil mixed with frankincense and myrrh to give it a sweet smell. Also, it has been blessed by ministers or other Christians. To Mike, anointing oil is a symbol of God's blessings and God's protection, going back to Old Testament times: "It's a symbol of God's power. I make it myself. I pray over it, and I have my Christian friends over, and we bless it to use it as the instrument of His protection. It's a faith aid, something for us to concentrate our faith on."

Mike Watkins is frequently asked how he reconciles ghost hunting with his Christian beliefs. He always refers to the Bible in his response: "I've studied the Bible. I've studied the Hebrew and Greek language. I believe in the Bible 100 percent, but I do know that there are minor translation errors, and I also know that we cannot put God in a box. To say that something in God's universe is not possible is wrong because with God, everything is possible. There are certain mysteries that God didn't see fit to explain in the Bible. There are certain things about life that He wants us to learn on our own. And there are certain things that don't need to be tampered with, and this is something I've dealt with for a while. Am I treading on an area that God never meant for man to tread upon? I've prayed for His guidance and understanding, and doors have kept opening, so I've taken this as a sign that He wants me to continue." Above everything else, Mike's mission is to show that there is life after death. "Plus," he says, "ghost hunting is just plain fun."

Paranormal Investigators of Georgia

LAWRENCEVILLE, GEORGIA

Angie Madden

A ngie Madden's life was changed forever after reading a book called *Unexplained Mysteries of the Universe*: "I enjoyed reading about sightings in places like the *Queen Mary* and sightings over in England and in different castles, stuff like that. I've been interested in it for a long time, and now I'm getting a chance to check into it more."

Angie joined a paranormal group for a while, but then she and two other members splintered off and formed their own group in 2002. "We've got one person who's an electrical engineer, and he can explain what's going on with our camera equipment and everything," Angie says. "His wife is a sensitive. She has a third eye. She's not really a psychic. Things just come to her. She doesn't really have to work to get them to come to her. Psychics ask questions, but she will just be sitting there and WHAM! She's got it in her head, and she can see it." Angie's training as a graphic artist has enabled her to discern the difference between lens flare and a real orb: "I can pick apart pictures and videos. If I can't explain it anymore, then it's probably paranormal." The Paranormal Investigators of Georgia also has a Yahoo group with a large number of members. As a rule, though, only three members go on investigations.

The equipment the members have purchased on their own is standard for ghost hunting: four digital cameras, one digital camcorder with Nite Shot vision, an EMF meter, and two non-contact infrared thermometers. Angie also has a small set and a big set of dowsing rods: "I'm trying to get into that a little bit more. You've got to keep your hands really still because any movement from your own body can cause a false reading. I've experienced them turning on their own and my hands going numb to the point where I've got to drop them."

Lawrenceville is a suburb north of Atlanta, and the group concentrates on the smaller surrounding towns. The members have not investigated very many private homes. "A lot of people don't want to acknowledge that they've got something going on," Angie says. "They don't want a lot of strange people walking around. Right now, we've only done four." Angie has found that a large number of the historic places that have contacted the group want publicity, like bed and breakfasts: "We've gone to some places and kind of debunked them a little bit on some of the activity that was said to be there, but we've gotten other activity that nobody knows about." In addition, many of these old homes and forts have already been investigated by other groups. "So for us, a home is something new because a lot of people don't want it known, but when they do, it's because they're really interested, and they want somebody to come check it out," Angie said.

Two members of the Paranormal Investigators of Georgia visited the Myrtles but were unable to conduct a full investigation because of the restriction against taking photographs at night. They did, however, manage to record some EVP's. "There were the two members and another couple staying on the first level," Angie said. "It was a slow night. They were from Georgia, and they all went out to eat. On the tape, I can hear them all leaving and walking through the door to go out. Downstairs, they have a little security door chime. You can hear the door chimes, and you can hear them all leave, and after everybody's gone, you can hear some faint footsteps from out of the blue and whistling." The two members were disappointed to find out that the owner of the Myrtles would allow night investigations only if the media are present.

Another historic place the group visited was Stumphouse Tunnel in Walhalla, South Carolina. In 1836, former vice president John C. Calhoun led a group of businessmen who planned to build a railroad linking Charleston, South Carolina, with Knoxville, Tennessee, and Cincinnati, Ohio. The never-completed tunnel was dug in 1854 by Irish immigrants using pick axes, dynamite, and dray horses as part of the Blue Ridge Railroad project. Construction ceased due to the impending Civil War and was abandoned completely in the depressed postwar economy. Although the tunnel does not have a reputation for being haunted, one of the group's members who had grown up in the area had heard tales about mysterious noises emanating from the tunnel. As the investigators entered the tunnel, they soon noticed that the farther they went, the darker it became. Once the group was completely enveloped in darkness, the member who had grown up in the vicinity started laughing hysterically. Then she screamed, "They're coming! We've got to get out of here! They're coming!" The girl grabbed Angie's arm, and all the members ran out of the tunnel as fast as they could.

The group also investigated the historic Tunnel Hill in Georgia. Construction of a tunnel through the Chetoogetta Mountain was completed by the Western and Atlantic Railroad on May 9, 1850. During the Civil War, the tunnel was strategically important to both the Union and the Confederacy. At least five, possibly seven or more, skirmishes were fought here in 1864 and 1865. Angie took a large group with her on the investigation of the old tunnel: "We went in there, and I turned around, and where the gate had been closed behind us, I could swear that I saw someone walking back and forth in front of the gate. One of my members said, 'What are you looking at?' and at about the same time, four other members turned around, and they were looking at the same thing I saw. All I saw was a shadow, like a profile shot. I could see what looked like a soldier's cap and a profile of a man with that hat on. There were about four or five other people who saw the same thing I saw. Part of me wanted to go down and take a picture, and part of me said, 'No, you need to stay where you're at.' My heart went straight up my throat. I know I wasn't imagining it because four other people saw the same thing." The group stayed in the cold, dank tunnel the entire night.

Angie's most memorable investigation was conducted at the Andersonville Civil War prison camp. Andersonville Prison was built in 1864 after Confederate officials decided to move a large number of Federal prisoners who had been kept in and around Richmond. During the prison's fourteen months of operation, more than forty-five thousand Union soldiers were incarcerated there. Approximately three thousand prisoners died from disease, malnutrition, overcrowding, poor sanitation, and exposure to the elements. Angie went down there with the first group she joined. She had a very strange experience when she was standing off to the side of the Star Fort area: "For some reason, something kept calling me up there, so I went. There's a little bridge that goes up to the Star Fort area. And right when I got to the top, I could hear all the locusts and the trees going nuts. And when I walked up the little path, everything just stopped. Dead silence. No wind, no birds, no bugs. When I got in there, I got a warm sensation up my arms and the back of my neck." While Angie was standing up there, she turned her camera toward a place where defensive cannons were set up: "Every time I looked through the viewfinder of my camera at one of the cannons, I could see something moving back and forth, like a soldier. Then I moved my camera away, and with my own eyes, I couldn't see anything. I must have done that about twenty times before I started taking pictures. The first picture didn't capture anything, and the second one had a real bright ball right in front of me. Then the next one right after it didn't have anything. There was nothing there to cause lens flare because it was at dusk. It was turning dark. There was no metal around there. I took the picture, and something just took the breath away from me. It was like my heart went up in my throat. When I turned around, I felt more warm breathing up my back. Something crossed my arms, and every little hair stood up on end. All the crickets and locusts and birds started up, and I high-tailed it down the bridge." When Angie rejoined the rest of the members, they remarked that she was as white as a ghost.

The members of Paranormal Investigators of Georgia would love to photograph a full-body apparition some day, but for now, they have to settle for orbs. "What we look for is a real orb," Angie says. "A real orb is like a cell in nature because the outside is a hard shell, and the inside is like a nucleus. Orbs show up where you were last at, where you last felt good. Part of your energy from your spirit stays in that one spot because it loves that area. Orbs change colors when the flash bounces off of them. I've gotten some that are blue, purple, pink. Some of them look like they have faces in them." Although Angie has developed some theories regarding orbs, she concedes that she does not totally understand them.

Like most directors, Angie has had to deal with opposition: "We haven't really gotten opposition from religious groups, although some people look down their noses at us. Some people say it's the devil's work." She has had more success changing the opinions of her coworkers, many of whom giggle when she tells them about her strange hobby: "Then they say, 'Oh, really?' They want to know more about it, so we usually direct them to our Web site, and when they look at the stuff, they say, 'Oh, wow! It's so cool!' And then they start opening up and telling me stories about what has been happening to them."

Paranormal Investigators of Georgia does not charge for investigations. "I don't see how we could," Angie says, "because we can't make anything go away. You do the research and tell them what you feel you've captured. But how can you say, 'Give me five hundred dollars, and I'll tell you what you've got?'" Angie and all the other members of the group believe that they derive more from investigations than the homeowners do: "We do it for the thrill of going out there and being in a situation where we can record stuff and try to figure out what's going on."

West Central Georgia Investigators of Paranormal Activity

TALLAPOOSA, GEORGIA

Scott McClure, Founder and Director

Most of Scott McClure's members had had paranormal experiences before they joined the group. Scott's occurred at the age of eight when he and his family moved right across the state line to Alabama: "All my relatives either raised hogs or chickens. We didn't have central heat or air conditioning on hot summer nights. All we had was an attic fan. With that humid air circulating through those pig houses and hog wallows, you want to close your window. This one night, I hadn't really gone to sleep yet. I was going to bed, so I went over to close my window so I could go to sleep without that awful smell. I happened to glance at the front yard where my dad had a garden, and I saw cows. So I woke my dad up. He went out with nothing but a shotgun, a smile, and his underwear. And there were no cows. I know I saw those cows." Scott got up the next morning to check for himself. He found no hoof prints. Nothing was disturbed. Not a single plant was broken. In the absence of a rational explanation for what he saw, Scott has concluded that he had a paranormal experience. As he grew older, his fascination with the supernatural was nurtured through hours of watching television programs and reading books on the subject.

Scott McClure's group has only been around since August 2004, but all of the members have been interested in the paranormal for many years. In nine months, the group has had four full-fledged investigations. "We've done the city jail in Tallapoosa, Georgia," Scott says. "There were supposedly a few inmates who had died there in the 1920s and 1930s, and there was also a police officer killed in that area. We investigated that and actually got some fairly interesting sightings on that one on our Web site. Most of the places we've investigated aren't private residences, but we've got three of those planned. We've got one in Anniston, Alabama, actually. [The homeowner is] a nurse who works in a local hospital here in Georgia where I'm at. She had something grab a hold of her and scratch her leg. She moved out of that house. She still owns it but doesn't live there."

The members of West Central Georgia Investigators of Paranormal Activity hold a wide variety of day jobs, including two police officers, a dispatcher, and an EMT. Scott is a paramedic. The group also includes a married couple who goes along on investigations. On big investigations, the members divide into groups. "We have one with the digital and 35 mm35 mm camera and one group with the thermal thermometer and the EMF meter," Scott says. "That way, one can be taking pictures while the other is taking readings. We have two cameras rolling at all times from different locations. The cameras are usually not manned." Following each investigation, the group returns to Scott's house, where they process their findings on his computer.

Scott's Web site is affiliated with quite a few other sites. Scott is one of the Web masters of "Haunted Voices.Com." Most of the members buy their own equipment, but the group buys additional equipment through the sale of T-shirts. "We have two different types of shirts," Scott says. "We have one for staff that is not available to the general public. It's for our protection. If someone claims to be part of our group and doesn't have one of our T-shirts, it ain't them." So far, the equipment used by the group includes three EMF detectors, five camcorders, five digital cameras, and three 35 mm SLR digital cameras. Some of the members have their own digital voice recorders and infrared thermometers. Scott favors digital cameras because they photograph in infrared. He also believes that digital cameras capture more anomalies than 35 mm cameras, but it is difficult to verify these images because there is no negative to examine.

Scott believes he has captured a full-body apparition on film with a digital camera. He and his group were out at an old cemetery one night. After a few minutes, he turned around spontaneously and took a picture. When Scott looked at the image in the photograph, he noticed that it was his cousin's tombstone. She had died at the age of eight of Reyes Syndrome: "It appeared to be like an angelic type of apparition right at the headstone. It looks like it's got little wings on the back of it, and it's floating in a little white dress."

The most convincing evidence for Scott is not the images captured on film but rather the sounds captured on voice recorders. He believes that, with the exception of those spheres that are actually in motion and emit their own light, most orbs are just moisture and dust. Orbs are not iridescent, transparent objects, like many people think. However, Scott truly believes that EVP's are real: "I've got several on my Web site. I'm as skeptical as they come. If I hadn't done it myself and known it wasn't doctored, I wouldn't have believed it. I've got three really good EVP's. We got one of them at a local cemetery. It says, 'Why won't you turn around?' It sounds very evil and malevolent. I just wonder what I would have seen if I had turned around." The other two EVP's were recorded at a local funeral home. "We were walking around upstairs kicking a few boxes around because it was kind of cluttered up there. We were recording during that time, and you can hear a voice say, 'I can help you.' And then a box opened when we walked into a room, and a voice on the recorder said, 'I moved it.'" This investigation was the only time Scott has actually seen something move on its own. One of the five members present was so awestruck by the sight of the box moving that she fell backward and hit the wall. This was, by far, Scott's most memorable investigation.

Scott has personally experienced activity at another funeral home: "It is an antebellum house. The business has been family owned since 1912. I used to be stationed on an ambulance there. That's how I know there's something going on. When I first became an EMT in 1992, doors would open and close. I would hear folks walking around upstairs when there wasn't anybody there. I've never been able to determine the identity of those spirits."

So far, Scott's group has received very little criticism from the community. "Some people at work think it's cool," Scott says, "and some think I'm stirring up a hornet's nest." The group has received no criticism from religious groups in the area. His step-father, a minister, has not said much about Scott's hobby. Personally, Scott does not feel that being a paranormal investigator conflicts with his religious beliefs: "I believe that in order to be a Christian, you've got to believe in the paranormal because we believe in a God that you can't literally see. I believe I can feel His presence, though. So in order to be a Christian, you've got to believe in the paranormal."

Scott estimates that half of his group's investigations have encountered paranormal activity. He attributes a great deal of this relatively high success rate to the time when the group investigates: "I prefer to investigate after midnight. A lot of times, though, my wife won't let me be out that long. We always try to investigate under a new or full moon. It's even more wonderful when solar activity is high because they say that solar activity tends to fuel the spirits." Scott says he is not disappointed when he finds an alternate or scientific explanation, even though his clients might be. "I don't want people to want me to make the house haunted for them," Scott says. "I want to show them that it's not and that there's usually a reasonable explanation why it happened."

Like many directors, Scott McClure has one eye fixed on the ongoing investigations and the other on future investigations. There are several houses in Tallapoosa, Georgia, that he is going to investigate, once he finds the time to pin them down for an interview. Scott is especially excited about an investigation at Bremen High School in Bremen, Georgia, with Jimmy Lowery, the producer of an ASPR radio show: "A wrestler was killed there back in 1981. He broke his neck in a wrestling tournament. They say he haunts the library and the gymnasium. There's a also a girl's ghost that the principal and a couple of other teachers swear they have seen walking on the second floor of the school, but nobody knows anything about her." When asked what the future holds for him as an investigator, Scott replied, "I plan on doing this as long as the Good Lord will let me. I really enjoy it."

Kentucky

Appalachian Ghost Hunters Society

WEST LIBERTY, KENTUCKY

Danny Akers, Founder and Director

Danny Akers says he was transformed into a ghost hunter between 1990 and 1993 when he lived in a haunted house: "The house was built in the 1920s or 1930s. I always felt like I was intruding on someone upstairs. My bedroom was originally the living room with the stairway to the second floor in it. I once awoke to the sound of voices. I knew it was the old man and woman who once lived there. He was trying to tell me something about the house." Danny had a personal encounter with one of the spirits in the house when a spectral visitor appeared in his bedroom: "I woke up and opened my eyes and saw a little boy about five or six years old looking at me. I yelled, 'Hey, little boy! Come back here!' I wanted to talk to him. I knew he was a ghost. I was curious. He ran back upstairs. I tried to sit up in the bed, but I felt something holding me down. I fought and broke free and forcibly sat up. He was gone." Another time while sleeping in a waterbed in the same room, he awoke to feel the bed moving violently. "It was like someone had jumped from the stairs onto the bed. I thought to myself, 'I hope it was the cat!' even though I knew it wasn't. The next morning, I found the cat outside the house."

Danny says that this was his most frightening experience in the house.

A friend of Danny's named Jack purchased the house in 1993, and within a few weeks, he began asking Danny if anything strange had happened to him when he lived there. After listening to Danny's experiences, Jack proceeded to tell his stories. He said that his children talk about an invisible friend of theirs named Bobby, whom they play with in the house. Once Jack was watching television in the front room, and a lamp came on by itself. He laughed and told his wife it was Bobby who had done it. On a whim, Jack said, "Bobby, turn that light out," and the light turned back off. The cord was unplugged from the electrical outlet at the time. A few weeks later, Jack fell asleep watching television in the front room; his wife was asleep in their bedroom with the door partially open. Awakened by the sound of children playing outside her door, she called out to Jack to put the children to bed. Jack woke up, walked up to the bedroom, and found nobody outside the door. He went to check on the children, and they were asleep in their beds. Jack went on to say that he, too, had heard the old man and woman talking in the front room. The similarities between Jack's stories and Danny's made Danny curious about ghost and paranormal activity. "I guess that is what made me want to form a ghost-hunting society for this area," Danny said.

Danny started the group in 2004 along with his brother Paul. His members include people he works with and friends from the community. "We have eight members and four reserve members that we can use from time to time," Paul says. "We've got a wide variety of occupations. We have a lady who works with the local health department. She counsels young first-time mothers on how to take care of their babies. We have one individual who's a janitor. We have a social worker who investigates abuse cases. We have another individual who works at a gas station and one who is a maintenance-type person. We have a male who is a home-maker. He helps elderly persons clean their houses and runs errands for them at the grocery." All of the members of the Appalachian Ghost Hunters Society have the same goal, which is to investigate the paranormal with a skeptical mind so that they can find the exact source of the disturbances. "We try to explain it if we can," Paul says. "If not, then there's the possibility of true paranormal activity there. Only 25 percent of our investigations enable us to say, 'Yes, there is something there.'" These "success-ful" investigations include situations where several different sci-entific devices indicate that something supernatural is going on.

The group started out investigating the truth behind some of the local folklore. "We thought we'd check out a few of these things," Danny said. "It turned out to be more than we thought. We had a lot of activity in the surrounding counties." Some of these places are historic sites that are open to the public, such as a Revolutionary War battle site (the Battle of Blue Licks) and the site of a Civil War skirmish in Sandy Hook. "We want to check those out," Danny says. "We haven't checked out any battlefields yet. We hesitate to go out until the weather warms up. We don't want to go out when it's cold and get false readings, like our breath. We want to be very careful about how we document such things."

Some of these folklore-related sites are cemeteries. One of these is an old graveyard located on top of a hill. The story goes that years ago, a man and his two sons were deer hunting in the area when the younger son looked up toward the graveyard and saw three individuals—a male, a female, and a girl—holding hands up there. He told his dad, "Look at those people up there.

They're all dressed in white." The father couldn't see them at first, and as he scanned the graveyard with his eyes, he finally saw them. Feeling the hair rise on his arms, he took off running toward where his second son was hunting in a different location. He yelled, "Come on, let's go!" Meanwhile, the older son was wondering what they were running from. The youngest son kept looking back, and he saw the three individuals at the graveyard come together in a ball of light and disappear. The Appalachian Ghost Hunters Society investigated the site on a stormy night. "It was a bad evening when we went up there," Danny said. "We didn't see anything. One of the things we want to find out is to look closely at the gravestones and see if a family is buried up there because, according to the legend, they were all together holding hands."

After an unsuccessful investigation at another graveyard, one of Danny's members drove home that night, which was not far from the graveyard, and went to sleep. The next morning, he asked Danny if anything strange had happened to him during the night. When Danny replied that it hadn't, the member said, "Well, I was asleep in bed, and it felt as though something sat down on the bed with me. It actually went so far as to move a pillow. I got so scared that I jumped up and left the room." The member speculated that something had followed him home from the graveyard. "He was really scared," Danny said. "He believed this in his heart. He almost quit the team because he was so scared. I thought he was going to quit, but he hung in there."

The group also does indoor investigations, especially at old, abandoned houses, which offer easy access. "It's usually quiet," Danny says. "We can go out there and set up our equipment. We can check out to see if we can see anything. You can have all this equipment, but you can literally feel it with your own senses and emotions if something's going on out there. It's a creepy feeling, like somebody's watching you." Before going out to one of these old houses, the group always does historical research to find out what happened there in the past.

Danny's workplace is ideally suited to his hobby: "I work at a hospital. There's a lot of death and dying in hospitals, so there's a lot of activity there." Danny has taken his members there on several occasions, and each time, they have gotten significant EMF readings. "Several times when we went out there on investigations, we ended up chasing an anomaly down the hallway from room to room. We got readings. We got pictures. That's why we kept going back." Some of the members speculated that an electrical source was causing spikes in the electromagnetic fields, but they eventually dismissed this as a possibility because the fluctuations occurred in different locations. Because the members could not find a logical explanation for the phenomena, they believe that spirits might be responsible: "We came to the conclusion that whatever this was, it did not want to communicate with us. We did not feel threatened. We decided that we probably shouldn't take this any further because it did not want to talk to us, so we pretty much left it alone."

Despite the fact that the hospital might be haunted, Danny does not feel threatened when he goes to work. In fact, Danny enjoys moving with one entity from room to room. He believes that the ghost is comfortable in his presence because neither he nor his group acted disrespectfully during the investigation. The group adopts this same approach at every location they visit: "Whatever is out there, be it a graveyard or a house, we don't want to do anything that will upset any sort of entity. We do not want to disturb it. We don't want to do any harm to the people who live in those locations." The members always ask permission to be able to film or document or record any activity they find on site. They attribute the above-average results they routinely get on investigations to the fact that they are respectful to the dead. "I'm not going to say that this is an individual who lost his way," Danny says, "but something is there, and it could have been human at one time, so we have to be respectful."

Occasionally, Danny and the other members of the Appalachian Ghost Hunters Society have encountered criticism from religious groups in the community. "We have run into individuals who really object to what we do," Danny says. "One lady came to me and said, 'What is your definition of a ghost?' I said, 'It is some sort of an activity.' She asked, 'Do you think it is a spirit?' I replied, 'Well, I'm not sure.' In an angry voice, she said, 'Well, how can you believe that God would allow an individual to get lost on his way to heaven or hell?' I said, calmly, 'Well, I'm not going to say that it's the spirit of a deceased person. It's energy.' We went around and around with this. I finally said, 'I don't want to get into this with you.' She started getting into negative energy and demons, and I said, 'If I think it's something demonic, I'm not messing around with it. I'm not going to do anything to bring any negative energy on me or in my home. I don't want anything to do with it.' She said, 'But that's what you're doing.' And I said, 'No, no. I investigate to see if there is some kind of activity there. There might not be, but if it is, we want to prove it scientifically.' This one particular lady really laid into me about demons and evil spirits. 'You're messing around with something you really shouldn't be.'" As a rule, Danny and his fellow investigators try to avoid any discussions of religion or demonology with their clients. Their primary goal is to see if there is real paranormal activity going on that they can record scientifically. If there is, they let the homeowners know about it. "We want to make our clients feel more comfortable in their home," Danny says.

Even though the Appalachian Ghost Hunters Society is located in a part of the South that is rich in history and lore, the one place that Danny is eager to investigate is the house that spurred his in interest in ghost hunting in the first place. Since moving out in 1993, Danny has talked to a number of people in the community about the history of his former home. The information he received generated more questions than it answered: "It was probably built in the 1920s. It had moved several times. Actually, there was an older house that was there first. There was a cellar dug. There has been an addition added onto it, and it has been bricked. I really can't confirm this, but the lady I talked to said that she had heard that a young child had drowned in a well on the property. We drank from that well. This could explain the activity, but I can't back that up. I don't have any evidence of that." Some day, Danny would like to take his team to Jack's house, but Jack's wife opposes conducting an investigation in her home: "We are trying to find a time when she is gone, maybe visiting her sister, and investigate the house," Jack says.

Ghost Chasers International

BARDSTOWN, KENTUCKY

Patti Starr, Founder and Director

Patti Starr claims that she has always had a heightened sensitivity to the unseen world: "All my life, I've had experiences. Of course, when you're little, they tell you it's just your imagination, or you had a bad dream. As I got older, I had children and became more sensitive, I began to think, 'There's something more to this.'" When Patti's children were little, she took them on little "ghost hunts" through old abandoned houses to see what they could pick up. In 1995, she began taking pictures at haunted sites, and she began looking closely at the anomalous images that occasionally surfaced. What had started as a hobby became much more than that after she set up her Web site: "It helped an awful lot when I went on line because to my surprise, there were a lot of other people there that had done what I had done, and they'd gotten pictures like I had."

In 1996, Patti became manager of the Old Talbott Tavern in Lexington, Kentucky. Built in 1779, the Old Talbott Tavern is the oldest western stagecoach stop still in operation today. The old inn has had a number of famous guests over the years, including King Louis Phillipe, Daniel Boone, General George Rogers Clark, Abraham Lincoln, John James Audubon, and General

George S. Patton. For a budding ghost hunter, working at the Old Talbott Inn was a dream job: "I had a tremendous number of experiences while I worked there. The ghosts would tease me a lot, and it got in the way sometimes. They would tease some of my customers, and my customers would come and get me and tell me something strange was going on." On one occasion, Patti went upstairs to her office to get some menus. After unlocking both locks on the door, she grabbed the menus. When Patti was ready to leave, she walked over to the desk where she had laid her keys. She was surprised to find that her keys were gone: "I looked everywhere. I stared getting furious because I couldn't leave the room unlocked. I peeked my head out the door and saw my keys lying at the end of the long hallway. There was no way they could have gotten there. I started screaming for someone to come see what had happened so I would know I wasn't going crazy. Stuff like that would happen all the time."

After working at the Old Talbott Tavern for three years, Patti decided that she wanted to make ghost hunting her profession. In 1999, Patti began teaching at Lexington Community College: "I taught an introductory class, and it went over very well, so they asked me to teach an advanced class." Patti began offering two ghost hunts per class. Over the years, she and her students have been to many area locations, such as White Hall and the George Clarke House. Patti also offers introductory and advanced courses on the weekends: "It's the same thing I teach at LCC except that we do it all in one day, so I have Saturday classes going on. Some of the restaurants in town hire me to come in [and talk to different groups]. I think the largest group I've ever talked to is sixty-five. Then I do a ghost-hunting presentation with a big screen."

One year after beginning her teaching career at Lexington Community College, Patti recruited students from her advanced class to form the nucleus of a ghost-hunting group: "In 2000, I got my company name, 'Ghost Chasers International.' I trade-marked my logo, and now I am set up as a corporation." Patti's members, who number between forty-four or forty-five, pay a membership fee of twenty dollars. The group includes schoolteachers, bank employees, civil servants, lawyers, and musicians. When they meet every second Thursday, the members share all of their experiences on their investigations, and then they set up new investigations. "We try to keep three to four going a month," Patti says. "We keep pretty active. I have a Power Point presentation and a big screen. We meet at the library. They furnish us with a room with a huge screen that we pull down, and I have a projector. People bring me their findings that they caught on film or audio or photographs. Then I put it on a CD and pop it in the computer and project it on the screen. Then we talk about it. We examine it. We look for other possibilities. So it's like a continuing education for them as well."

Unlike many paranormal investigators, Patti includes dows-ing rods in her arsenal of equipment: "Sometimes when I'm dowsing when I'm with a group in a haunted location, I'm ask-ing questions, and I'm using my dowsing rod to answer yes or no questions. The dowsing rod will point to someone, and all of a sudden, I'm coming up with information about that person, and what happens is that someone wants to get in touch with that particular person, and they come through." Patti insists that not every entity she contacts with her dowsing rods is a ghost: "It might be a spirit guide or a protective parent [who] has come back. So if we get something at a location, that doesn't mean the location is haunted."

Patti's dowsing rods produced dramatic results while she was conducting a seminar for the cast of the musical *Miss Saigon* when it was performed at Lexington several years ago. The manager asked Patti to wait until the show was over before beginning her seminar in the Holiday Inn North, so she did not begin until midnight. The seminar lasted until 4:00 A.M. She did a full presentation with the Power Point, and then she invited a couple of the cast members to come up and try the dowsing: "They were amazed at how well the dowsing worked," Patti said, "and all of them had cameras, so they were taking pictures of us as I was doing demonstrations, and we got all types of unexplained lights in the room, and we got shadows behind us. It was just unbelievable."

On one investigation, Patti's groups discovered that dowsing is not the only way through which one can communicate. They were walking through a house when they heard a strange sound coming from above them. They looked up and noticed that the globe in the chandelier was jingling. Patti said, "I asked if there's a spirit in the room that could communicate with me by jingling once for yes and leave it alone for no, and I carried on a pretty good conversation."

Unlike most ghost hunters, Patti Starr does not prefer conducting late-night investigations: "I have done investigating as early as ten A.M., but I do most of them between two P.M. and six P.M. If people can't do them during the day, then I'll do them between six o'clock and eight o'clock. Usually, I don't do anything after eight P.M. I really don't want to be out late at night, and you can get just as good of results. We think we have to be at a place at midnight, and it has to be spooky or dark. It makes for a better story, but that's not the case. You get the same results in the day as in the night." Three o'clock in the afternoon has proven to be a prime time for sighting spirits because, as she explains it, "I found that some scholars of the Bible claim that Jesus Christ was crucified at three P.M."

Patti insists that no one has ever been scared on her investigations. One reason why they show no fear is the courses she requires them to take as part of their training. One of her primary goals in her introductory and advanced ghost-hunting courses is to dispel the myths created by Hollywood: "I want them to know what they're dealing with. It's nothing like the horrible demonic energy that Hollywood would lead you to believe because it doesn't exist. It's not out there. I ask them to name someone they know who's evil or demonic. I always have smart alecks. I had one lady ask, 'Does that include ex-husbands?' I ask them how many know a serial killer, and most of them don't. But that's what television projects. The world is full of sadists and murderers and serial killers. We think the spirit world is the same way, and it isn't." Patti also insulates her group members against fear by reciting prayers for protection before and after the investigation to ward off any malevolent spirits.

One of Patti's favorite places to take her students and her ghost team is the George Clarke Bed and Breakfast. On one occasion, one of Patti's students took a picture of her walking through the living room and into the dining room: "In the picture, you can see the outline of a woman," Patti said. "That was awesome. We got lots of faces in that place. We got a face in a mirror, and it looked like an old Colonel Sanders. It had a white mustache and a goatee." Thinking that the face in the photograph looked familiar, the student ran upstairs to look at the picture of George Clarke, who had built the house in the 1800s. She was amazed to discover that George Clarke had a white mustache and a white beard, just like the figure in the photograph.

In 2001 Patti Starr received word from the head groundskeeper that the Mansion at Griffin Gate was haunted. Built in 1854 by David Coleman, the antebellum mansion is now a popular local restaurant that seems to have some "permanent" residents. After talking to the manager, Patti received permission to conduct a scientific investigation of the restaurant during the off shift. Her first investigation took place at 1:00 P.M. and lasted until 4:30 P.M. As soon as she began setting up her equipment, she noticed that none of the five cameras she had brought along were functioning. "I was having a terrible time," Patti said. "I thought my batteries were dead. My tape recorders weren't working either. My husband was trying to get our video camera to work, and it wouldn't turn on. The manager suggested that we plug in our equipment, but that didn't work either. After going downstairs to make sure that the current hadn't been turned off in the room, he said, 'I can't understand it. We had a meeting in this room last night, and they used this room for their projector.' During all this confusion, my cameras started clicking away, and my recorders started working." After Patti returned home and began listening to the tape recordings she had made in the restaurant, she heard an angry, spectral voice say, "Get out!"

Shortly after the problems with the equipment, Patti set a couple of tape recorders in the hallway. She and some of her fellow investigators were standing in the hallway talking when one of the sconces in the hallway started blinking on and off. "You have to remember that they were turned off," Patti said. "So we were pretty amazed by this. One of the managers came up to me, and I told him about the lights." When she returned home and listened to the recording tape, she discovered that at the very moment that she told the manager about the sconce, a little girl's voice chimed in: "Daddy was causing the light."

Because of the little girl's message, Patti began to suspect that there was probably more than a single ghost haunting the restaurant. Her suspicions were confirmed when she played the tape for the manager. "Oh, my goodness," he said. "A year ago, a lady came to have lunch here, and after lunch, she came up to me and said, 'I'm a psychic, and I'm feeling very strongly that there's a presence upstairs. Can I walk around up there?' I said, 'Yeah, go ahead.' So she went upstairs and walked around. Then she came back downstairs after twenty minutes or so and said, 'Oh, my gosh! Do you realize you have a whole family of ghosts living upstairs?'" The psychic's revelation led Patti to conclude that the little girl's voice was one of Coleman's daughters and that the grumpy male voice that said, "Get out!" might have been a grandfather's voice.

Patti Starr picked up the voice of another male member of the ghostly family while following her dowsing rod into the office of one of the managers whose name was Laurie: "It started moving erratically, and I said, 'Do you have a message for Laurie?' Later when we were listening to the tape, we heard the word, 'Secret.'" Patti connected the word to a previous owner of the house who belonged to a secret order called the Masons.

During Patti Starr's three-and-a-half-hour investigation of the restaurant, she captured the voices of seven males, three females, and a single child. She also caught the image of an orb on the video camera. Both Patti Starr and the restaurant manager Leigh Hendrickson are convinced that the Mansion at Griffin

Gate is a very active site. "If I had the time, I could tell you twenty different stories about the restaurant," Patti Starr said. "There's activity constantly going on there."

Despite the fact that Patti Starr and her group are already very well known in the Bardstown/Lexington area, they still do what they can to get the word out. One method that works well for them is wearing their ghost-hunter jackets with their logo on the back. "A lot of times, I wear this vest, and it's got 'Ghosthunters. com' on it," Patti says. "People come up to me and say, 'You're a ghost hunter?' They say things like, 'I know a great place. My brother's place is really haunted.'" Besides joining the Chambers of Commerce in Lexington and Bardstown, Patti advertises ghost walks and seminars through e-mail messages and brochures, which she passes out at metaphysical shops and at the junior college. "I hand out leaflets at the job place, and people put them in the employee lounge," Patti says. "They can tear off a number at the bottom and give me a call if they want to take the course." Still, though, there is no substitute for word of mouth and her Web site: "People e-mail me from all over. I've been to Chicago and Alton, Illinois; to Atlanta, Georgia; to Charleston, South Carolina—I've been all over."

Patti does not charge for investigations, but she admits that donating her time this way does place a financial burden upon her. The problems have intensified because of the popularity of television shows like *Ghosthunters* and *Medium*: "I'm getting more and more calls. My investigations are free. People are becoming insistent that I [investigate their house], but my husband said I've got to make a decision because it's taking up so much of my time. If you charge, people accuse you of trying to cheat them or take advantage of their situation." Patti says that a short investigation lasting only one or one-and-a-half hours costs her $75. A full investigation—fifteen hours—costs her $250: "This includes film and equipment and coming home and hours I spend putting it all together. Most people don't realize how expensive it is. At the end of the year, I can easily call myself a nonprofit organization."

To subsidize her investigations, Patti has been conducting ghost walks in Bardstown, Kentucky, for two years. Her tours begin in June and end in October. As a rule, she takes her tours to the homes and businesses she has investigated and explains what the disturbances were. Patti encourages people to bring their cameras because they occasionally capture spectral images on film. "They capture faces," Patti says. "One woman captured a full apparition coming out of the kitchen doors when we went to one place. I've had other people capture faces in windows." At the end of the tour, Patti takes her groups back to the tourist center and shows videos of past investigations.

In addition to conducting ghost tours and teaching classes, Patti Starr runs a "Ghost Shop" out of her husband's art gallery: "I have equipment and lots of books about things like dowsing and smudging. I sell different types of meters. I also sell a ghost-hunter's vest. It's really a photographer's vest. We need those pockets because that's where we put extra film and batteries and camera—35 mm and digital. We use thermal scanners, too, so our pockets are full because we don't want to keep running back to our suitcases."

Patti Starr estimates that she has conducted over five hundred investigations, and she has no plans to stop anytime soon. "I've been so blessed. The people I've met in this profession are open-minded." Her ultimate goal is to inform, not necessarily convert, skeptics who do not believe in the spirit world. She is encouraged, though, by the rising numbers of young people who are trying to lead a spiritual life: "I read that 85 percent of teenagers pray. Isn't that amazing? I was shocked at that because we only see the bad. Edgar Cayce predicted we'd become more spiritual, and I'm glad."

Louisville Ghost Hunters Society

LOUISVILLE, KENTUCKY

Keith Age, Founder and Director

Keith Age credits a girlfriend for instilling in him an interest in the paranormal. When he first met her, he had been on the road with his band playing across America. He was troubled by her reluctance to introduce him to her mom and dad: "I figured it was because I had hair down to my butt and a beard and was a rock and roller." The real reason became clear after returning her home one night from a date: "I tried to kiss her goodnight, and something threw me through the door. She was pretty upset. At first, I thought her dad had gotten a hold of me. Her dad was sitting in the Lazy Boy chair. He was ten feet away. There's no way he could have touched me. From my elbow to my wrist, I had a hand print. I was bruised. I thought, 'This is cool! She's got a ghost in her house!'" After Keith's relationship with the girl ended, he became kind of the adopted older son, returning to the house many times. "Finally, they sold the house," Keith says. "They couldn't get anybody to live in there very long, and it burned down about twelve years ago. And there hasn't been a house put back on that spot yet, probably because of the reputation of the house."

Keith started his group in 1996 with ten people. While many of his founding members were recruited through word of mouth, some of them were students in a noncredit course he was teaching at a small college. His active members, who number fifty, include doctors, lawyers, police officers, stay-at-home moms, and arm-chair investigators. Keith himself is the promotional manager at the Derby Park Traders Circle Flea Market. Foremost among his various duties is the booking of concerts at the flea market. He has a much larger group of on-line members, a few of whom might be deranged: "We've got the crackpots who are a little flaky. Out of seven hundred members, you are going to have one or two [who are a little nutty]. They don't interfere because, though, I have over seven hundred Internet members. They're vastly outnumbered!" Occasionally, Keith also invites outside experts from related fields on his investigations. For example, in 2005, he invited a couple of meteorologists to accompany his group on a visit to the Waverly Hills Tuberculosis Sanitorium, which has been abandoned since the 1970s: "They were scratching their heads and saying, 'How come it's fifteen degrees colder five feet from right here, and why is it moving? That's not a weather pattern.'"

All of the members of the Louisville Ghost Hunters Society are required to take training workshops because of an incident that occurred in a century-old private residence on Third Street in Old Louisville: "They were restoring the places, but it still looked like the Munsters' house. As we were walking through, the lady was telling us about things that had happened in the house, and I keep hearing this noise, a sound like chopping wood. She led us back to the small kitchen in back of the house. There was only room for one person at a time on the stairwell. It opened up into the kitchen. When we walked into the kitchen, everyone was walking behind me, and as I was getting to the kitchen, the noise was getting louder and louder, and I saw gore and blood. I was trying to put the brakes on, and all these people were cramming up behind me. As soon as one person saw the blood and guts, she freaked out and ran out the front door, down the steps, and across the Third Street road. She almost got run over." It turned out that the lady's husband had shot a deer, and he was gutting it in the kitchen. This incident taught Keith and his fellow researchers about the risks of investigating somebody's home: "You research a place as much as you can, but you might be walking into a place where somebody's nuts. That's why it's easy to be scared in places like this." The female researcher who was so terrified refused to participate in another investigation.

The Louisville Ghost Hunters Society receives hundreds of invitations to investigate private residences each year, many more than it can accept. Because the Louisville Ghost Hunters Society is the oldest and largest group in Louisville, publicity is not a problem. People get in touch with the group through its Web site. Keith promotes the group through public appearance. For example, in March 2005 he served as a motivational speaker for the Louisville Police Department. A shop within the flea market sells T-shirt with the group's log emblazoned on the front. Raising money for charitable organizations like the Crusade for Children also keeps the group in the public eye.

Even though most of the Louisville Ghost Hunters Society's investigations are held at private residences, the members' favorites seem to be the historical places they have visited. There are many historical places in the Louisville area, but the Old Talbott Tavern in Bardstown is one of the best-known haunted sites. Built in 1779, the Old Talbott Tavern is the oldest western stagecoach stop still in business today. In 1998, the old tavern was severely damaged by fire. While the Old Talbott Tavern was being restored, Keith and his group were called in to investigate strange activity that had just started up. Keith claims that one of three actual orbs that he has captured on film was taken at the Old Talbot Tavern: "The orbs I find interesting are the ones that are not completely circular, or you can't see through them, or they are showing some kind of movement, and this is what I got at the Old Talbott Tavern."

Probably the most haunted building the group has investigated is the old, abandoned Waverly Hills Tuberculosis Sanitorium. The sanitorium opened in 1911 with only eight patients. By 1924, the hospital was expanded to house four hundred patients. Many people died at the sanitorium, and their bodies were removed from the hospital complex through a steam tunnel. The old hospital closed its doors in 1961. Unlike the orbs Keith's group captured at the Old Talbott Tavern, the ones his members photographed at the tuberculosis hospital cannot be presented as reliable evidence of the paranormal: "You know, we had thirty people tramping around in an old building that isn't cleaned regularly, and if [the anomaly] is round and you can see through it and it looks like you have a pattern in it, it's more than likely dust." However, during one investigation, the researchers encountered cold spots and recorded some intriguing EVP's: "Everyone was sitting around taking notes, marking down every noise. We recorded it and listened to it again, and then we broke it down in the computer to find out what range it's in. If it's in the two hundred or three hundred megahurtz range, we can't hear that, but the tape can. On this one particular trip out there, we recorded the sound of heavy breathing, and I know that none of us were making any noise."

Although Keith's group has never photographed a full-body apparition, they did capture a human-like shape that might be the ghost of a little boy who is reputed to haunt the Waverly Hills Tuberculosis Sanitorium: "Twin Talks Entertainment just shot the movie *Death Tunnel* up here. They had so many things happen that they also did a documentary called *Spooked*, which we're a major part of. So Halloween night, we let five winners do an ongoing investigation at Waverly Hills all night. Basically, we were just walking around all night. We took a fluorescent light—break 'em and shake 'em—and set it in the hallway. We put a camera on it, and we watched this thing move across the hallway to the other side. It went up and down. It was really cool!" The group did not know they had captured the strange image on film until after the investigation. Shortly thereafter, Keith had a personal encounter with the little boy, who is known by a variety of names, including Timmy, Johnny, and Tommy: "He runs and plays ball with a little leather ball, the type they had in the 1920s or 1930s. The first year I was giving tours out there on one of the lower levels. I was in the habit of walking backwards, and I tripped over something and landed on my butt. And when I got up, it was a round, leather ball. This was the last tour of the night, and we put it somewhere and sure enough, we went up there again, and the ball was gone. We were the last people in the building. We let the people out and went up straight to look for the ball, and come to find out, it was on the fifth floor."

Another moving figure made an appearance in 2004 when Keith's group tried to capture what has become known as "the shadow people" on film. The group set up laser grid in the rooms on the fourth floor. The laser beams were emitted by motion detectors placed in the corners of the rooms. "As we were watching it on film, these shadow images started moving through the lasers and broke the beam, and the motion detector went off," Keith says. "That tells us that these things have mass."

Keith had a much more violent encounter with the ghostly inhabitants of the Waverly Hills Tuberculosis Sanitorium one night while conducting a tour: "I was standing there talking to twenty people, and something hit me in the head—POW! It was a chunk of concrete." After Keith regained his composure, he led his group out of the building just as another group was coming in: "As they opened the door, I was standing there blood-soaked, and those people screamed. It was great!" Keith blames increased adrenaline flow and heightened imaginations for the group's extreme reaction to his startling appearance. This same combination, Keith says, can affect the judgment of ghost hunters as well.

This writer accompanied Keith Age and Troy Taylor, president of the American Ghost Society, on an impromptu investigation of the Waverly Hills Tuberculosis Sanitorium during the Mid-South Paranormal Conference on September 27, 2003. At 11:30 P.M., the three of us were walking up the stairs. It was totally dark except for the moonlight coming through the broken windows. When we reached the third-floor landing, Keith extended his hand to open the heavy iron door, and the door opened and closed very fast. At that moment, Keith yelled, "Oh, my god!" I must admit that I thought we would find a member of his group standing on the other side of the door laughing. What we did find was a single wet footprint, probably a woman's footprint because of its size. It was then that goose bumps began to pop up on my arms. Keith explained that his group has found the wet footprints before: "With those footprints, what we found is they are fifteen to twenty degrees colder than your footprint, and they will last three times as long as yours will."

Another historically haunted site that the Louisville Ghost Hunters Society enjoys investigating is Bobby Mackey's Music World in Wilder, Kentucky. This 1850s slaughterhouse was used as a gambling casino called "The Primrose" in the 1930s and 1940s. In 1978, the old two-story building was purchased by Bobby and Janet Mackey, who converted it into a nightclub. Big-name entertainers like Redd Foxx have drawn thousands of people to Bobby Mackey's Music World. However, the building is also famous for a vicious murder that was committed here in 1896. Two Satanists beheaded a young woman named Pearl Bryan and used her head in their ceremonies. After they were arrested, they never revealed the location of Pearl's head. According to legend, they threw the head in an old well. The well was filled in years ago. "It's like a big sunken depression," Keith says. "The old wooden boards are still there. It's really interesting."

On one of the group's investigations at Bobby Mackey's Music World, they had a very unpleasant meeting with some of the club's more unsavory customers: "When we went to Bobby Mackey's, a group of thugs was going to terrorize us from outside. We were inside listening for every little noise, and there were these idiots banging and pounding and acting like fools."

Fortunately, Keith, who is a biker himself, has a friend who happens to live on the hill right above Bobby Mackey's. This friend is also a member of Hell's Angels. "I asked him to do us a favor," Keith said, "so sure enough, he had about fifty of his buddies cruising up and down the street outside of Bobby Mackey's. We didn't have any more trouble after that."

Once the investigation finally got underway, Keith asked Bobby Mackey to turn off all of the electricity. The group did not collect much significant evidence, mainly because of the electromagnetic interference produced by the nearby Lincoln River. "We caught a light mist on the stage where a female spirit is supposed to appear and lots of camera malfunctions, but not much else," Keith says. Because the temperature outside was only ten degrees, Keith suspects that the mist they saw might have been produced naturally.

Not long after their investigations at the nightclub, several of his team members returned to take a tour. Keith says that while they were there, "they got a little bit rattled because there's a stairwell that leads to nowhere. They were standing there. Bobby, one of our members, was with them talking, and the next thing he heard was these footsteps. Bobby is so inquisitive. He doesn't believe it until he sees it. He never gets spooked, but he said he got spooked on this one."

Unlike most of the groups interviewed for this book, the Louisville Ghost Hunters Society has been criticized by religious groups: "They have said we are the devil. It's not people picketing or rioting, but you get the hate mail. We're part of the Bible Belt, and a lot of people's views are stuck back in the 1800s. That's the way they grew up, and that's the way they're going to believe." Keith says that his group receives much less criticism from the younger generation, which is much more receptive to the idea of ghosts.

Keith takes pride in the fact that the Louisville Ghost Hunters Society is, in his words, "nonmetaphysical." Even though some of the members of his group claim to be psychics, he does not use them on his investigations: "Most of the people who claim to have psychic abilities are there for three reasons: one, for money; two, to get their name out; and three, they're nuts," Keith says. His attitude toward psychics is due in part to a live radio show his group did at the Waverly Hills Tuberculosis Sanitorium in 2003. The radio station had brought in a world-renowned psychic, who was asked to give his psychic impressions of the old sanitarium: "The way it started, the announcer asked him how he felt about the place he was in now, and he said, 'Oh, Lord! So much death! Oh, Lord! So much pain! I can't breathe!' He walked into a room and said, 'And there was so much death in this one room!' Of course, they put the mike to me and I said, 'This room here?' The reporters were going nuts because this guy was running around waving his arms like Mr. Chicken. They gave the mike back to me, and I said, 'You're sure about this room?' He said, 'Yes!' I then asked him, 'You're sure about this bathroom?' The psychic just stopped and looked at me, and the announcer walked over and smiled and said to me, 'That was cruel.' I said, 'I just gave him enough rope to hang himself.'"

Keith added that he is not saying that there are no real psychics out there, but he has only met a few of them who are legitimate and are not in it for personal gain.

In Keith's many years of investigating the paranormal, he has found that places that are active are few and far between: "Ninety percent of the time, you will go to historic places that are regionally haunted. This just means that there have been rumors about it for many years. Most of these rumors are just legends and nothing more. Or you will go to a place where someone is extremely lonely or is out of their mind. The 1 percent is where you go and something genuine actually happens. Out of one hundred and twenty-two investigations we did last year, we had two—two—that I would say have the possibility of having some sort of paranormal anomalies happening there."

Although Keith Age says that he would like to investigate the Myrtles some day, he does not really have a dream investigation anymore. Some days, in fact, he finds his responsibilities as director to be overwhelming: "With everything that goes on here, with my involvement with the media, out of the one hundred and twenty-two investigations we went on last year, I got to go on two. My role has become that of paper pusher or liaison." His situation is even more frustrating because he believes that the field of paranormal investigation is on the verge of a breakthrough, and he would like to be there when it happens: "I'd love to have Satan himself tap dancing in front of me as long as I've got a camera in my hand. I think we are on the verge of finding out about it, but I don't think we will in my lifetime."

Southern Paranormal Research

BURNSIDE, KENTUCKY

Roger Johnson, Founder and Director

Death has been Roger Johnson's business for most of his life: "I used to be a coroner. I was a volunteer assistant chief of the fire department. I worked as a medical technician, and for many years, I taught people to be instructors in American Red Cross courses. I've done it all. And a lot of it was done at the same time. I've seen a lot of things. I've [observed] over two hundred and fifty autopsies." He now calls himself a "full-time" ghost researcher.

Roger became inspired to start a ghost-hunting group as the result of a trip to a cemetery in 1996: "I took a small tape recorder and some friends, and I decided to go to a small cemetery where my family's buried. We went out and turned our recorder on and placed it on a gravesite. I got a few voices, but nothing from my family. It was from other parts of the cemetery that we got it, and that pretty much started it." In 2003, Roger changed the name of his group from "Southern Ghost Research Group" to "Southern Paranormal Research" to better reflect the members' broad range of investigations.

Southern Paranormal Research is divided into two chapters, the main chapter in Pulaski County, Kentucky, and another group in Sevier County, Tennessee. The more research Roger did into the way other groups are set up, the more he realized that both chapters needed to be better organized: "I found out that you've got to have good continuity to your research, a good backbone. I looked at other groups and found that they each had their own rules to keep things going in Pulaski County, Kentucky, and also in Sevier County, Tennessee, and I wanted continuity so that the other groups would be doing the exact same things we were doing. So it's about keeping the standards up at all times. I can take a group down to Sevierville and Robin Cunnagin, my director of operations down there, would be able to conduct the investigation in the exact same way we would here. So as we talk and do research, we figure out what we want to try out, what experiments we want to do, and integrate that into the group as we go along." In the past, the two groups combined have had as many as thirty-three members. Recently, though, he has reduced that number to twelve. "I found out that if we have a large group, we're constantly playing catch-up, trying to get everybody together and scheduling training," Roger said. "It's better to have a few people who are knowledgeable and committed than a lot of people that you have to baby-sit and train in different areas. We're looking for new members all the time, but we're trying to keep the group small in order to keep ourselves from constantly having to train everybody." The mission of both chapters is to prove scientifically that spirits, or ghosts, exist. At the time of this interview, Southern Paranormal Research had logged well over fourteen thousand hours of investigation time.

Unlike most groups, Southern Paranormal Research does not require its members to buy their own equipment. "I've got the equipment here in Pulaski County, and Robin's got her equipment down in Sevierville," Roger said. "I purchased all the equipment for myself, and Robin, whom I've known for many, many years—she's a good friend of mine—she decided to purchase her own equipment, too. She's really committed. So we've pretty much got the same type of equipment." The equipment the group uses ranges from the simplistic (e.g., digital thermometers and 35 mm cameras) to the high-tech (e.g., Nite-Shot camcorders). The investigators also use a laptop computer on site to edit their digital voice recordings and determine if the voices are those of actual spirits.

Southern Paranormal Research always investigates during the night, but not because of the folk belief that the period between midnight and three A.M. is the "Witching Hour." Like most directors, Roger prefers the nighttime because it is quieter. Also, he finds night-vision camcorders to be superior to regular camcorders: "Night vision eliminates the possibility of dust particles, not entirely, but it's better. In daytime, if you have a window that the sunlight's coming through, you can see the dust particles. They're all over the place. You can't get rid of them. But Night Vision with the infrared has a very good way of filtering it out to where—unless it's really big dust particles—it's more than likely going to be orbs, especially if it has purposeful movement."

Roger takes orbs more seriously than many directors do because he believes they are spiritual energy: "We believe that spirits can manifest in different forms, depending on the amount of energy required. Orbs are the most basic energy forms, and full apparitions are the most uncommon because of the tremendous amount of energy required." For Roger, seeing an orb is not proof that the group is in a haunted location; it simply means that energy is present. Moving orbs are even more significant: "There have been several times when the spirits have tried to communicate, and the orbs have moved or stopped and changed directions. I've got that on video. It's really cool to see something like that." Roger cites as an example an investigation his group conducted at an old farmhouse in Sevierville. On the viewing screen, one can see an orb emerge from a wall and pause in the center of the room. When Roger asked if there were any spirits present, the orb moved in his direction. He has observed that moving orbs are easier to see on large television monitors than on the small viewing screen of a video camera.

The dramatic impact of orb photographs notwithstanding, Roger puts more stock in EVP's: "Orbs could just be energy within that area. Basically, they are direct answers to questions. To me, an EVP is something that's actually taking place or a residual haunting from the past. Under certain electromagnetic conditions, there might be a playback mode. It's not a residual haunting exactly." Roger believes that there is a correlation between the amount of electromagnetic energy in a building and the close proximity of limestone, high-tension lines, or underground springs. "The higher the levels of electromagnetic energy, the more the spirits seem to manifest themselves," Roger says. For example, the Alton Penitentiary in Alton, Illinois, was constructed of limestone blocks in 1832. After serving as a Confederate Civil War prison, the building was abandoned, and the limestone blocks were used by contractors in a number of nearby houses. Roger cites the presence of paranormal activity in these houses as proof that limestone increases the levels of electromagnetic energy.

Roger trains his new members in a few specific cemeteries that have proven to be hotbeds of paranormal activity. The more experienced members accompany Roger on trips to private residences, which now constitute the bulk of the group's investigations.

Roger has tried promoting the group through fliers and interviews on local television stations, but the group did not get much of a response. Like most directors, Roger has found word of mouth and his Web site to be effective ways of generating interest in the group.

One private residence the group visited was an old funeral home that is now inhabited by two families. The members placed a tape recorder and a lollipop on a boulder in the unfinished basement. A video camera was positioned in the direction of the boulder. "There was nobody close to the rock, and the tape recorder was on the rock for some time," Roger said. "One of the investigators asked for some type of proof, and the tape recorder and lollipop moved. This was captured on video."

The investigators have visited some houses that definitely instilled fear in them, despite Roger's efforts to make his team members impervious to fear: "My number-one rule is, 'Never let your imagination get the best of you' because once you do that, it will have a domino effect on the rest of us. If they see something, then it's mass hysteria. I've had plenty of people frightened, but I think 90 percent of it is the imagination factor, especially for the newer people." Some of Roger's members have felt nauseated when they entered a house, but they recovered quickly when they stepped outside. He attributes this phenomenon to the person's ability to sense the presence of spirits.

Roger himself fell prey to the very fears that he tried to insulate his members from when the group investigated an old abandoned house in Sevierville. "The owner allowed the police to use this house for training," Roger said. "They shoot tear gas in it. From what I have been told, some of the cadets who have been trained there have refused to go back in. Although I can't say that I actually saw or heard anything that frightened me, it was a feeling. I got sick to my stomach. I started sweating. I was anxious. I was frightened. Every emotion that could possibly happen happened, and I just had to get out of there, and I remember that my camcorder was hooked up downstairs with a microphone attached to it upstairs, and I said, 'I gotta beat this,' so I went in there, and I actually retrieved the camcorder and everything and the whole time I was there, I was filled with an overwhelming cold fear of getting out of there." He thinks the old building is a "restless" place because a number of murders and suicides occurred there back in the days when it was used by bootleggers as a hideout.

Roger can truly say that he is a full-time ghost hunter because he lives in a haunted house. He inherited the house from his mother, who passed away in October 2003. "One agreement we made when the house was put in trust was that I was to live here and take care of everything," Roger said. "I haven't changed any of her decorations or anything like that. Her bedroom stays locked. Once in a while I'll open it up on a real cold night just to circulate the air. She's got light-up carousels all over her bedroom." One night, he turned the TV off, turned the lights off, and rolled over and began to fall asleep. About two minutes later, one of his mother's carousels started playing. Other strange things have happened there as well: "I've had lights burn out prematurely. It's a whole new electrical system they've put in. I've had plumbing problems, things that are pretty standard for hauntings." Roger has even conducted a formal investigation in his house. His members photographed several orbs and the image of his mother's face in the hallway. "I talked to a friend of mine who's a psychic, and he said she's going to be around for a while," Roger said. "She's just making sure everything's all right, and then she'll gradually pull away." In October 2004, a local television station did a story on Roger's house.

On March 11, 2005, while I was interviewing Roger Johnson on the telephone, his mother made an unexpected appearance.

R: You know what? Something's just happened here.

A: Really? What happened?

R: I have a Golden Retriever, and he sleeps on the floor of my bedroom. And she is looking in the hallway. [Pause.] She's looking in the hallway as if she's looking at something.

A: Oh, my god!

R: She's also making like a rumbling noise, too. I'm used to it. She's done it before.

A: She has?

R: I've got my digital camera right there and my EMF detector handy. I might do a little recording. She hasn't done this in a while.

A: Oh, my!

R: If I'm in my family room watching TV, she'll be watching in the kitchen. She just stares in the kitchen. One time, I turned the camcorder on and turned everything off in the bedroom, and although the camcorder didn't catch anything on video, you could definitely hear something like feet shuffling in the kitchen and cabinet doors opening and closing. It's cool. I love this stuff, man!

A: Does it freak you out when she acts like that?

B: No, it makes me want to [get all of the equipment]. If you ever get up this way, you're welcome to go on a ghost hunt with us.

At the time, I was talking to Roger on the speaker phone, and my wife, Marilyn, listened to this interchange as well. Both of us are convinced from the quavering tone of his voice that Roger really was experiencing some sort of traumatic event on the other end of the line.

Southern Paranormal Research has not really encountered any opposition from religious groups in the community. However, Robin Cunnagin elicited a critical response when she wrote a letter to Billy Graham. "One of his staff members wrote back and said that what we're doing is not in God's acceptance," Roger said. "The letter quotes from chapters of the Bible that mention spirits and ghosts." Even though Roger has been dealing with death for most of his life, he still has not found all the answers to such metaphysical matters as the afterlife: "I haven't really formed an opinion about that. It's natural for human beings to be curious. If we weren't meant to do this, then we wouldn't have it in us to be that curious." What keeps Roger going is his burning desire to get all the answers, even though he knows he probably never will.

Western Kentucky Ghost Hunters Society

PRINCETON, KENTUCKY

Jason Brooks, Founder and Director

J ason Brooks's interest in the paranormal was sparked by books he read on mythology and demonology as a young man. After he married, Jason and his wife began going to areas that were supposed to be haunted and took photographs, some of which showed some strange anomalies: "We were getting some things. We went on the Internet and started talking to people and showing them some pictures, and a group just formed." The Western Kentucky Ghost Hunters Society, which started in 1995, now consists of seven members. Jason, a deputy jailer, believes that his profession makes him a better investigator: "Like most law enforcement, you're nosy. You've got to get all the answers. It becomes a way of life. If there's a question, you want an answer."

Because the Western Kentucky Ghost Hunters Society investigates mostly historic or outdoor sites, security has become a primary concern of the group. For that reason, Jason has selected members who he knows will not run off if trouble arises: "We need to have people we can rely on because we never know what kind of situation we're going to find ourselves in, especially when you're outside and there's wildlife. You need to know there's somebody around who will help you out." He also enlists the aid of local police if his group is investigating in an unfamiliar location. He cites as an example a Civil War cemetery they visited in Dover: "We had to have permission to be there after hours. We gave the police a few weeks, and they checked out our Web site and our employers. When we pulled up, we had officers coming in off-duty asking us questions. They came to stay with us, but they also wanted to satisfy their curiosity." Jason does carry a knife with him on investigations, but he uses it only when one of his members becomes tangled in the brush.

Although outdoor sites, like cemeteries, offer easy access to ghost hunters, they offer other challenges. Some of the orbs Jason's group has photographed outside are extremely unreliable because of environmental factors: "There have been times when we got something we thought was an orb, but it was the glare off a streetlight or a piece of glass lying out in a field. One of our members will spot orbs as he's filming with our camcorder, and he'll point it out, and we'll go look, and a lot of times, it's light reflecting off a car going by." The members always bring along at least one EMF detector to use for verification if an orb or some other evidence is picked up in a certain location.

Jason has found that he actually enjoys the few investigations his group has done in private residences the most: "It's more of a concentrated area. You can walk in, and you get that feeling that something's not right. You can talk to the people. You can get the history." Children, he says, are an excellent source of information regarding hauntings, not only because they tell the investigators exactly what they have seen, but also because children tend to see more than adults: "You can find out what's going on through the little kids. They're great ones to talk to because they don't sugarcoat anything. They tell you exactly what they see. Also, they tend to see more than adults. It's like my dad told me, 'The only reason you don't fly is because you're told you can't.' When you're growing up, you're told ghosts don't exist, so you don't see them anymore."

Of course, private residences also present problems. Aside from the presence of the inhabitants of the house, the electro-magnetic fields created by electricity in the house can also cause interference. The ideal situation, of course, would be a private home where there were no people or electrical wiring. Several years ago, the Western Kentucky Ghost Hunters Society was asked to check out a house that the owners had just recently moved from and were trying to sell: "They were buying a second house, so they turned the power off. We were getting voltage readings, and we didn't have any equipment in the house yet." Because no electrical equipment besides the EMF detectors was present in the house, the group suspected that the energy in the house might have been paranormal in origin.

Before visiting a private residence, Jason's group conducts extensive historical research on the building. Their attention to research came in very handy when the Western Kentucky Ghost Hunters Society was investigating an old house in Corinth, Mississippi: "It was built on the foundation of an old Civil War hospital where the Yankees were conducting medical tests on Confederate amputees. The little girl who lived in the house said she could see a wounded soldier sitting in a corner. Also, there are eight Indian burial mounds in this area that you can see. It was a highly death-oriented area." Jason believes that the spirits in the home become active after the family started remodeling.

The Western Ghost Hunters Society's most memorable investigation took place at a local home. One of his members, Troy, walked into one of the rooms with a walkie-talkie. In the room, a micro-recorder had been set up to record EVP's. While he was standing in the room, Troy attempted to tune his walkie-talkie to the same frequency as Jason's. Jason was listening to Troy's attempts to tune his walkie-talkie when, all of a sudden, Troy ran into Jason's room: "You could hear him do his little test. Then he came out of this room, and he was pale-white, as white as someone could get. He said, 'Did you say anything on the radio a minute ago?' I said, 'No.' He said, 'Something told me to SHHHHH!' So we got the micro-recorder and played it back, and you could hear the SHHHHH! as plain as day. That kind of spooked him because he wasn't ready for it. He was all by himself at the time." Jason himself had a very weird experience in the same house: "I was going up a flight of stairs, and it felt like a hand hit me in the chest. It stopped my momentum. I had to step down a step and start over again. That was kind of fun."

Strange activity continued to occur late into the night. One of the members, Patrick, photographed several orbs and heard voices while everyone else was asleep. The voices were so loud that they could be heard above the sound of the generator. After Jason woke up, he heard somebody banging on the door. Jason went outside to check that area, but there was nobody there. Jason says other strange things occurred that night: "We have EVP's of cabinet doors slamming, but they were closed. We were all outside. We had our micro-recorder moved. We had it in a room, and the next thing we knew, it was in the room, and none of us were inside. There was nobody else there."

Jason prefers to stay all night at a location and return in a month or two. "I stay up all night naturally," Jason Says. "I'm a night person. I've worked second and third shifts all my life, so I'm used to it. Also, it's cooler then." Unlike some paranormal investigators, he does not prefer to work at night because the spirits are more active then: "Ghosts have no sense of time. I figure that because it's dark, you can see more in the dark than you can in the light. In the daytime, shadows play tricks, and the light can be refracted." However, the length of his group's investigations more often than not depends on how much free time the members have and how long the owners of the property are allowing them to stay. Jason claims that 80 percent of his investigations have produced some sort of evidence, but he maintains that the success of a "ghost hunt" is determined by more than just orbs or EVP's: "We judge the presence of spirits by how tired we are. Spirits need energy, and they'll take ours."

Jason admits that the Western Kentucky Ghost Hunters Society has received criticism over the years, especially from members of local churches. Because he believes that most of the hostility he has faced over the years stems from ignorance, he tries to convert their negativity into something positive by enlightening them: "The little towns we live in, it's more personal, face-to-face. But as people get to know my wife and me, it goes from criticism to questions and more questions. It's like they're trying to put up a front to their friends, but you get them one-on-one, and they're asking questions. Besides having investigative skills, you have to have quite a bit of PR too. But it's fun." He has found that projecting a "no-care" attitude when people mock him at work often has the same result: "At first, the people I work with laugh. When they see that it doesn't bother me and I don't care, then it becomes,

'Hey! Did you ever check out this area? Where have you been? What have you seen?' I answer their questions. People laugh at what they don't understand, and then later on, they think, 'This has happened to me. Maybe he can help me out.'"

In order to dispel misconceptions about the group and to make their presence known in the community, the Western Kentucky Ghost Hunters Society has focused on public relations. "On our Web site, we had a little store where you could order stuff from," Jason said. "We had an 800-number that went to a pager, and we'd call people back and answer their questions and talk to them. But we had to cancel that because of the money." Like most groups, Jason's has found that the best way to publicize their group is through their Web site and word of mouth.

Despite all of the equipment and experience that an investigator brings to a site, his greatest liability, as well as his greatest asset, is his own personality. Many ghost hunters are just as susceptible to a "spooky" setting as the average person. Jason and his members have had to combat this tendency in themselves: "Just because something doesn't feel right to us, we're not going to say it's haunted. It could just be you're just in a bad mood, or the environment is new and strange." Jason believes the ghost hunter's most effective weapon is the doubt lingering in his mind during every investigation: "We try to eliminate all that's possible, and what we're left with is the truth. The only way to do it is to go into an investigation with a skeptical mind."

Louisiana

South Louisiana Ghosthunters

PRAIRIEVILLE, LOUISIANA

Pam Gates, Founder and Director

Pam Gates comes by her psychic abilities "honest," as they say in the South. When Pam began having psychic experiences at the age of five, her Cajun grandmother, who was a clairvoyant herself, told her she had a gift. Pam's gift became apparent to the entire family at the age of seven when she contracted scarlet fever: "I was very ill. I was lying on the couch in the living room, and my mom came in to check up on me. I sat up and said to her, 'Barbara's here.' And she said, 'Who? What?' And I said, 'Barbara's here.' She said, 'Barbara who?' And I said, 'Barbara Richardson, Mom. She's standing in the corner.'" At the time, Pam was unaware that her mother had received a telephone call thirty minutes earlier from one of Barbara's family members, informing her that Barbara had been killed in an automobile accident. Not only did Pam not know this lady or her family, but it would also have been impossible for her to have overheard her mother's telephone conversation because she was in a totally different part of the house. Since becoming a ghost hunter, Pam's psychic abilities have come in very handy on investigations: "I sense presences. Sometimes, I can see them. There are times when they have conversations with me. I have gotten EVP's, too. If I go into a strange place where I've never been before, there are times when they actually have conversations with me."

Pam founded South Louisiana Ghosthunters on October 20, 2003. Prospective ghost hunters apply by filling out an application on the group's Web site: "They must interview with my co-director and me," Pam says. "We have two other members on our team who are the next in the chain of command. The four of us will get together, review the application, go over the interview, and make the decision whether to accept them as a member or not." At the time of this interview, South Louisiana Ghosthunters had just become affiliated with The Atlantic Paranormal Society (T.A.P.S.) network of paranormal investigating groups. Pam feels that her group will benefit immensely from the increased exposure: "As the result of becoming a family member [of T.A.P.S.], we will be getting a lot of referrals from Jason and Grant. I'm trying to gear up right now in training people because I've got a feeling that we're going to be getting an influx of requests for investigations outside of Louisiana." Because the group will probably be expanding its coverage area, she is considering changing the name of the group to something more regional like "Southern Paranormal Investigations."

The first investigation that Pam's group conducted as part of the T.A.P.S. family was at Georgia Plantation in a little bayou town called Labadieville, Louisiana. South Louisiana Ghosthunters was accompanied on the visit to the old sugar plantation by Jason Hawes, Grant Wilson, and several other members of the T.A.P.S. paranormal research team. The members focused their investigation on the overseer's house. The main part of the house is over two hundred years old; the addition is one hundred years old. The stories told by the homeowners regarding the ghostly activity in the house led Pam to research the Civil War history of the house. She discovered that in 1862, between 250 and 300 soldiers were killed on the property. Evidently, the tragic legacy of suffering and death has made an indelible impression on the ground itself. "The homeowners told me that because it's still a working sugar-cane plantation, there's a plot of land where anytime the machines come near it, the engines totally cut down." Pam said. "So among all these rows of sugar cane, there's this one spot where nothing grows. They can't farm it. They can't get any equipment near it because the equipment won't work. We're not sure if it's a mass burial site." Pam speculates that the property could also have been used as a burial ground for a tribe of Native Americans who had lived there centuries before the whites settled there. Unfortunately, Pam's group has been unable to investigate this particular spot of ground: "We haven't been able to get anywhere near this space because every time we've gone out there, it's rained, and we'd be knee-deep in mud out there."

On the group's first trip to the plantation, Pam took full advantage of her Cajun heritage to communicate with the spirit of a little girl in the overseer's house: "In this particular house in the upstairs, the first time we met, I sensed the presence of a small female child. I tried communicating and couldn't get any communication. The second time we went, I realized this child spoke no English. So my co-director and I began speaking to her in Cajun French. The dialect in different areas of Louisiana is different, so saying one word one way in one part of Louisiana, some Cajuns wouldn't be able to understand. After I spoke to her in Cajun, then she responded to me."

The second time the South Louisiana Ghosthunters visited the plantation in Labadieville, Pam received sensations from the site's Civil War past: "The last time we were at Labadieville, we were on the grounds, and there's an old barn out there. I looked, and I saw about five soldiers standing around in a semi-circle, like they were standing around a fire. So I told my team members there was a group of Confederate soldiers standing over there, and they all began taking pictures in that direction. They got some very, very bright blue and green orbs when they analyzed their pictures." Although the movement and the color of the orbs has convinced Pam that her group has photographed energy on the property, she will not go so far as to swear that these balls of light are ghosts. During this same investigation, Pam also made physical contact with one of the spirits in the house: "I was pushed. One of my members was standing behind me when this happened, and he got pretty shook up. He didn't leave. In the guidelines, it states that if you run or you cry or you scream, you are done for in this group. He just said to me, 'I think I've got to go outside and take a breather,' and I said, 'O.K.'" The young man was totally unprepared for what he might encounter on an investigation because he was a relatively new member, and it was the first time he'd ever seen anything like this.

Pam returned to the sugar plantation with one of her group's members, Michelle, for a segment of the *Ghosthunters* television show that first aired on the Sci-Fi Channel on August 10, 2005. "T.A.P.S. had secured Brennan's [Restaurant] and the Hotel Monteleone, and they had another group in New Orleans that supposedly had another residence for them to do, but that fell through, so they found us on the Internet and got in touch with us," Pam said. "They didn't make reservations in time in New

Orleans, and the Crescent City Classic was going on, so the only hotel they could get was in Gretna. We met them in Gretna, and from the time we started filming at the hotel, the film crew had to be back to the hotel room in twelve hours, or [Sci-Fi] would have had to start paying them [the crew] mega bucks overtime. So we did not spend enough time at the sugar plantation. We got there at five o'clock and left about nine-thirty." Pam believes that because the T.A.P.S. investigation lasted just four-and-a-half hours, the only piece of evidence the group collected was video footage of a door opening and closing by itself. She also credits the paltry evidence to the fact that too many people were crowded into the house at a single time: "They had a twenty-one-member film crew, there were seven members of T.A.P.S., there was the producer and the location manager, there were the two residents, and Michelle and me."

Disappointed by the T.A.P.S. investigation of the sugar plantation, Pam returned there with her own group and a documentary filmmaker on August 20, 2005. This time, the spirits were much more active in the room where the door had opened by itself during the T.A.P.S. investigation: "We put a camera in that room, and we got some very interesting light anomalies. The light bulb hanging from the ceiling started swinging back and forth. My tech-support guy stopped it, and we decided to try to get [the spirit] to do it again, and it did."

The spirits in the house were much more aggressive in the attic: "When you enter [the attic], there are two rooms hidden off to the side. We believe they may have hidden valuables or Confederate soldiers there because the plantation was taken over by Union soldiers at one time. I was showing the filmmaker one of the hiding rooms, and something grabbed me from behind and started dragging me into the room. It took Michelle and two of my guys to drag me out of the attic because the harder they pulled one way, the harder [the entity] pulled the other way." Once Pam's group had rescued her from the grasp of the ghost, it began attacking her physically: "Twice, I felt hands on the back of my head. Then [the ghost] pushed my head into a windowsill. It also pushed my head into a beam." Moved by concern for Pam's welfare, her group escorted her down the attic stairs. As they were walking through the front door, Pam was overcome by a sensation of icy coldness. Then she fell face-forward on the ground: "At that point, my team said, 'You've done enough. That's it. No more. We're gone.' I didn't want to pack up and leave, but they made me." Pam promises to return to the sugar plantation someday and rid the house of its menacing phantom, which she believes is the ghost of the little girl: "It has become very evident that I am the catalyst. She does not like me. I'm going back until I get rid of her. That's my ultimate goal, and that's why she fights me. She knows I am the only one who can get rid of her."

Pam brought away more than just photographs and recordings from a private residence where the homeowner's sister had committed suicide. "This lady's sister had killed herself, and she and her children were seeing things in their home," Pam said. "We got some really good EVP's from that. It also seems as though the sister attached herself to me and is still to this day communicating with me. When she's talking to me at my house and telling me things to say to my sister, she's attached herself to me." The deceased woman's spirit made a startling revelation to Pam during one of these conversations: "One day, she said something to me. I didn't know what it meant. I said it to the sister, 'You're for the milkman.' And when I said that to her, she totally lost it and broke down in tears." Sensing that the statement held a special meaning for the lady, Pam asked her for an explanation. "My sister used to say this to me when we were little because we looked so different. She had olive-colored skin, dark hair, and dark eyes. I have white skin, blonde hair, and blue eyes." Pam also learned that the two women were from a Cajun settlement known as Momou: "Mamou is the original site of Mardi Gras, where they still do Mardi Gras on horseback," Pam said. "So they are very, very Cajun. 'You're for the milkman' is exactly the way a Cajun would talk." This was one of many messages the spirit has given Pam to relate to her sister.

South Lousiana Ghosthunters also has the distinction of being one of the few ghost-hunting groups in the United States to have investigated the Myrtles Plantation. "The Myrtles is like my spiritual home," Pam said. "I'm out there at least once a month or so. There's never been a time when I've been to the Myrtles that I did not have some kind of experience." Even though the group was only permitted to investigate for a few hours on a Friday afternoon, the members still managed to collect some intriguing photographic evidence: "I do have a picture of a face in the front door of the Myrtles. There's the front door and two glass panels on the side of the door. No one was there but the staff, myself, and my co-director. I had her go through the house and make sure there was no one there because I could see someone looking through the window at me. She came back and gave me the all clear. I took the picture, and there is definitely a face in the window. We also got a picture of a vortex."

Pam considers the group's investigation of the Myrtles to be incomplete because of the approach the members usually employ when they investigate a location. "We do an initial tour of the facility in the daytime, but we do the main investigation at night," Pam says. "We find that the quieter the house is, the more you can hear and record. And I do feel that there are specific times and hours and circumstances that make for more activity." Pam admits that she also prefers to investigate according to the phases of the moon, but doing so is not always possible: "I've got so many investigations lined up that it would be silly for me to schedule them during certain moon phases. But I do find that I do get a little bit higher activity during certain moon phases."

Pam has learned from experience that "hype" and "hauntings" do not always go together, especially in Louisiana. The owner of the Myrtles, for example, is not entirely comfortable with the mansion's reputation as one of the most haunted houses in the United States. "A lot of these old homes are state historical sites, and they don't like for them to discuss it," Pam says. "That's why the Myrtles [personnel] will only discuss it on their mystery tour at night. If you ask about it during the daytime tours, they won't say anything. I know Tina Moss personally, the lady who owns the Myrtles. She doesn't allow her employees to discuss anything they have seen." Like the Myrtles, Destrehan Manor tries to downplay its ghost stories, even though many investigators, like Pam Gates, believe that it is truly haunted. Oak Alley, however, does not quite live up to the reputation it has with ghost hunters and locals. "I've been to Oak Alley a few times because it's not very far from my home," Pam says. "It's not the most active plantation I've ever been to. The only presence I've ever sensed at Oak Alley is the lady who was the first owner. I've sensed her presence really heavily in the bedroom. But other than that, they don't really promote it that much as being haunted."

In addition to directing South Louisiana Ghosthunters, Pam has collected her conversations with the ghosts she's encountered in a book called *Stories from the Spirit*: "For example, when I was in Labadieville, I had a very long conversation with a soldier. The way it came about was my technical director at the time had his night-vision camera and saw something in the field pacing back and forth. Then I approached the spot and began a conversation with this entity. [The soldier's spirit] told me what happened to him, why he was there and what he was looking for. I have several stories like that, and it's basically what they have said to me."

Pam admits that she has earned a reputation for herself as being a taskmaster in the mode of Jason Hawes of *Ghosthunters* fame: "A lot of disgruntled former members have called me 'the female Jason.' We took a picture of the both of us in the 'mad-Jason' pose. If we are on an investigation and I give you a task to do, you need to get on the task and stay on it. I don't allow people to do their own thing." Most directors agree with Pam that structure is an essential element in any investigation.

Pam Gates regrets the crass commercialism that has seeped into South Louisiana's best-known city, New Orleans. "I was born and raised in New Orleans, and I don't like the fact that it has been turned into a vampire mecca. There was never any mention of vampire activity in New Orleans until Ann Rice became famous, so I take offense to this. I hate that people have turned New Orleans into a freak show." Resisting the temptation to "cash in" on Louisiana's haunted reputation is not difficult for Pam because she is not in it for fame or fortune: "I don't want to be a TV star. We do this for the pure love and passion we have for it, not for money at all. If this could be my full-time job, believe me, I'd be in heaven."

Mississippi

Mississippi Paranormal Research

CARROLTON, MISSISSIPPI

Sonia Lindsey, Founder and Director

Sonia Lindsey developed an interest in the paranormal after she and her husband moved to Mississippi from Dallas, Texas. They moved into an old house out in the country in Lexington. "I was told that the house was about one hundred and twenty years old," Sonia says. "We had heard stories from people who had lived there before. It took a little bit of time before we began noticing anything." The first indication they had that the stories might be true was the sound of blues music playing when neither the radio nor the television was on. Then they began noticing things disappearing and other things showing up in their place, like dishes, glasses, certain glasses: "We're big NASCAR fans, and I have a set of NASCAR glasses, and they kept disappearing one at a time," Sonia said. "I was thinking, 'Well, someone's taken off with them in the car.' We never could find them. We came home one day, and we had a bowl sitting where the NASCAR glasses usually were. I'd never seen it before in my life. It was dirty. It had old dirt caked on it."

Eventually, Sonia and her husband began searching for answers on the Internet: "We learned a lot, photography, EVP's, EMF meters, all that kind of stuff. So we started buying equipment.

A digital camera was the first thing we bought, taking pictures. A lot of pictures turned out with orbs. Then we got a lot of pictures with a mist. An ectoplasmic mist is what I guess the proper term would be. It's not in the same shape or form as cigarette smoke. And most of the time there would be a bright, bright orb associated with that. We found that in a couple of rooms in the house." When Sonia and her husband walked through the house with an EMF meter, they began getting strong readings from a room, which turned out to be the same place where they were getting strange images in their pictures.

After satisfying themselves that the photographic evidence was genuine, the couple decided to begin collecting audio evidence: "We bought a couple of cassette recorders. The very first one, we hooked up a regular microphone to it—I'm a singer, so we have several microphones—and we left it at the house. We locked everything up. We let it record. When we came home, we listened back to it. There was nobody home except the cat. We have two doors—front door and back door. They were locked. The doors were both closed because I don't allow the cat in the bedroom. So we listened back to the tape, and it was really weird because the first thing you could hear was a door slam, and it doesn't sound like any of our doors. It sounds like a big door. And the next thing we heard was somebody running across the floor, maybe in heels or something. It came up on the cat. The cat did its little hissing thing. You can hear that on the tape. And then you hear the footsteps run back, and the door slams again." This recording was the first EVP Sonia ever recorded.

On their next investigation of the house, the Lindsey's attempted to interact with the spirit in their house. They started asking questions, like, "Is anybody here?" or "Is there anything you'd like to say?" while the tape recorder was running: "A lot of the time, we didn't get anything, but a good bit of the time, we did. We didn't get names or anything. We got sentences, weird sentences. We had one particular one that was really good. We listened back to it, and you could hear a voice coming in and trying to speak, but you couldn't make out what they were saying. And then another voice, a definite voice, came on top of that and just as plain as day, [said], 'Not you, you dead spirit.' It sounded to me like a young black man."

Sonia and her husband asked the spirit its name, but with no success: "When we ask questions, we very seldom get names. A lot of times, I think they have something they'd rather say instead of giving their names. Maybe they feel that their names aren't important." Convinced that the other presence in their house was a former occupant, Sonia tried to find out the spirit's identity in the library: "I did some research and learned that there was a house there before that one, and it was a huge house. The man who built it was Jeremiah Coleman. He built it in 1845. The man who built the house we moved into had died. His name was Samuel Coleman, and he was a black man. I think the story goes that Jeremiah had a black mistress and brought her there, and it turned out to be a black family."

Sonia formed Mississippi Paranormal Research three years ago. Her members range from businessmen and -women and construction workers to housewives and teenagers. However, most of them have had experiences themselves of some kind and actually believe in the paranormal. Sonia and her husband have artistic backgrounds: "I've sung all my life. I've been in bands. I had my own band for seventeen years in Dallas. My husband's a drummer. We play every other weekend at a little club up the road up here.

During the day, I write, if I'm not painting. My husband paints. We paint houses sometimes here and there. I write fiction. I have written a couple of children's fantasy stories for ages nine and up. I've got a romance book I'm working on now." Mississippi Paranormal Research also has members on their group site on Yahoo who live out of state. All of their new members are required to read and sign their on-line handbook before they can go on investigations: "They learn about what you can and can't do, how to take pictures, [how to record] EVP's, things like that. All members must wear I.D. badges on investigations. We also tell them to have homeowners sign release forms so we can post their photographs on the Internet. This is protocol that we learned from other ghost-hunting groups." Sonia's members are required to buy their own equipment: "We have our digital camera and our Sony Nite Shot camcorder, motion detectors, two-way radios, infrared thermometers, EMF meters, tape recorders, voice recorders. Most of our members bring digital cameras or tape recorders."

Unlike most paranormal groups, Mississippi Paranormal Research has been able to photograph apparitions: "We've gotten pictures of people that you can only see half of them, or we've gotten a full figure standing behind a tombstone that you can see through. I got one at an old cemetery here in Carrollton, dating back to the 1700s. It was after a tornado came through a couple of years ago that messed up tombstones and the fences they put around them. I was pointing my camera down at an area you couldn't drive through because of the debris, and there was a lady standing down there. If you zoomed in on it, you could make out her head, her hair, her blouse. From her knees down, there was nothing. I took the picture, and there was nobody there when I took the picture." At this time, Sonia was using a digital camera, but members of her group have also captured apparitions with 35 mm cameras.

Mississippi Paranormal Research's most memorable investigation was the Bearmash Cemetery. Sonia admits to feeling uneasy the moment they walked into the cemetery and separated: "I heard footsteps crackling in the leaves behind me. I got a little scared because there was nobody behind me." The members collected audio and visual recordings and returned home. When the members analyzed the evidence, they were amazed by what they found. In addition to several orbs and a "twisted light" form that defies classification, the group recorded some fascinating EVP's: "One was a woman whispering, but you couldn't make out what she was saying. Another one was 'Adam!' Those that pop out like that are the ones I'm really interested in. I'm trying to figure out what they're saying and why they're saying it. We had one that we recorded in front of a little girl's grave, and the only thing we heard her say was 'Bear.' It was as plain as day. That was pretty interesting." Sonia laments the fact that one of the most interesting EVP's was barely understandable because one of the investigators was talking too loudly. Still, Sonia believes the EVP is the voice of a little boy saying, "I'm up here."

Approximately 40 percent of their investigations reveal genuine hauntings. "Most of the investigations we've done, something was happening in the house. Most of the times, we turn up something." The group's relatively high success rate reflects their mission: "A lot of groups try to disprove things, whereas we try to prove things." The group also puts more emphasis on orbs than other groups do: "But the ones we consider are true orbs are the ones we've had something else happen around them, like sudden temperature drops, maybe a voice, or felt a breeze or had a door shut behind them. And usually they're brighter and denser. We have gotten some that are actually moving from one place to another in a certain direction." Someday, Sonia would like to take her group to Yazoo, Mississippi: "There are a lot of places I'd like to investigate, like Glenwood Cemetery in Yazoo—the witch's grave. They have her grave surrounded by a fence. I'll bet we could get a lot of orbs there."

Orbservations

MERIDIAN, MISSISSIPPI

Gigi Ahrens, Director and Founder

Gigi Ahrens was raised to believe that nothing is truly weird. "The paranormal was not considered to be something odd or off the wall," she said. She maintained her interest in the paranormal after marriage but did not really act on it until she found other women who shared her fascination with the unseen world. "Most of us are bored housewives," Gigi says. "We'd sit around and talk about goofy phenomenon, stuff that's unknown and mysterious, and one day, I said, 'Instead of just sitting around talking about it, why don't we do something about it?'" In 2004, she and her friends began structuring themselves into a bona fide group. All five of the active members are female.

Gigi's group decided from the beginning not to charge for the investigations or do fund-raising. Consequently, financing their hobby is a constant problem: "Everybody has their own equipment. We all cram into one car. Because gas prices are so high, we just can't do the traveling that we'd like to. We're not looking to make money. It's for our benefit."

The group's original reason for setting up its Web site was to find a safe way to keep records of the investigations. As the number of hits on the Web site increased, Gigi decided to make it more attractive. After a few weeks, the group gave itself a name: "It just dawned on us that we had structure and were an actual group, even though we aren't professionals. [Investigating] is just something we love, and if you are going to do something you love, you ought to do it right."

Orbservations' Web site gives the impression that the members only investigate cemeteries. Actually, the members do visit private homes, but they feel compelled not to publicize these investigations. "A lot of people don't want pictures of their homes shown to the public on the Internet," Gigi says. "Either their house isn't as clean as they would like for it to be, or they don't want other people to know that they've seen a ghost. Some people look at it as a stigma."

Gigi can certainly sympathize with people who do not want to look foolish on the Internet. In fact, she and her members are very selective about the photographs that appear on their Web site because they do not want to risk ridicule: "We have a lot of fabulous pictures that we haven't used because we know people would think we were crazy. It would seem like we were grasping at straws. We don't want to convince anybody, but we don't want to look like crackpots, either."

One of the greatest unknowns involved in investigating private residences is the way the homeowners will react if the group finds a logical explanation for the disturbance. "Some people are disappointed," Gigi says. "You can see it in their faces. Sometimes we get people who are so worked up their minds, they know we're going to tell them their home is haunted. If we tell them there's nothing here to write home about, it really hurts their feelings." Gigi believes that a large number of clients do not understand why her group conducts investigations of private homes: "We're not trying to prove that a place is haunted. We are trying to see what we can pick up and try to explain it. We are more inclined to disprove something than to prove it."

Gigi's first investigation was generated in response to a strange incident that occurred when a real-estate agent was showing them a house. The house had been vacant for years, and the power and utilities were turned off as well. The real-estate agent was reluctant to enter the house when it was almost sunset, and no one had brought along a flashlight. "She wanted to come back during the day, but we were on a rushed schedule. We told her we really wanted to see the house so we could get back to what we were doing." Fortunately, Gigi had a light on her video camera, so she led her husband, her son, and the real-estate agent through the house. They were walking in the back hall when something very strange happened in the bathroom: "In the very back is a bathroom, and in the bathroom, they have one of those old metal coil heaters in the ceiling. We were in the hallway, and she was describing something that was done to the house a couple of years back, and about that time, the heater fired up. She said, 'O.K. I'll meet you outside.' My son has been around spooky stuff all his life, so he wasn't fazed at all." After Gigi's family finished their tour of the house, the real estate agent apologized for being frightened. Gigi's reply was, "I think we want the house."

After Gigi and her family had lived in their new home for a while, their son had an encounter: "My son told me one night that he had seen a little kid about five or six years old out of the corner of his eye in the house, and I thought, 'Whatever,'" Gigi said. She asked the previous owner if her son's sighting was just a figment of his imagination. Gigi was shocked by his answer: "Oh, no, no. There was a little boy who died in the house. He fell in a well and broke his neck." He went on to explain that when he was growing up in the house, he was often awakened at night by strange noises. The man's story reminded Gigi that they had discovered a straight-shaft well in the basement shortly after moving in, but they had not given it much thought. Gigi's husband suggested that she check out the well to see if it was the origin of the paranormal activity, so she took her first ghost photographs. "I figured this house would be a good place to start [our first investigation] because there had been nobody living in the house for years, and we hadn't started working on the house, and there was nothing in the house. That's what started the whole ball rolling." Gigi credits the incident with the real-estate agent with making her want to learn more and share her knowledge and experiences with her friends. She said the haunting of her own house also impressed her with the importance of researching the history of the buildings they investigate.

Orbservations' most humorous investigation was conducted at Stuckey's Bridge, which is the oldest iron bridge in Lauderdale County. The groups was attracted to the old landmark by the legends about a member of the Dalton gang who robbed and murdered people who visited his inn and buried them around the bridge. Gigi says that one night the group decided on the spur of the moment to go out to the bridge and take some still pictures. "We drove across the bridge, and it made a spine-tingling squeal. I wanted to crawl out of the roof of the car. It really shook me up. The others thought it was funny." The group had just unloaded the equipment when the sheriff showed up. The sheriff told the women that he and his deputies were trying to arrest teenagers who were down there drinking. "I said we weren't drinking, and we certainly weren't teenagers. He saw all our equipment lying there, and he thought we were crazy. I told him what we were doing, and he asked if we needed any help." The group's flashlights were not powerful enough to illuminate the entire structure, so the sheriff aimed his spotlights on the bridge, enabling the members to take photographs. To dramatize the arrival of the sheriff's car on the Web site, one of the members videotaped the sheriff's car arriving with its flashers and blinkers on. With the help of the sheriff, the group captured some intriguing images on film: "We got a mist in one of the pictures, and nobody was smoking that night. We sat in the car and had our last cigarette and then went out there. It wasn't cold, so the temperature didn't cause the mist. It was warm out. It wasn't humid. We got a mist and a couple of good orbs. I think that spine-tingling squeal just put everybody's nerves on edge just that much more." Gigi was so shaken up that one of the other members had to drive her car back over the bridge.

Other historic sites in Lauderdale County have also yielded some tantalizing evidence. On May 19, 2005, this writer accompanied the group on an investigation of an old abandoned cemetery in the Broadmoor area behind Temple Beth Israel in Meridian, Mississippi. After climbing over fallen trees and stepping around several sunken graves, the investigators managed to photograph some orbs, most of which hovered around the grave of John

Franklin, one of the few marked graves in the entire cemetery. Gigi conceded, however, that the orbs could have been made by insects flying around the woods that night. That same week, Gigi and another member of her group, Brandy Smith, investigated the second story of Peavey Melody Music in downtown Meridian. In the aftermath of the tornado of 1906, fifty bodies were carried up the stairs to the second story of the building, which, at the time, was being used as a funeral home. This time, the investigators photographed orbs and what appeared to be a cluster of faces in a mist.

Orbservations collects photographic evidence primarily because of problems the members encountered while trying to record EVP's: "When we did get an EVP, we had trouble getting it off the digital recorder without compromising the integrity of the sound. I need to get equipment that's right for the job. We don't analyze videotape too deeply, so I don't know if we have captured any EVP's on videotape or not." Because the group investigates outdoor locations primarily, background noise has been a problem. "Also, there are very few places where we can leave our recorders safely," Gigi said.

Gigi admits that security is a very important consideration for an all-female group. Usually, the women avoid "questionable" areas altogether. Once in a while, though, the women bring their husbands along: "It's not always safe for a bunch of women to walk around in the dark. This is when we get our husbands to go with us from time to time."

S.P.I.R.E.

PONTOTOC, MISSISSIPPI

Jeff Harris, Founder and Director

Jeff started reading about the paranormal in the 1980s when he was in college. His interest waned for a number of years. Then in 2001, he began investigating on his own. In 2002, he began recruiting members for a group: "I put a random e-mail out on a message board saying, 'I want to form a group.' You'd be amazed how many people responded. But I was picky. 'If you do drugs, you're out of the group.' 'If you're too young, you're out of the group.' I wasn't trained to throw people out, but you've got to have a believable witness." Jeff has two sensitives in his group, both of whom come in very handy during investigations: "One is ghost bait. She'll say, 'Shoot a picture now' or 'Go over this way.' And every time she says something, there's something in the picture, or the meters will go off. The other one is an empath, who seems to be able to tell where to set up. By combining the two, we don't rely on them as evidence, but they seem to lead us to the right places constantly without error. I can't use them as evidence, but I can use them as bloodhounds."

The members of S.P.I.R.E. come from a variety of backgrounds. Jeff is a house painter during the day and a musician at night. The eight other active members are musicians as well. The group also has six or seven inactive members, who just "come and go." The group conducts investigations all year round: "We try to get together twice a month, although it slowed down to once a month in December. I had to give it a break. I'm getting burned out. I'm also handing leadership over to another person." S.P.I.R.E's Web site generates twenty e-mails a month requesting help with a haunting, but Jeff rarely responds to more than two: "After you read through, you get a sense of the ones that are legitimate and the ones that are really 'out there.' We also investigate public places. We investigate the history and legends the best I can and try to confirm or deny what is supposed to be there."

S.P.I.R.E. has found it difficult to get access to some local sites because of objections from some of the Christians in town: "I approached the chamber of commerce about it and said, 'Why don't we do a haunted tour at Halloween because of all the haunted places in town?' One of the members said that the idea offended him because of his Christian beliefs, they don't want the town associated with that kind of thing. Now don't get me wrong. I'm a Christian, but the closed-mindedness of this town is really surprising." The fear of ridicule has made some people reluctant to talk about the ghosts in their homes: "Even people who do have haunted houses here don't want anyone to know they have had ghost experiences here. Even when they call us to help stop something, they don't want anyone else to know who they are or where their house is." S.P.I.R.E. has also had difficulty getting permission to investigate the local cemetery at night: "The cemetery in Pontotoc is now closed at night, so I went out there early one morning before it was light. I ended up with some fantastic pictures, high readings, EVP's. It's a very active spot, and I have yet to track down all the legends about the place. They put an announcement in the newspaper that they didn't want anyone in the cemetery at night."

The investigators have found that the best way to produce indisputable evidence is to go into an investigation in a dubious frame of mind: "We measure all the electrical magnetic fields. We trace them down. We try to look for the logical or scientific cause of the phenomena. We need something to confirm everything we have. If we have a great picture, but we don't have any EMF readings to confirm it or video to go with it, we can't count it. If our meter picks something up and we see it but we don't have a picture of it, we don't count it. We have to have two non-personal confirmations." Jeff admits, though, that he is the only genuine skeptic in the group: "If I watch a video with an orb flying by, I say, 'Wow! But do we have anything to back it up?' If not, we have to throw it out." In fact, Jeff's primary objection to the *Ghosthunters* television show is the fact that they are too eager to believe: "They might catch something on video, but they don't back it up. And then they will get an EVP with nothing else there, and they will say it's reliable, and that's wrong."

Sometimes, though, the group has disproved the haunting of a private home a bit prematurely. "One time, we were in a little house, and we said, 'There's no way this place is haunted!' And while we were there, the bathroom door shut and latched from the inside. So what it boils down to is that it's only our opinion that the place isn't haunted."

Jeff Harris has collected some expensive equipment over the years, but he has found that the most effective equipment is often the cheapest: "I'm sitting here looking at Geiger counters and large EMF meters that are just collecting dust. I use a small

Wal-Mart twenty-nine-dollar recorder to collect EVP's. It works great. I also use just a little hand-held meter. I just use the basics. You don't have to spend a lot of money to do an investigation. You need a pair of eyes and a notebook. You also need a witness for confirmation." Jeff's group uses 35 mm and digital cameras as well, but he prefers digital: "If you take the TV remote and push down the button, you won't see anything, but if you hold it in front of a digital camera and do this, you'll see a white dot. This is because it's picking up infrared. Most of the older digitals can pick up infrared. Most people don't know this."

Before S.P.I.R.E. undertakes an investigation at a private residence, the homeowners are interviewed. The psychologist in the group asks them such personal questions as "Do you do drugs?" or "Is there a history of insanity in your family?" Afterward, the entire group watches the videotape of the interview in order to determine whether or not the homeowners are telling the truth. "If they are telling the truth, we go in, even if they are a little nuts—you know, not completely out there on drugs," Jeff says. "After we do that, I'd say out of every hundred, we might pick up something on 5 percent of those. And out of that 5 percent, maybe one might actually have something. It's like 1 percent, or half of 1 percent. It's not like there are ghosts everywhere. We are pretty picky." The members of S.P.I.R.E. are always excited if they can verify a haunting, but it is almost as satisfying if they can disprove one by finding out that it's an air vent causing that cold spot or a pipe causing that moaning. If homeowners ask Jeff to stop a haunting, he refers them to people who do that sort of thing.

The Faxton House sticks in Jeff's mind as S.P.I.R.E.'s most memorable investigation. The old house was the home of

Dr. Faxton, who was one of the founders of Pontotoc. In the town museum, we have Dr. Faxton's original office down there, and they build him up some kind of great hero who set up this town. The house's legendary past piqued Jeff's interest: "The old-timers have different stories about Dr. Faxton. They say he was the mayor of the town. He was a doctor. He was the sheriff. He was the judge. He was the jury. And he was the executioner. Supposedly there were five or six lynchings on his property at this old tree. Apparently, he was like Judge Roy Bean. I don't know which story to believe. There is no written history on the man." At the time S.P.I.R.E. visited the house, it was abandoned. The last resident lived there in the 1970s.

"They found the old man cooked under an electric blanket," Jeff said. "He passed out while it was on 'high.' He basically got roasted. His relatives pulled his body out onto the porch. There were about five or six people present. And there was lightning flashing all around. The power went out. And when the lights came back on, there were only two people left. The rest got scared and ran off. No one ever wanted to go near this house. It had a reputation for years and years and years." Of course, once the members learned of the house's tragic history, they were eager to investigate it.

The group received permission from Mayor Faxton to spend the night at the old house. "The owners live in Texas and let the town use it. They use it as a tax write-off," Jeff said. Jeff usually keeps the number of investigators small when visiting a house to prevent crowding. After the four members of the group got settled in the house, Jeff split them up into groups of two. For the first few hours, the group found no evidence at all of paranormal activity. The place seemed to be dead. However, at 9:00 P.M., the situation changed dramatically: "Every meter went off at once. We got video of things moving. There was a coat hanger stuck on one of the walls on a nail. One of our people said out loud to the entity, 'Can you make that move if you are actually here?' And I swear, the thing actually started swinging fast." Aside from a variety of orbs, the group also got some incredible EVP's, including one voice that said, "Go away!" and another that said, "Monster!" The flurry of activity lasted until 10:45, when it stopped abruptly.

A few days later, the group returned to the Faxton House for a second investigation. Expecting something to happen at 9:00, the group arrived at 8:30. "At nine o'clock, sure enough, it started happening again," Jeff said. "This time, it stopped right after ten o'clock." The investigators collected more evidence, but not as much as they had on their previous visit.

Ironically, the only member of S.P.I.R.E who has ever panicked during an investigation is a male, who ran out of one house almost screaming. Most of the females in the group, though, are rock solid, even when something exceptionally weird has happened. Jeff recalls one young woman who stayed on site, even though she did not want to: "At a place in Jackson, one of the girls wanted to leave. She sat there shivering, panicking, saying, 'I can't stand it!' Finally, I told her to leave, and she did. We allow that. If somebody's uncomfortable, it's best to go outside, get in the car, and go home. We always set up a backup. We don't want to pressure somebody to have to stay." Jeff wants to avoid a situation where he tells the homeowner there is nothing paranormal in the home, and then one of his members runs screaming out of the front door.

One of the group's most startling investigations took place at an old factory. Before the group went out there, the owner of the building had told Jeff about an incident that occurred one Halloween night when it was being used as a "Haunted House" for a community organization. The owner said that one group was taking the circular route through the factory, and they saw an old man. He was wearing coveralls and a hat, and he just stood there, smiling. Several young people told the owner about the strange man, and he matched the description of the ghost that is supposed to haunt the old factory. Apparently, the ghost was enjoying the "Haunted House" as much as the kids were.

When S.P.I.R.E investigated the old factory, the members began collecting EMF readings, photographs, and EVP's not long after they arrived. Suddenly, Jeff discovered that his wife was missing: "She goes along with me on investigations. She was on the far side of the factory. We could see her with her flashlight. Then her flashlight goes out, and the lights above go out. We were sitting there doing EVP's. We try to keep it dim. Then everybody froze. We started hearing this clawing, scratching noise. It sounded like somebody was gouging or scraping the cement." Jeff became concerned because his wife was alone. As Jeff ran in the direction where he had left his wife, some of the members began yelling, "Oh, my god! Oh, my god!" When he finally caught sight of her, she was bending over, and then she seemed to disappear: "I went over to her, and she had bent down and was petting a puppy that had come in underneath the floor. It was scratching its claws on the cement. It panicked the whole group, even me. We thought she had disappeared, but she was just bent down petting the thing."

The group also spends a lot of time in cemeteries. "There's a lot of emotional energy left in cemeteries, so it's a great place to train people," Jeff says. "I wouldn't bring somebody new into a

private residence, so we investigate a lot of cemeteries." Not only
are cemeteries are a great place to go and have a picnic, but they
are usually beautifully maintained. "Plus, no one bothers you,"
Jeff says. "I imagine that if there are any spirits there, they enjoy
the company."

Even though the only full-body apparition the group has ever
photographed was captured in Pontotoc Cemetery, Jeff does not
believe that most cemeteries are haunted: "They're 'dead,' if you
will pardon the pun."

Even though S.P.I.R.E goes to great lengths to collect evidence
that holds up to scrutiny, he is fully aware that it is impossible to
prove a haunting: "Modern science does not accept videotape.
Modern science does not accept electromagnetic field readings. It
doesn't accept photographs because it cannot be reproduced. And
if it cannot be reproduced, it cannot be called a scientific fact, even
with all of the historical evidence." However, the fact that every
culture in the world has ghost legends has convinced Jeff that there
has to be something to the paranormal. Jeff can never envision a
time when he will stop investigating; hunting is in his blood: "I
don't hunt [deer]. I hunt things that are already dead. If I'm going
to hunt meat, it's got to be wrapped in plastic."

North Carolina

East Coast Hauntings Organization

BATH, NORTH CAROLINA

Christine Rodriguez, Founder and Director

Christine Rodriguez is, first and foremost, a writer. She started out by writing a book on the effects of feral dogs on wildlife. It was picked up by Tufts University Veterinarian School as a textbook. It took her five years to sell the book because it was so bizarre, but after it finally sold, she went on to other things: "I have written fiction and nonfiction. I wrote a fiction horror book in the same vein as Stephen King. Then I wrote collectible guides for a number of years. I coauthored with my twin sister. I did some collectible Sci-Fi stuff, motorcycle toy collectibles. We took all the photos for that. So we had to do studio photography for the models." Christine stopped writing for nine years. Then in 2003, she revamped some old manuscripts and sold one of them right away. Christine's second novel—a mystery—was published in April 2005. Someday, she would like to write a nonfiction book on the paranormal.

Before coming to North Carolina, Christine was founder and director of a group in Florida called P.O.R.T.A.L. The story of the evolution of P.O.R.T.A.L. reflects the instability of many paranormal groups. After leaving a subgroup of North Florida Paranormal Research, Inc., Christine started P.O.R.T.A.L. in 2002. The group consisted of four members, one of whom was an empath. The group experienced a high turnover in its membership during its two-and-a-half-year existence: "People on teams rotate quite a bit," Christine said. "They leave. One of the original members of P.O.R.T.A.L. had an impacted colon and had to go to the hospital fighting for her life. Different things happen. People get divorced. It's hard for people to continue doing this straight through on a volunteer basis, and I know all groups suffer from this problem." In January 2005, she founded a new group in Bath, North Carolina. By February, she had only two members, both of whom are still undergoing training. Actually, though, Christine is not looking to recruit very many more members: "I don't like a large group. Four or five are enough. If you can sustain four or five members for more than six months, you're lucky."

Since moving from Florida to North Carolina, Christine has had to change her group's name because another group in Tennessee was already using the name: "I contacted them and told them this had been my name in Florida for two and a half years, and it might be confusing for browsers to pull up the same name. They might think we're related, which we aren't. They agreed to take the dots out of P.O.R.T.A.L. but leave everything [else] the same. A browser doesn't know the difference. I wrote them and thanked them for considering the change. Then I went about changing the name." Changing the name of her group turned out to be a very expensive decision because she had already made a large number of T-shirts with the P.O.R.T.A.L. logo. The group's new name is E.C.H.O.—East Coast Hauntings Organization.

The members of E.C.H.O. buy only the equipment that fits into their budgets, such as infrared cameras, thermometers, EMF meters, video cameras, analog tape recorders, digital tape recorders, and 35 mm cameras. Of course, there are some very expensive pieces of equipment that Christine would love to be able to afford: "Some people use Geiger counters, but they're quite expensive. The average groups can't afford them. A thousand-dollar thermal imagery camera is really costly. Nobody's going to be able to buy that. There's a lot of equipment I wish I had." Even more important than the type of equipment the group brings along on an investigation, Christine believes, is timing: "If it's going to happen, it's going to happen. I don't care what kind of equipment you're carrying. If you're in the right place at the right time, you'll get something." Christine prefers that all her members have their own cameras, EMF meters, and thermal thermometers.

Christine also uses her psychic abilities on investigations: "I'm clairsentient. That means I feel electromagnetic energy. Sometimes I feel it even before my EMF meter registers it. Over the years, I've gotten more and more sensitive. I can tell right away when something is eight to ten feet ahead of me, an energy of some sort. I can feel it. I'm sensitive to whatever energy is roving around and making the EMF meters and the digital thermometers act up. I'm assuming that it's some sort of spirit presence. So that really helps me take photos. I also tell other people where to shoot."

Christine is particularly fond of the spectral photos that her group has taken in locations where she has sensed a surge of energy. She believes her group would take even more amazing photographs if she were not the only clairsentient in the group. Like many investigators, though, she is skeptical of orbs unless they can be verified by EMF readings or temperature fluctuations. "I do think there are true orbs," she says. "They are probably plasma. We don't know if they are spirits or an afterlife of some sort." As fascinating as photos or video footage can be, Christine believes that EVP's are the one scientific tool that really attracts attention: "People will even try to discount EVP's, but some are so clear that they can't be discounted. When questions are directly answered by EVP, that's a little more tangible evidence."

Only 2 percent of all the group's investigations have produced really strong evidence of hauntings, either crystal-clear EVP's or physical manifestations. One of these investigations took place at the oldest house in Boynton Beach, the Andrews House. After the Andrews House was renovated as a historic home, staff and visitors began noticing strange activity in the house. Witnesses have seen beds move by themselves. Two different apparitions have been seen in the house. During the renovation of the house, work crews reported that some of their tools were missing. People on the first floor have heard the sounds of footsteps and furniture being moved across the floor. Frequently, staff members who enter the children's playroom in the morning have noticed that blocks placed on the floor changed positions during the night. In the same room, the staff members have found toys stored in a child's cabinet scattered all over the floor when the house is opened up in the morning.

The night that P.O.R.T.A.L. investigated the Andrews House, the members placed a video camera in the children's room and let it run for two hours. "When we went up, we had packed everything else, and we went up to get the video camera," Christine said. "We had no sooner unplugged the video camera and put it in a bag when we witnessed the physical movement of the cabinet door opening four times, and three times at my request after I closed it. We did not have a tape recorder to collect EVP's." After the activity stopped, the group

broke down all their equipment because they did not have anything else to document. Suddenly, the door to the child's cabinet began to open very slowly. "When the door opened the first
time and hit me in the chest, even I did a double take," Christine
said. "It's amazing how your brain tries to rationalize things.
I stopped talking, and the members across the room were looking at me. I just thought, 'Who opened that door?' They all
watched me, and I thought, 'If I bolt, they're going to bolt.' I said,
'Is there somebody here? That's a neat trick. Let's do it again.
I'm going to close the door, and you open it again.'" Christine
closed the door very gently, snapped it shut, and waited five seconds. Once again, the door unsnapped and slowly opened against
Christine's chest. After she closed the door, it opened again. This
time, it took ten seconds for the door to open. Christine told the
spirit, "One more time." After twenty seconds, the door opened
again. "I thought it wasn't going to open again, but it did,"
Christine said. "I closed the door, and it did not open the next
time, so I assumed that energy was being used up in some way.
Then we packed up, and I said, 'Thank you for putting up with
us. We are going to leave now.' And we left. That was the first I
had ever seen a physical manifestation." Four members of the
group witnessed the activity at the same time, adding even more
credence to Christine's story.

Christine senses that it was not a child's ghost who was opening the door because the energy she was feeling to her right side
was very strong: "In fact, it worried me a little bit how strong it
was. And this is why I thought it was a male. My impression was
also that it was an adult with some sort of mental handicap. He
wasn't dangerous or anything. It was very focused energy. The
energy comes in pulses. Males of eighteen or nineteen seem to

have more constant, focused energy. Children, though, tend to hover around your waist."

Another one of Christine's 2 percent places is Stranahan House in Fort Lauderdale, Florida. "It's the oldest in Fort Lauderdale," Christine says. "The Stranahan House is the best place for documentation that I have been to for EVP's or EMF readings. I've been there three times. I'm going back to Florida to do it again." Christine says that unlike the Andrews House, where the physical activity seems to be trying to get a reaction from the investigators, the activity in the Stranahan House is very subtle, and it usually happens when the house is locked. On one of the group's investigations at the Stranahan House, Christine was trying to communicate with spirits through dowsing, and she made contact with a little Seminole Indian girl. "The Stranahan House was originally a trading post in the late 1800s and early 1900s," Christine said. "Just by asking 'yes' and 'no' questions for thirty minutes, we came up with this little girl. She was eight years old, and she told us her name. This was surprising because seven people had died in the Stranahan House— it's historically documented—and there was no mention of a little Indian girl dying in the house. So this very chatty little spirit answered the questions with great strength and ability. She told us how she died and the year she died. I transcribed the entire dowsing, which we filmed so you can see the rods move. I was asking the questions, and Marlene was using my rods."

Christine said that representatives of the Historical Society of Fort Lauderdale, which is in charge of the house now, were dubious about the existence of the Seminole girl. Then about five weeks later, Christine received an e-mail message from the director of the Stranahan House asking her to bring her group back for another investigation. The director told Christine, "I went to the Historical Society in Fort Lauderdale and asked for pictures of the seven people we know died in the house. I found in the diary of Ivy Stranahan—one of the spirits we believe is there—she talks about the death of a little Seminole girl and the trading post. We were told that one of the people who died in the trading post was a Seminole woman. She keeled over dead in the trading post, and they had to have her ceremony in the trading post because they believed you had to have the ceremony where the person died."

Since moving to North Carolina in January 2005, Christine and her new group have investigated two historically haunted locations. Christine and another member of E.C.H.O., Sonya, investigated the North Carolina State Capitol in Raleigh on June 25–26, 2005. "Anyone who wanted to go could go," Christine said. "The group that had the connections with the Capitol was the Ghost Research Foundation of Pennsylvania, and I found out about it through another investigator. It was a two-night overnighter, Saturday and Sunday."

While the Ghost Research Foundation spent most of first night investigating the library on the third floor, Christine and Sonya were in the Governor's Office on the first floor. After walking around the first floor for an hour, Christine received word that the group in the library needed her assistance. "They were a young group. They didn't have much experience," Christine said. "They heard that I was sensitive, and they wanted me to tell them about the entity that was responsible for the orbs in their photos." Christine walked through the library and discovered a large concentration of electromagnetic energy around a window on the west side of the room. Christine then told the group to begin taking pictures to the left of her: "They were taking flashes of me. As soon as they started with their flashes, the energy dissipated and I had to tell them to stop with the pictures and let this thing get closer."

When the energy in the library began to dissipate, Christine began using her dowsing rods. She soon discovered that she had encountered a female spirit: "I talked to the female for a while. She was really reticent, though. She didn't want to give any information." Suddenly, Christine sensed the presence of a male spirit. "He was very good at working the rods," Christine said. "I asked him if he would spell his name, and he said, 'Yes.' We went up to three letters—Z, E, and B." Before she went any farther, a videographer from the Ghost Research Foundation told Christine to ask the man if he had four children. When the spirit responded in the affirmative, the videographer identified the ghost as the spirit of Zebulon Vance, the first governor of North Carolina. "He said Vance was here when Sherman marched down the street here to take the capitol," Christine said. "Everyone else had gotten on their horses and left. Zebulon did not want to lose the capitol and surrender it to the Union soldiers, so he stayed until he actually heard the drums of the Union soldiers coming down the street. He finally jumped on a horse and got out of here. He was someone who would have very strong feelings about the capitol and not want to leave it." Christine also believes that the ghost of the first governor of North Carolina is haunting the capitol because Vance lay in state in the rotunda on the first floor after his death.

Christine and Sonya ran into another spirit when they walked downstairs from the library. When the women reached the bottom of the stairs, Sonya told Christine that he smelled cigar smoke. "I even know what brand it is," Sonya said. "It smells like a

Swisher Sweet." Christine still could not smell the cigar smoke, so she took four steps, turned around, and took a picture where Sonya was standing. Christine was surprised to see an orb in the photo: "I showed Sonya and she said, 'See, I really did smell it.'" Later, she learned that one of the security tapes had captured the ghostly image of a man with a cigar. Another security camera had caught a mist coalescing in a chair at a desk in front of the podium in the senate.

The next night, Christine and Sonya went into the women's bathroom. "I went in first because Sonya was taking pictures in the hall," Sonya said. "It's a tiny bathroom with two stalls and a tiny porcelain sink. I went in and put my camera and glasses on the left side of the porcelain sink by the water faucet. I went into the bathroom and was sitting there quietly for thirty seconds before Sonya came through the door. She started talking to me as soon as she got through the door. She said, 'I went over to this one big window on the right side of the stall and looked out over the capitol grounds through this one window. I came out of the stall and went over to pick up my camera and glasses. My camera was still on the sink where I had left it, but my glasses had been opened and moved so that the eye pieces were put by the wall with the nose part of my glasses on the faucet because it looks like a face. It was perfectly balanced on these porcelain knobs in the back. The faucet looked like a big nose." Christine started laughing because she thought Sonya had done it. When Christine discovered that Sonya had not, she began laughing again: "That was the first time I have had a spirit play a joke on me. It was very clever."

When the women went downstairs, they were told that the bathroom was reputed to be haunted by a female spirit who made the faucet turn on by itself. Christine began dowsing in the bathroom and learned the identity of the spirit: "She spelled out her name as Joan Adams, and she was a former clerk at the capitol. She said she had no intentions of leaving because she liked it there. The energy was all over me. Most of the time, that's a positive emotional response. We were interrupted when people started coming into the bathroom."

Christine also believes she had a paranormal experience at two historic sites on Mordecai Square in Raleigh. While taking a tour of the Mordecai House, Christine sensed a female presence. As Christine and the docent, Janet Manuel, walked past some portraits of the Mordecai family, she was taken with the painting of a woman named Mary. "I asked the docent if this was Mary's bedroom, and she said, 'Yes.'"

Christine and the docent then made their way to the Andrew Johnson House, which is located directly behind the Mordecai House. "Nobody has ever seen anything," Christine said. "But they felt that somebody is watching. It's a very uncomfortable place." When the women walked up to the door, Janet asked Christine to enter the house and tell her what she felt. Christine walked over to a large fireplace on the first floor and told Janet, "You've got a lot of electrostatic energy in this corner. It's the spirit of a woman, and she hangs out in this corner on the left side of the fireplace. This fireplace is really important for some reason." After the women walked out of the house, Janet said, "I have told nobody this, but I went in one morning and opened the door and went around to the side of the front door to deactivate the security system, and as I got to the security system with my back to the corner you were talking about, I distinctly heard a woman clear her throat, like, 'Unnhh!' It was just as clear as if a woman were standing there. I whirled around. It scared the heck out of me. I re-set the alarm and bolted out of there."

Christine believes that most of the spirits she has encountered are much more than the energy they seem to project: "I think spirits can move on when they want to. I think they choose to be right where they are. Whatever personality quirks they had in life, they still have. They're choosing to stay right where they are until whatever they want resolved is resolved, which may never happen." Christine says she has never encountered a demonic spirit, but if she had, she would not even go near it: "I don't need to put myself in the position where I'd be in the presence of something that's really bad news. There's a safety factor involved. I don't know if people who do that are brave or stupid. Of course, people who are experiencing this kind of problem in their house probably need somebody." Christine is concerned about the psychological toll of conducting demonic investigations. She compares investigators who specialize in this kind of investigation to police officers who see too much of the horrible side of life: "The psychological effects would be powerful. Your whole perspective on the world would be affected. I'd rather be around something incorporeal that doesn't have a lot of physical strength. Disturbing malevolent entities is tapping a deep well, as far as I'm concerned."

Even though Christine's most successful investigations have been conducted at historical buildings, her favorites are residential investigations because they involve people who really need help: "I approach it from a psychological viewpoint since psychology was my major in college. I want to help people with things they can't cope with because a lot of this stuff is very distressing to people." She is confident that she and her group will be able to help their clients even more after advances are made in the equipment they use: "Face it, today's technology is not close to where it needs to be to prove anything. We've scratched the surface, but that's it."

Foothills Paranormal Investigations

MARION, NORTH CAROLINA

Rena Harp, Founder and Director

Rena Harp has had paranormal experiences all her life. Her first experience occurred at the age of ten when her father died: "I had a seizure, and they pronounced me dead. The ambulance drivers had called it in. Then I sat up in the ambulance and scared everyone half to death. I didn't see any white lights." Afterward, as Rena's psychic abilities seemed to grow, she accepted the fact that she had a gift. "I was encouraged by a local psychic here—Angela Moore—to follow my intuition," Rena said, "and she told me that if I just started a group, it would grow, and interest would be abundant, and she wasn't lying. I started this group in 2004, and I put it up on the Internet and created a free Web site, and I started getting responses from local people. I registered immediately with Yahoo and Google." While she was starting her group, Julie Sugrue, owner of Rowan Tree Books, allowed the group to hold their meetings there once a month. She also had business cards printed up to help with exposure. Only a month after starting her Web site, she had people calling her from Wilmington, Charlotte, Asheville, and West Virginia. Within six months, her group was up and running. "It actually started as a place to meet and find out our interests with the paranormal, and it kind of exploded from there," Rena said.

The members of the group buy their own equipment according to what they feel they're expert in. "Everybody seems to have their own field, and we work well together," Rena says. "We have some pretty good equipment—EMF meters, digital voice recorders, laptops, cameras. All of Rena's steady members have specific roles. Richard Liebeck—the "tech guy"—has been on the Learning Channel and several television shows about ghost hunting. Kyle, who is actually a pharmacist tech, specializes in recording EVP's. The husband and wife team of Chris and Donna Ellis do a lot of the photography.

Rena and two other women, Phyllis Lowe and Tammy Lee, handle the nontechnical side of the investigation, including the use of pendulums: "I've worked with the pendulum for nine years now. It seems to give me good results. We have another girl who hasn't been around lately. She's a sensitive. Her name is Donna Wheeler. We have our resident psychic who comes in after the investigation is done and tells the homeowners what she's feeling and what she's getting. We all bring something to the group." Rena puts more stock in her pendulum than anything else because it has never led her wrong: "Anytime my pendulum has been active, my investigators and their findings go nuts. What it's finding is an energy force. I can also use the pendulum to communicate with spirits." It took Rena an entire year before finding a pendulum, or rather, before one found her: "You find the one that you're drawn to. You hold it in your hand, and if it starts burning the inner part of your hand, or a tingling sensation starts, it's more likely than not that's the one you're supposed to have. It's a cosmic connection, I guess. I found it in downtown Asheville in a little shop. There were two of them in a glass enclosure. It was crystal, and it felt cold. But the minute I put my hand on the other one, it felt like fire. And it's been with me every day ever since." Some people say it is a spirit guide that makes a pendulum work, but Rena believes that the user must have some sort of natural intuition. Practicing every day does not hurt, either.

The members consider themselves an amateur group, even though they have been paid for two of their nine investigations. "We only take donations at this point," Rena says. The group now has eight or nine members who come every month, but all together the group has an outreach of about thirty-five or forty people. "We have a chat room on the Web site for the members in Wilmington and Charlotte. We have a small newsletter, and we let them know when we are going to have the meetings and what time we're going to be on-line. We kind of discuss everything from the previous investigation and talk about when our next investigation is," Rena says.

Rena believes that promotion is crucial to the survival of her group. The group advertises at the bookstore where the members hold their meetings, which attract a number of drop-ins from the community. A typical example is a member of the chamber of commerce who told the owner of the bookstore that she would like to attend the next meeting because she had experienced strange activity in her former house. The bookstore owner also mentions the group in the cards she sends her customers regarding upcoming events. Thanks to the publicity the group receives, the meetings average between ten and twenty-five people. Rena refuses to promote the group through T-shirt sales, though: "We are not trying to make money off our group. We do this because it fits in with our personal interests. Everybody in the group has a strong love for the paranormal. I think that we don't want to go that route of some groups that put on cruises, seminars, hotel haunts. We want to keep it on a small, local level."

The group's first investigation was in North Carolina. "A lady contacted me from New York," Rena said. "Her sister lives in Little Switzerland, which is right above Marion. She asked me some questions and wanted to know if we could be discreet. We did an investigation up there in December." Because Rena does not believe it makes a difference if they investigate at night or day, the group visited the house between 1:00 and 4:00 P.M. The members took photographs and recorded EVP's and returned. Rena says the EVP's they got were amazing: "You can hear Donna, one of our investigators, ask, 'Is anybody here? Would you like to make contact with us? We're here for you.' Then about three seconds after her last comment, you can hear someone whisper right into the microphone. When we heard that, we thought it might be the homeowner downstairs talking, so we gave her another tape and another tape recorder and we sent her to another area. I was analyzing the first, and I couldn't believe it, because it sounded like someone was whispering to her. You couldn't make out what the whisper was. So I put it in another one of our tape recorders and slowed it down, and that same whisper after eighteen seconds was a woman screaming. I had everyone there to make sure it wasn't my imagination, and it was definitely a woman screaming." Realizing that living people speak at a certain speed, Rena speculated that because the entity they had contacted was speaking from another realm, the members might have to slow down the recording of his voice just to pick it up. Rena said that the same thing happened on the other tapes: "The homeowner didn't have any cockatoos or animals, and she lives on top of a mountain. There was nothing outside. It was winter. We went through everybody's notes to make sure. When we analyzed the second tape, we heard two birds. We slowed that down and discovered it was two men fighting. I realized that something was going on here. That was really good evidence for us. That got us excited." While they were investigating the house in Little Switzerland, the members also photographed a couple of mists.

Rena admits to being somewhat uneasy during the Little Switzerland investigation, but only when it dawned on her that Donna, the member responsible for EVP's on that particular investigation, was in the room alone: "If it had been something evil, it could have responded in any manner. We talked about it afterwards. We're not going to have anyone working alone anymore. We will always have two people." Rena also said that having men in her group tends to reduce the "fear factor" on most investigations.

Foothills Paranormal Investigations also investigates historic sites. One of these was the 17Hundred90 Inn and Restaurant in Savannah, Georgia. According to legend, the inn is haunted by the ghost of Anna Powers, who fell in love with a married seaman and threw herself from a balcony into the courtyard below just a few days before her wedding. The most haunted room in the inn is Room 204. Rena and Tammy, a friend of hers, stayed in Room 203: "As soon as we got to that room, the door handles shook relentlessly—they are those long metal door handles— when we entered the room. When I got close to the closet, I began getting these sharp pains in my head. It was like someone was poking me." Later that evening, the women were getting ready to go on one of Savannah's ghost walks. Rena was sitting on the bed watching television when she heard the door handle shake. She did not think much about it at first because ever since she and Tammy had checked in, they had heard the door handle rattle: "We thought somebody was at the wrong room and was trying to get in." This time, she looked over at the door to her right, and the handle was not moving. Rena assumed that someone was in the hallway because she could hear footsteps. To make sure she did not hear the door handle rattle again, she turned up the volume on the television. This ploy had the opposite effect: "When I turned the volume up louder, the rattling got louder, too. Eventually, I had the TV turned up so loud it was blaring, but I could still hear the door handle over the TV." At this point, the investigator side of her took over. She grabbed the digital camera and started taking pictures. Rena and Tammy were not surprised to see black orbs in all of the photographs. "We also got shots of mists as well," Rena said.

Strange things happened again early the next morning after Rena and Tammy returned from their ghost tour. At 3:00 A.M., they took a walk around the hotel using the pendulum. When the women made their way to the end of a window-less hallway on the second floor, Rena told Tammy, "We really need to go to bed. I'm tired." Then Tammy made a joke, and Rena replied, "You don't really need to be joking like that. They're probably right behind us sticking their tongues out going, 'Nanny! Nanny! Nanny!'" Tammy, who was standing in front of Rena with the pendulum, said that the pendulum was going wild. "I took the camera and held it over my shoulder and snapped the picture," Rena said. "The picture that came out was amazing. It was a skull with the eyes and nose, and you could see its tongue sticking out. It is quite amazing. I've had it analyzed by the local photographer, and I've had it analyzed in Asheville at one of their photography-developing places. They said there's nothing in that hallway that would reflect such an image."

The next morning during breakfast, Rena and Tammy were sitting in the little alcove by the window, talking about everything that had happened. They were sitting across the room from the closet where Tammy had hung their clothes. After a few minutes, Rena turned to Tammy and asked, "Is my shirt swaying back and forth?" Without waiting for a reply, Tammy walked over to the closet and said, "Well, your shirt was swinging. Now the light cord is swinging." Because there were no breezes in the room, Rena is convinced that something was trying to get their attention: "We're not exactly sure what it was."

Before checking out of the 17Hundred90 Inn and Restaurant, Rena and Tammy told the concierge what had been going on. He said, "Oh, I don't believe in such things." The women then interviewed one of the maids, who was cleaning Room 204 at the time. Rena asked her, "Have you ever experienced anything?" She said, "No, why? Are you planning on leaving?" Rena replied, "Oh, are you kidding? That's what we're here for." She shut the door and started telling Rena and Tammy what had been going on in Room 204 for the past ten years of her employment. Then the maid asked Rena and Tammy if they had heard what happened in Room 201." Rena said, "No. What happened?" The maid said, "Not even ten minutes before you got in your room, the other people checked in, and five minutes later, the woman came screaming and running out of the room. Her husband followed her, and they checked out."

While Rena and Tammy were in Savannah, they decided to go to the historic Bonaventure Cemetery to find a certain gravesite. Legend has it that a spectral dinner party is replayed on quiet autumn nights, at Bonaventure Cemetery, which was formerly a large plantation owned by Josiah Tattnall. Rena and Tammy had been walking through the winding roads for almost an hour when Rena decided to use her pendulum: "We were just talking, and the pendulum was not moving at all. Then it started moving like crazy. It started spinning out of control. So I stopped to the left and looked, and the pendulum stopped. I took five steps to the right, and it started spinning out of control. I turned around and looked, and about fell over. The gravestone was 'Pike'—and that's my ex-married name." Her first thought was that something had happened to her children, but Tammy believed the pendulum was telling her that she was on the right path. When they came to an intersection where the roads met, Rena asked the pendulum, "Do we turn right? Do we turn left?" The pendulum soon led them directly to the gravesite of little Gracie.

North Carolina has also proven to be a fertile hunting ground for ghosts. The Carson House, for example, is a very haunted site. Built in 1793 by John Carson, the Carson House was originally a log cabin. Several other sections were added around 1800. In the early 1800s, the Carson House was operated as a stagecoach stop, serving luminaries such as Daniel Boone.

In July 2005, Ann Swann, curator of the Carson, invited Rena's group to conduct an investigation there. Rena was particularly excited about visiting the old house because of a well-publicized photograph: "A young girl had come to see the house with her grandparents in the early spring and had snapped a photo that's hanging on the wall in the Carson House. You can clearly see a mist in the photo." Rena and the eight people she brought with her were not disappointed: "We had a lot of spikes in EMF readings upstairs on the second floor in the main part of the house. One of the investigators was taking readings while the rest of us were walking around. Four or five of us took pictures of her, and in each of those photos, we had a mist or orb going across the photo. You couldn't see anything on the film, but when I brought the cameras home and downloaded them on the laptop, you could see what looked like small orbs in the bottom-left corner of the picture. In a different room, I took ten or twelve pictures standing in the exact same place on a rug by a rocking chair. Each time, the orb moved to another location."

Rena returned to the Carson House a few weeks later to take more pictures in the room where she had shot the moving orbs. "We moved all the furniture around to make sure that I wasn't photographing a reflection. I stood at the same place in the room and took twenty pictures. In each one, there was either a blue or a white orb, and sometimes, both appeared in different spots. When we blew them up on the laptop, the forms of the orbs seemed to have a solid outer region. I can't say what's there in the Carson House, but it definitely moves."

Being sensitive has come in handy in family situations as well; for example, when Rena's grandmother died of Alheizmer's in 2004. Just before her grandmother's death, Rena pleaded with her, "Please, come back, and let me know you're O.K." So after she passed away, Rena waited for a sign from her grandmother, but nothing happened. Then five months later, Rena was sitting at the computer in the kitchen, and suddenly, she detected the scent of the rose perfume that her grandmother used to have in her bedroom where she had played as a child. Later when Rena and her family moved into their new house, she and her sixteen-year-old daughter got into an argument: "We were in different rooms. My daughter was lying on the couch yelling at me, and then all of a sudden, she started screaming, 'It's Mamaw!' I ran in there, and I got close to her, and it was like someone had poured rose perfume all over her. I said, 'See that! Your grandmother does not want you talking to me that way.' She ran into her room, telling me to tell my 'Mamaw' to stop it. When she ran into the room, the smell went with her. It was no longer on the couch in the living room."

Considering that Foothills Paranormal Investigations operates in the Bible Belt, Rena is amazed that her group has not received much criticism from the religious community: "We're in the middle of the Bible Belt. I have counted over one hundred and twenty churches in this area alone. It's a very religious area; amazingly enough, they know we're here. It hasn't had any kind of effect one way or the other." This is not to say, though, that everyone in the area feels comfortable in the midst of the paranormal. In February 2005, the group was contacted by a family from Old Fort, North Carolina, who believed they had "something" in their house. The group verified that the family did indeed have an entity in their home. Afterward, though, the family was reluctant to discuss the possibility of an investigation with anyone because of the stigma attached to living in a haunted house. They were even approached by the television show *Sightings* to come out to their house and film, but the family refused because they were afraid their neighbors would talk.

The paranormal is very much a part of Rena Harp's life, even when she is not on an investigation. For example, in 2004, she felt herself drawn to a cottage-like house in town when she and her husband were house hunting: "We just purchased this house here in town. The ex–owner's husband had died a long time ago. And after we closed the deal on the house, I found out the husband had been killed right in front of the house where we used to live. Now that's too much of a coincidence because we lived way out of town." She believes that spirits are all around everyone and that they are trying to get in touch with us. "But unless you accept that it's possible, I don't think you'll ever get a chance to communicate with loved ones who have passed on."

Haunted North Carolina

CHAPEL HILL, NORTH CAROLINA

Jim Hall, Founder and Director

One could say that Jim Hall was destined from childhood to become a paranormal investigator: "There are stories of hauntings and strange things happening in our house. Some people in the family have said, 'Yeah, I remember that. It didn't happen exactly that way.' But when you're a child, you believe everything, so that's what got me interested in the paranormal." Jim's career as a ghost hunter began almost as soon as he got his own car and license and was able to drive around to places of interest, chasing down folklore and legends. He became interested in the scientific aspect of investigating in 2000. "That's when I started taking it really seriously and studying and applying the scientific method to research and joining up with an organization that conducted that kind of research." The group's original name was Seven Paranormal Research, but the members changed the name to Haunted North Carolina in 2004. "We changed the name to match the Web site," Jim said. "What happened was the person who founded Seven Paranormal Research left the group last summer. She moved down to South Carolina and just wasn't going to be around anymore. The name 'Seven' had personal significance to her. It was a question that came up anytime we did any media interviews. They'd ask us, 'What does Seven mean?' and none of us could really answer that question because we didn't know. So just because we grew tired of answering that question and because the name of the Web site was already 'Haunted North Carolina. com,' we decided to change the name to match the Web site." The members believe that their new name better connects them with the state.

Currently the group has twelve active members. "Six of those are brand new," Jim says. "They are people we've brought in from different disciplines. We are looking to diversify our membership base so we can get a lot of different perspectives. We brought in a person who does sound work with musicians, so he's great with audio. He can take any type of audio clip or evidence we've produced and run it through software and do a spectrum analysis. We brought in a policeman who is very experienced in interviewing witnesses to crimes. He's great for conducting interviews with witnesses to paranormal phenomena. He can sort of get at the things that people are not saying." The membership also includes a computer software designer and two people with history degrees. Before enrolling at the University of North Carolina as an education major, Jim was a property manager. Although Jim wants to capitalize on his members' strengths, he also wants them to maintain their outsider perspective.

The group is now exploring new ways of doing what they have always tried to do. "Traditionally, our mission was to collect and analyze evidence relating to paranormal phenomenon," Jim says. "We just recently have been having deep, late-night philosophical discussions about changing the way we've done things. There are ten thousand groups out there getting the same kind of evidence, and that evidence isn't convincing anybody. It's not even convincing all of us. The field is slowly coming to the realization that we are going to have to focus less on trying to get pictures and focus more on more traditional scientific methods, like statistical analysis, doing prolonged studies, things like that. That's what we're looking to do now." The group would like to conduct experiments someday, but because they do not operate in a laboratory environment, they would find it extremely difficult to incorporate controls.

The members find the places they investigate in two ways. The most common way is to have the people come to them. "They say either, 'There's something strange happening in my house' or people from other groups come to us and say, 'There's this one location we went to, and you might want to check into it yourself.'" Jim says that only 10 percent of their cases are self-generated: "There's one member or another who says, 'I've always heard this legend about this one place out in X county, and I've always wanted to go there, so let's put it on the schedule to do an investigation.' Maybe one out of ten investigations are like this." Thanks to the group's professional reputation, some of the historic sites in the area, like Stagville and Mordecai House, approach them first. Michael finds this development to be especially gratifying because his field in education is history and social studies.

The "ghost hunter's tool box" used by members of Haunted North Carolina includes the standard pieces of measuring equipment, most notably EMF meters and digital thermometers. However, they also bring along devices used to measure environmental factors, such as barometers, air ion counters and geomagnetometers. "We're trying to catalog environmental factors so we can do a statistical analysis and see if there's a correlation between certain environmental factors and reports of the phenomenon," Jim says. "Other groups use that equipment for other reasons, like a strong electromagnetic field is the sign of a ghost. Anecdotally speaking, that might be true, but the problem with that is because we can't say what a ghost is, it is impossible to ascribe characteristics to it, so it's impossible to say that fluctuations in the electromagnetic field are a ghost or that drop of temperature is a ghost. Correlation is not causation." He believes that the inability of ghost researchers to prove that fluctuations in the electromagnetic field are directly responsible for such phenomena as a chair moving across the floor opens them up to criticism.

Jim shares the disdain held by many of his colleagues in the field for orbs, primarily because they can be caused by environmental factors, such as dust, moisture, and insects. Only a few orbs really catch his attention: "There are some orbs we've seen that we caught on video that displayed characteristics that are interesting, such as moving in the foreground and the background, so that gives you some sense of scale, like the object moving behind somebody and in front of them." Even though orbs such as these might be significant, Jim is reluctant to post them on his Web site: "People don't read the disclaimer stating that orbs are not irrefutable proof of the existence of ghosts. They just see the orbs. The next thing you know, you've got pictures of orbs flooding your e-mail. So it is frustrating because people will take any type of photographic anomaly and say, 'Hey! What do you think this is?' Even if it was a ghost, we couldn't verify that because we didn't take the picture."

Haunted North Carolina's investigations go on all year round. However, because everyone in the group has a day job, Jim schedules most of the investigations for the weekends, with the exception of media opportunities that are scheduled for a certain date. As much as possible, the members try to put themselves in a position to witness an event as it happens. "It's like blindfolding yourself and throwing darts," Jim says. "You have no accurate way of predicting when events are going to occur except for anecdotal accounts by previous witnesses who say this activity happens at night or when there's only one person here, so we try to duplicate those circumstances as much as we can." For example, if witnesses report that activity occurs three times a month and always at noon, Jim tries to schedule the group's investigation for noon. Someday Jim would like to conduct an experiment to see if there is an ideal time to experience supernatural activity: "There's a long-held belief in the field that most paranormal activity occurs at night at three to four A.M., but no actual study has been done to verify this. So we're looking into doing a study surveying people who report these events and the times and doing a statistical analysis to find out if it's really true." The places Jim's group has investigated have been active at various times during the day.

Haunted North Carolina receives many more calls for help than the members can possibly respond to. "Most of the time, we get in the neighborhood of two to three investigation requests a day," Jim says. "We have to go through a process of elimination to determine which ones are most likely to have some sort of credibility to them. So there are probably a great many opportunities we've missed out on that are actually legitimately some sort of paranormal activity going on." Jim estimates that only one out ten of the group's investigations has revealed genuine paranormal activity: "Most of the time we are able to go out and find whatever the events are that are being described, but we can usually find another explanation for it. Just because we found another explanation for it, that does not mean that is the correct explanation." Jim cites as a hypothetical example a private residence where the occupants have reported hearing voices in their home. If the investigators go out there and discover animals living under their house that make some sort of vocal noise, they can surmise that the homeowners are interpreting these sounds as human voices. "This does not mean that is what it is, but that is the most likely explanation," Jim says. He added that most people who report that their house is haunted are disappointed when the group disproves it.

Finding a rational explanation for a disturbance does not mean that an investigation is a dismal failure. "I'd have to say that the longer I do this, the less disappointed I become," Jim says. "I'm sure there was one point when I was disappointed, but now that my focus has turned toward getting at the truth and looking at things objectively, disproving a haunting has become just as important as proving one." Jim becomes more frustrated when the group can neither prove nor disprove a haunting because nothing happens while the members are there.

One investigation that produced evidence the group considers strong was conducted at an old plantation in the western part of North Carolina. "The farm is still there," Jim says. "It's on Edwards Road. The farm has no name. The creek that runs through the farm is Payne Creek, so it stands to reason that the people who owned the farm were named Payne. One thing we turned up in our research is there was a former first lady from Stokes County, and her name was Payne. The land is still there. Some of the original farm buildings are still there. The only thing that burned down is the main farmhouse. The property is unoccupied." When the group examined the historical records of the past fifty years, they discovered that an incredible number of deaths by misadventure or through some kind of foul play took place on the farm. "There were murders there," Jim says. "There were suicides. In this one location, we have picked up some of our clearest EVP's. We collected photographic evidence, not just of orbs, but other types of anomalies, like human-shaped mists that were taken at a time when people were actually seeing an apparition. It was at this location where we've had members actually physically grabbed. One member was walking up a slight slope, and he started falling backwards, and we looked to see why he was falling, and you could literally see the backpack being pulled off his back. That lasted for a few seconds, and whatever it was let go, and he stumbled forward."

Then there are other locations where the members have had to return several times before collecting any evidence at all. A good example is the Mordecai House in Raleigh, which is reputed to be haunted by a woman in a long, black, pleated skirt, wearing a white blouse and black tie. "At Mordecai, we went out two times and got nothing, and we were ready to close the case," Jim says. "We went out one last time because a local news station wanted a story run on Halloween, and we needed a place we could get into on an hour's notice. We called them up, and they were willing to let us do it. That night, we went out there, and we had the news crew with us, and it was extraordinarily active. We got a photograph of an apparition, we got an orb video where you can see an orb moving behind and in front of the person we're interviewing, so that one was successful as well." The full-body apparition matches photographs of Mary Turk Willis Mordecai, who has been identified as the Lady in Black. "We took a picture outside of the house looking into the living room, and there's a woman standing in the window," Jim says. "The figure is very clear. It's hard to make out individual features of the face, but just from a cursory examination of it, if you hold it next to a photograph of Mary, they do look very similar." Jim Hall returned to the Mordecai House in 2005 with T.A.P.S. to film an episode of the *Ghosthunters* television show. Unfortunately, Jim and the other researchers were unable to conduct an investigation. "We got food poisoning at the Mordecai House," Jim said. "But the scene they showed of us eating at a restaurant was set up. We actually got [food poisoning] from a place that catered. Everybody who had the salad with bleu cheese dressing got sick."

Before T.A.P.S. and Jim Hall visited the Mordecai House, they did a two-day investigation of the battleship *North Carolina*. "We are fortunate that a lot of activity got caught on camera. Nothing on the actual investigation [which aired on August 17 on the Sci-Fi Channel] was fake. They assigned us a camera crew and followed us around. All of the conversations [that were filmed] are real." The most frightening segment of the program depicted Jason Hawes's and Grant Wilson's pursuit of an elusive shadow in the brig. While they were making their way in the dark, they heard objects being thrown in front of and behind them. While Jason and Grant were chasing the shadow, Jim Hall and two members of his group, Justin and David, were walking through the galley, where they heard a banging noise. No one else was present at the time. "A battleship is like a maze," Jim says. "It's not a place where somebody could easily flit in and out of."

Jim and the members of Haunted North Carolina had another strange encounter as they were climbing up out of the forward turret: "One of the team members—the one who was going first off the ladder—saw an apparition. He was trying to get his camera that was slung over his shoulder. The apparition peaked around the corner, then sneaked back. He said it was human in form but very pale. It had a transparent quality. It didn't look like a flesh-and-blood person standing there." Jim's first thought was that they had to find out who or what this was. "We have protocols for this sort of thing," Jim says. "If one of us was coming up the ladder, one of us would have said, 'Hey, everybody. It's me! I'm in this room.' So I wanted to find out which of our team members wasn't following protocol or if someone was messing with us. We went into the part of the ship where he saw it and realized that the figure would have had to run past us or down into the area where it couldn't have gone anywhere else. It couldn't have gotten away from us without going past us. The intruder would have had to unlock the padlock and taken off the chain, opened the hatch by undoing six levers, gotten through the hatch, and closed it."

The most startling piece of evidence featured on the *Ghosthunters* episode was an EVP collected by Jim and a member of T.A.P.S., Dustin. "We were standing on the ship," Jim said. "We were kind of wired and weren't ready to turn in. Dustin said, 'Do you want to check out the brig where Justin and Grant

saw that thing?' I said, 'Yeah. Since we're going down there anyway, we might as well take a tape recorder and have it running
while we're down there.' The digital recorder was on my belt.
We had it running the entire time we were down there." After
Jim and Dustin rejoined T.A.P.S., they were surprised to hear a
spectral voice on the recording: "The voice you hear on the
recording is actually closer to the microphone than I was. You
can hear it say something about 'the ship,' and then you hear my
voice on top of it, the [ghost] voice is actually louder than my
voice. I was speaking about one and a half or two feet from the
mike. Dustin was behind me. He wasn't talking while I was going
down the hallway, and we reached a place where we could go left
or right or down a ladder. We didn't know which way to go. I
said, 'Oh, we've got our choice of directions.' What you hear on
the recording is that voice right before you hear mine."

Haunted North Carolina's most frightening investigation was
held at the historic Stagville Plantation, which was founded in
1776 by Richard Bennehan and remained in the Bennehan family for nearly two hundred years. By 1860, the family owned
almost thirty thousand acres and nearly nine hundred slaves. In
2004, the group visited the old plantation: "In the main house,
there is a long sleeping loft at the top," Jim said. "One other team
member and I went out there, and he took a picture standing in
one of the rooms at the other end. When he took the picture,
in the flash of the camera, you could see someone or something
in the other room dart across the room from left to right. As soon
as that happened, we hit our flashlights and tried to figure it out.
Was it some sort of funky shadow caused by the flash? We sort of
mentally logged it and continued with the investigation." Two
weeks later, Jim and the other member returned to Stagville.

Another team member had set up cameras in that same sleeping loft. The whole night passed uneventfully. Nothing was collected. Nothing was witnessed. Convinced that the spirits were not going to cooperate, one of the members was sitting on the floor breaking down his equipment when someone radioed him to say, "Hey, David. Be quiet up there. We're trying to tape record, and we hear you stalking around up there." He replied, "I'm sitting down. I haven't moved." About the same time he said that, he saw a shadow move across the wall. This was the same room where he and Jim had seen someone dart across the room. "It was dark in the room, but he had been there long enough that he had night vision, and his eyes had adjusted," Jim said. "Then the shadow came off the wall and started moving toward him. He described it like a black cloud. He took off out of there so fast. By that time, the two people who had radioed him to be quiet were coming up the steps to see what was making all the noise, and he about bowled them over trying to get past them on the stairs. He left his equipment upstairs and everything."

Jim says that most of the time when his members get scared on an investigation, they freak themselves out: "It's almost a sign of how long people have been doing as to how visibly scared they are. When people first start doing this, they're excited and they want to do it and they're interested in, and they go out on their first investigation, and somebody steps on a twig, and they're darting for the cars. In terms of being frightened on an investigation, it's happened to everybody, myself included. Now being frightened by the paranormal, that has happened, too, but not as often."

Promotion is a top priority for Haunted North Carolina, as it is for so many other groups. "Our main connection to the world is through our Web site," Jim says. "Over the Web site, we sell

T-shirts, we advertise on other Web sites, we do media whenever we can, not for the purpose of becoming famous, but to get the word out and to increase our name recognition. When people think of paranormal research in North Carolina, we want them to think automatically of 'Haunted North Carolina.'" The group's community outreach efforts also include presenting programs at historic sites, doing ghost walks, and reading ghost stories at schools or libraries during Halloween.

The North Carolina state capitol is number one on the group's list of places to investigate. "It's reported to be haunted," Jim said. "They've had other groups out there at least on two other occasions. At one time, we had an open invitation to go out there. For whatever reason, our director at the time decided we didn't have the time or manpower to do it, so we didn't take advantage of the opportunity. Most recently, we were discussing it, and we said it's a crime that we call ourselves Haunted North Carolina and we've never investigated one of the most famous hauntings in the state." Recently, Jim tried to set up an investigation at the capitol but was told that because of budget problems, the capitol did not have the manpower to stay out there all night with them.

Jim believes that the group has not encountered any opposition groups because his members take a scientific approach to investigating the paranormal: "I've never come across any criticism, and I think it's because we are trying to do it scientifically. We're not spiritualists. We're not going out there with Ouija boards, and we don't get into angels or demons. Now we have encountered criticism from the skeptical community, but that just comes with the territory." Jim does admit, though, that his mother worries about his soul constantly.

Jim Hall says he will continue investigating until his group finds absolute proof of what causes paranormal disturbances or until they disconnect him from the iron lung: "I love it. I'm fascinated by it. Our mission right now is not to prove the existence of ghosts. It is to change the way the field approaches the study, to make it more in line with scientific methods." Haunted North Carolina would like to get the assistance of other scientific disciplines, but that will never happen until the scientific community begins taking groups like Jim's seriously: "If we're all running around with our Dr. Gauss meters saying we got a ghost, they're not going to do that. If we can produce studies where we say we examined hundreds of different reports of paranormal phenomena and we found common factors in all of them, we established a statistical correlation, and we did a controlled study of these locations, we might be able to move the field forward a little bit."

South Carolina

Coastal Spirit Chasers

MURRELL'S INLET, SOUTH CAROLINA

Jennifer Latka, Founder and Director

Jennifer first became interested in the paranormal when she lived in a haunted house in Myrtle Beach: "It was a rental. I moved in when I was twenty-one and moved out when I was twenty-five. A Civil War soldier appeared in my room one night, and he actually took me back to the war, and I got to see everything that was happening, and I saw everything he was feeling. Before he left, he told me his name. The next morning, I got on the Internet and looked up his name, and sure enough, he was in the Civil War. That was confirmation enough." Jennifer also used to have a tanning bed in her room. While she was tanning late one afternoon, someone whispered "hello" into her ear. "That kind of freaked me out for a minute," she said. Other strange things happened during Jennifer's four-year stay at the house: "At first I was scared because a lot of different things were happening. The doors would lock from the inside and things like that, but after a while, I got used to it. I started to read up on ghosts and started chasing them, actually."

Jennifer started her group in 2002 through a Web site called "Meetup.com": "I registered there, and everybody around the town could get together and talk about it, and I ended up forming my group this way. We don't have any educational qualifications except that we want them to read." Each member of Jennifer's group plays a specific role: "Chris loves to read, so she researches any location we go to. Then we have our technician Chris. He knows everything about equipment. He's good with analyzing everything. Darrin is another dedicated member. He likes to get involved in anything and everything. Jeremy is a photographer here in town. He is a major asset to our group because of spirit photography." Aside from leading the group, Jennifer puts her psychic abilities to good use on investigations: "I sense spirits as well as my mom. It was passed down in my family. If I go into a place, I can actually feel—it all depends on the situation. When I have those feelings, I point the other members in that direction. It usually pays off in the form of orbs or high readings or EVP's."

Unlike most directors, Jennifer can devote all of her time to running the group: "I have no day job. My fiancé works, so this is all I do." She admires directors like Jason Hawes in the Sci-Fi Channel television show *Ghosthunters* who enforce discipline on an investigation, but she does not approve of Hawes's methods: "I think Jason is very professional. He keeps everybody in line. I don't think [his way] is the way to do it, though."

Most of the Coastal Spirit Seekers' investigations are conducted outdoors, usually at cemeteries, because of their easy access: "We tend to go to cemeteries in the day because it is easier for everybody to go out there, but night time would be best. The energy is different, and you get better footage at night than you do during the day. Also, there's a possibility of glare [showing up on pictures]." At one local cemetery, one of Jennifer's team members picked up two fascinating EVP's. Not long after the group arrived, he was having trouble finding a switch on his tape recorder. In frustration, he said aloud, "How do I fix this?" When the tape was played back, he heard a very clear voice respond, "It's on the back." He looked on the back of the tape recorder and, sure enough, found the switch. Later on that evening, the same team member was walking through the cemetery, and he accidentally knocked over a vase. He picked up the vase and continued on his way. On the recording, he heard a voice say, "Thank you very much." Groups like Jennifer's who do most of their investigations outdoors do not go out much when the weather is cold and wet. "Now that it is getting warmer, we will probably be doing investigations twice a month, and we'll have meetings, also," Jennifer says. "We'll get together after our investigations. We'll discuss all the photos and the happenings and fill out a report."

The group's most memorable investigation, however, was at an indoor site, the Litchfield Plantation Manor on Pawley's Island. Located on six hundred acres, the 1750s manor house has been converted into a popular bed and breakfast. The Carolina Spirit Seekers were drawn to the old house by stories of the ghostly image of a man who has been seen by employees and owners alike. Once they arrived at the plantation, Jennifer learned that waiters have had trays knocked out of their hands by an unseen force. On several occasions, little boys have been tripped and even flipped over. Not surprisingly, Jennifer's group collected some tantalizing evidence at the bed and breakfast: "We were doing a promotion for a radio company. We were taking people and putting them in the haunted plantation for the night. I felt the coldness. You could feel the energy in that whole room. It was unexplainable. We got photography and EVP's. We also got a black vortex in some of the photographs. I want to go back someday."

Even though the Coastal Spirit Chasers have had some very weird encounters over the years, Jennifer says her members have never been frightened on an investigation: "My members have never been frightened. That is one of my major concerns. We always pair up in teams so nobody is alone. I have never felt really scared. The main thing we look for when we are interviewing people is the absence of fear. The wife of one of our members had said she wanted to go on an investigation, but she attended one meeting and said, 'That's it. I don't really want to go.' She was too scared."

The Coastal Spirit Chasers promote themselves in ways other than their Web site: "We are listed in the back of *Ghost Magazine*. We plan to sell T-shirts to the general public. We are also going to get a Dickey shirt with our logo on it just for the investigators." All proceeds from the T-shirt sales will be used to buy new equipment for the group. According to Jennifer, the group has not been criticized by any religious groups in the area. "Everyone I have spoken to seems to be fine with it," Jennifer says. "They could be saying something, but they don't actually speak to me about it."

Although Jennifer's dream investigation would be in Scotland, she would also like to take her group to Georgia, Florida, and Virginia someday. Jennifer's fondest wish, though, is to discover more sites that are really haunted: "I'd say that 20 percent of our investigations reveal genuine hauntings. I am disappointed when we find a logical explanation for the phenomenon, but you've got to keep moving on."

Ghost Takers

CHARLESTON, SOUTH CAROLINA

Gordon Small, Founder and Director

Ghost Takers is unique among southern paranormal investigative groups in that it has only one member. Gordon Small is the business manager in a floral decorating and events coordinating company called "Celebrations by Appointment." Gordon says he became interested in the paranormal after reading a book about Edgar Cayce: "I read the first book about him. This just makes sense to me, the universal mind concept. When you read about Edgar Cayce, the man with such minimal education, and the things he could do, and everything is so well documented. There has to be a great deal of validity to it."

Ghost Takers also stands out from the other groups in that its sole activity is capturing orbs on film. Gordon says he first became interested in orb photography in the four months he worked as a tour guide for Anna Blythe's Ghost Walk tour company in Charleston: "I had just gotten my temporary license to be a tour guide. I went on a tour with her [Anna Blythe]. She was the actual guide; I just walked along, and I took my camera with me. I really don't know why I did because at that point, I really didn't know very much about orbs. I was just taking a bunch of pictures." On those occasions when he accompanied Anna's tour group in an official capacity, he ventured into those residential areas that tours cannot enter after 6:00 P.M. He routinely left the group for a minute or two, took the pictures with his digital camera, and caught back up with the others.

Anna Blythe recalls Gordon's fascination with orbs: "Night after night, he stays out until one A.M. and captures orbs. The most recent ones have six sides. One night, he was over on the street behind me where there are two graveyards, and he took a picture and moved; took a picture of the same thing and moved; took another picture and moved. The orb seems to have a tail, and it's moving. It's the same orb."

After one of these tours, he and Anna returned to her house and downloaded his pictures onto her computer: "That's when it was discovered that one of the pictures had two orbs in it," Gordon said. Anna asked Gordon the name of the graveyard where he took the pictures. Gordon could not remember, so at 11:00 P.M., he and Anna retraced his steps through downtown Charleston until he found where he had taken the picture: "It turned out to be the south graveyard of St. Phillip's Church. If you're standing across the street facing the church, it'd be the graveyard on your right. We were standing there looking at it. We had printed off the picture. We were looking at the picture and the graveyard, and I said, 'This is it!' Then I said, 'Anna, are you ready for this?' She said, 'Yes.' I said, 'See where the edge of the picture cuts off?' She said she did. I then pointed out that my parents' gravestones were just off the edge of the picture. The orbs were close to them." Gordon suspects that the orbs hovering around his parents' graves might have been their spiritual energy.

Since then, Gordon has taken quite a large number of stills in a variety of places: "I started off in graveyards. Then it will come and go in spurts. I will get some and then not get any for a week or two. Then I'll start getting orbs again. For some reason or another, I got off on a slightly different tangent. I started taking flash pictures at night of church steeples, and you get a whole different photographic effect from using a flash effect at night. And what I started noticing in those pictures is that you get orbs up high. I had been taking pictures at eye level, and now I started aiming my camera up."

After that experience, Gordon began expanding his search for orbs throughout the entire city. He has very good luck photographing orbs around churches, such as the Circular Congregational Church, St. John's Lutheran Church, St. Phillip's Episcopal Church, the Second Presbyterian Church, and the First Scott's Church." However, he has not had much luck photographing orbs inside churches or anywhere else. In February 2005, Gordon found he was getting pictures of orbs wherever he aimed his camera, including historic sites such as the Old Exchange Building and some of the old forts on Sullivan's Island. One of the most productive sites has been a piece of property that Anna owns about thirty miles south of Charleston. On one occasion, though, his eagerness to capture orbs clouded his judgment: "It was a large Confederate campground. I get hundreds of pictures of orbs down there, and that's where I'm getting orbs that have the delta-shaped center. I showed one of them to Anna, and she looked at it and looked at it and looked at it and said, 'That's a moth.' And it was. It had gotten caught in the flash."

After a few months, Gordon found ways to eliminate other false orbs. One recurring anomaly that is often caused by people is a mysterious mist that shows up on photographs on cold days: "Most of the time, this mist is the photographer's breath. What I do now is, when I put my finger on the shutter, I inhale and hold my breath about two seconds before I take the picture. That way I eliminate that possibility that it's my breath, so that if I get a mist, it's something else." Other possibilities for artificial mists could be cigarette smoke or a light source like a street light that is off-picture: "You might be taking a picture of something, and you won't notice the street light, and it will leave a curve that looks like a mist. It is particularly prevalent in high humidity. And they will be different colors. Sodium vapor lights will be yellow in color, and mercury vapor will be greenish in color. So you can tell from the color of this thing." To help eliminate temperature interference, Gordon purchased a two-thousand-dollar camera in March 2004: "It's the Minolta Maxim 70, a digital camera. This new camera I have is so high tech that I can tell it Kelvin temperatures, and it will eliminate that color. If I get a green light in it, I'll tell the camera this color, and it will eliminate that temperature and that color."

In May 2004, Gordon took what he says is one of his most amazing—and baffling—photographs. At the time, he was on one of Anna's tours: "That's when I took the picture of the angel rod. You could see it on the viewing screen in the digital camera. I told the people in the group, 'In the course of my life, I've taken thousands of pictures, and I've never run across anything like this.' Gordon showed the photograph of the sticklike object to several experts, but none of them could explain what it was.

Although most of Gordon's orbs have been photographed at night, he has taken pictures of orbs in broad daylight: "They don't look any different than the ones I take at night. For example,

I photographed a spot on a tree that appears to be the size of a quarter. I was maybe thirty-five to forty feet away from that tree. I've seen this tree hundreds of times, and there's no white spot there on that tree, but there is in that picture."

Like many ghost hunters, Gordon believes that "genuine" orbs have a sort of nucleus: "Some of them have almost a donut-like shape. They appear to be round, but the hole is not complete. I came up with the analogy of a mini black hole. They appear to be spiraling, and the spire goes into the center." Gordon has noticed that when he blows up the orb pictures on the computer, a dark spot in the center is noticeable. In one particular location, all of the orbs he has photographed have a delta-shaped center. After capturing an orb with a distinctive center in several locations, he decided to use fingerprint software to determine if he can identify these orbs as the same orb: "It could be like snowflakes. Every snowflake is different, so each snowflake is identifiable. If the orb is an entity, it will be easier to study than snowflakes because orbs don't melt." Some of the other orbs Gordon has found have centers that are five-, six-, or seven-sided. Anna Blythe, who has just started taking orb photographs of her own, has captured orbs with shield-shaped centers. A few of the orbs Gordon has photographed appear to be moving: "An analogy would be the Apollo spacecraft coming back through the atmosphere. You see something that appears round on the leading edge, but it has a trail behind it."

Gordon has also found that some orbs do not show up at all until he enhances the photographs on his computer: "I change the brightness and the contrast, and then the orbs show up. For example, one sphere showed up on the steeple on the Circular Congregational Church after I enhanced it on the computer."

Another time, he took sixty pictures, and there were orbs in about forty of them. They were all visible on camera. However, when he changed the brightness or the contrast, he was able to see the orbs on the other twenty pictures as well.

When Gordon captures an orb that is atypical, he takes the photograph to a local camera store and asks the owner to analyze it for him: "I'll try to get them to tell me what they think it is, what photographic or light phenomena caused this to appear on my camera." By letting experts express their opinions, he feels that he is approaching orb photography from a negative standpoint: "I'm trying to disprove my own work, and in that sense, I can tell you what it is not. I guess you could say I am trying to be scientific." Even though Gordon has a degree in biology with a minor in chemistry and physics, he is very receptive to metaphysical explanations that are not explicitly stated in the Bible: "I definitely believe in ghosts. I believe we're not alone in this world. There are hundreds of references in the Bible as to the passing on to the other side, crossing over the River Jordan. These are all phrases about your soul, if your body has died and has not 'crossed the River Jordan' or 'gone on to the other side.'"

Gordon is trying to make contacts among the caretakers of the graveyard in town because all of the cemeteries in Charleston are locked up at 6:00, thereby preventing him from doing any night-time photography: "I need to get into these graveyards at night. Usually when I do get in at night, it's really nasty weather because whoever is supposed to unlock the gate just doesn't want to do it, so they don't. So those are the nights I go out and I get in the graveyards."

Right now, orb photography is nothing more than a serious hobby for Gordon. Although orbs seem to have nothing in common with the flower business, his photographic skill did come in handy when his partner asked him to develop a Web site for the business: "We needed pictures, so I took them," Gordon said. Someday, he plans to set up a Web site for his orb pictures so that they will reach a broader audience.

Tennessee

Memphis Paranormal
Investigations Team

MEMPHIS, TENNESSEE

Michael Espanjer, Founder and Director

Although Michael Espanjer has been fascinated by the supernatural since he was a boy, he did not really get into the field seriously until October 2003, when he started his group: "At that time, I noticed that [the paranormal] was starting to get more popular on TV and in movies. I knew that we had something that a lot of groups didn't have, so I guess that makes us more successful. I don't mean to brag or anything. We focus more on the spiritual end of it." The group's reputation has grown to the point that the members are occasionally asked by the local police department to serve as consultants on murder cases.

The group has ten members, but only six of them go out on investigations. The number is even smaller when the group goes to houses. "We get better results if there are just two or three of us," Michael says. "It's just too much energy. I am trying to fine-tune my psychic ability. Sometimes when I'm in a place, I pick up on one of my members, and I don't need that. Some of the houses we go to are really small, so we can't have a lot of people bumping into each other."

Michael's membership can best be described as a "hodge-podge." His lead investigator, Ginger, is working on her master's degree in psychology. "We also have a retired nurse, we have two members who are professional pet sitters, and we have a single mother. I am a retired hospice nurse, so I do this full –time," Michael says. "I helped people cross over. There are few places that unnerve me because death was part of my life." He often goes to private residences by himself to meet with families and to get a feel for the house, but he never goes to cemeteries by himself: "I'm worried about real people, more than anything, although you can figure that a cemetery is the last place a crack head's likely to knock you over the head for your wallet. Also, you need to have a witness. I know too many people who went to a cemetery by themselves and saw the best stuff, but there was nobody there to verify the story, and that can be really frustrating."

Michael is uniquely qualified to explore the Other Side because he had a near-death experience shortly after his grandmother died: "I had a heart attack, and everything started coming in clear after that. It's like a door was opened. I didn't see a white light or pass through a tunnel. In fact I had collapsed on the floor. I was on my knees. I had one arm on the bed, and I was slumped over. I saw my grandmother in the identical position I was, and she was probably fifteen or twenty years younger than when she died. She said, 'I'm not ready for you yet, baby. You've got to go back.'" Although Michael's near-death experience does not conform exactly to the popular image, he does agree with those survivors who claim that relatives or friends are there to help the deceased person cross over.

Michael has also been an automatic writer since he was fifteen years old, although he did not know it at the time: "I used to write poetry, and I would write [the poems] about people. I wrote one for my aunt on her birthday one year—she lived in Wisconsin—and she said, 'I don't know how you know me like that. You sound like you know me from my childhood.'" The poem discusses experiences she had as a child. At the time Michael wrote the poem, he was in his early twenties, and she was sixty-five.

When Michael does automatic writing, he is conscious of his surroundings, but he is usually so focused on his pen and paper that he tunes everything else out: "I've always told people it takes a tremendous amount of electromagnetic energy for a spirit to communicate, and if it takes that much energy to communicate with me, it's my obligation to pass the message on, whether it makes sense or not. I tell people, 'This is what I wrote down. You can tell me if it makes sense or not.'"

Michael's psychic abilities have brought him closer to the spirit world than most investigators ever come. He cites as an example an incident that occurred late in February 2005. He went to the local insurance company to buy a new policy for his car: "A little girl behind the desk was typing up something, and I said, 'I know you're going to think this is weird, but did you just have a male relative die recently?' She said, 'Why would you say that?' I said, 'Because there's a rather large, tall man standing in the lobby.' I described what he looked like, and she said, 'Oh, my god! That's my stepfather.'"

Several weeks later on Valentines' night, Michael went to bed, and the phone rang. He let it go to voice mail, but had second thoughts and called the lady back. She said, "My daughter said you might have some information about my beloved." Michael took out his pad and said, "The first thing he shows me is a blue birthday cake with blue candles, and he keeps saying, 'Blue, blue, blue. Lots of blue.'" The lady replied, "He had beautiful blue eyes like Paul Newman. We buried him in a blue suit in a blue-lined coffin and blue flowers." "Apparently, he really likes it," Michael said. "The next message he sent me was, 'I'm sorry. Tell her I'm sorry. I just wasn't loved. I didn't know how to do it.'" The lady told Michael that the man had been severely abused when he was a child. She added that even though he loved her, he could not marry her because he had not divorced his wife. After telling the woman that her lover appeared to have been married twice before, Michael had a vision of the man holding a bouquet of petunias. Through her tears, the woman told him, "He planted me a garden out back, and it was filled with nothing but petunias. He'd come into the house, and he'd be holding petunias behind his back, and he'd use his Popeye voice. Popeye used to give petunias to Olive Oyl, you know." After hearing these words, Michael began to cry, too.

Michael often uses his skills as an automatic writer on investigations. Sometimes, vibrations come through to him in telephone conversations with clients, as they did during his late-night talk with the woman on Valentine's Day. Working on the assumption that an entity might communicate with him on an investigation, Michael always brings along a pad and pencil. Michael also attempts to record EVP's: "If I ask a question, and I get a response, I consider it to be genuine," Michael says.

Despite the group's success with communicating with the other side, the members concentrate most of their efforts on photographing spirits. Michael believes apparitions remain in a particular location because this is the place where they know they can be seen. "I've always believed that most ghosts deny death," Michael says. "If you can see me and take pictures of me, I'm not dead." In other words, nobody wants to be dead, not even the dead.

On many occasions, the group has taken some amazing photographs while he is doing automatic writing, including two full-body apparitions. "One of our full body apparitions is an adult male, and the other one is a male baby," Michael says. "It looks like a male, but it's hard to tell. It's maybe one or two years old. We captured it in a cemetery." One of the group's newest members has even photographed an orb that appears to have an eye in the middle. The strangest pictures the group has ever taken, though, are of one of their own members: "Whenever one of our members is in a real active spot, we take pictures of her, and her face looks just like the Elephant Man's face, and there's no explanation for it. It's a digital camera. The rest of the picture is clear as a bell, but her face is so distorted that you can't even tell who she is."

The group does a large number of outdoor investigations, especially cemeteries. Their favorite cemetery is the local potter's field, where approximately seventy thousand indigent and nameless people are buried. The cemetery's most distinctive ghost is Arthur. "We nicknamed him 'the Cucumber Man,'" Michael says, "because when he meets you, it's like you walked in a wall of fresh-cut cucumbers. The spirits all have their own way of letting people know, 'This is me.'" Arthur seems to be especially fond of a couple of the group's female members. A reporter from one of Memphis's local newspapers also attracted Arthur's attention. After walking through the cemetery, the reporter told Michael, "I just don't know how to discount [your story about the cemetery ghost] after experiencing it. You know, in the middle of January, you're not likely to be smelling cucumbers, at least not around here."

Michael attributes the large number of haunted cemeteries in the Memphis area to the yellow fever and meningitis epidemics of the nineteenth century: "There were two bouts of yellow fever, one in the mid-1800s, and the other was in the 1870s. The last bout was the one that took everybody. A lot of these people died very suddenly, and they didn't know they were dead. We also got hit by viral meningitis, which took out almost every child under the age of ten." Apparently, a large number of yellow fever victims still have not crossed over. Michael believes these lost souls tend to flock together: "Some of the cemeteries are communities of a sort. It's a bunch of lost people. They don't really know what to do."

One of the group's favorite nineteenth-century graveyards is Salem Cemetery. While the cemetery was undergoing an expansion, workers accidentally dug up a mass grave for slaves. A sundial now marks the location. Michael's experiences in the cemetery have led him to conclude that it is "not a very nice place." The first time he went to the cemetery, he heard someone running up the hill. He tried to follow the sound of the footsteps up the hill, but to no avail. The next morning, he had an egg-shaped knot on his forehead. Through automatic writing, he was able to draw a picture of the figure he saw on the hillside. Three new members also experienced the terrifying side of Salem Cemetery. "I think they lasted five minutes, and that was it," Michael said.

Some of the more modern gravesites in the area have yielded results as well. "We were communicating with a World War II vet in Raleigh Cemetery," Michael said. "It's a really active cemetery. It was Veterans' Day. While Ginger was taking photographs, I stood over the grave, saluted, and said, 'You served your country well, sir.'" When Ginger showed Michael her photographs, he was shocked: "There's a before and after picture. You can see a huge beam of light coming down from the sky at a ninety-degree angle right onto his headstone."

Before entering a cemetery, Michael tells his new members that graveyards are not really "dead" places: "You don't ever have to say a word when you're in a cemetery. They know every word you're thinking. It's one of the gifts of being dead. They know your thoughts too. If they know that you've got bad intentions, you're not going to get a thing. It will be just a quiet night in a spooky place. If you're honest, and you have great intentions, you'll get great evidence."

The Memphis Paranormal Investigations Team also visits indoor locations, such as the Orpheum Theater, which is reputed to be haunted by the ghost of a twelve-year-old girl named Mary. Witnesses describe her as having brown, braided hair and wearing a white dress and long, black stockings. While the group was filming an episode for the Travel Channel, the investigators discovered that Mary is not the only spirit in the old theater. "We got a lot more than that," Michael says. "We made it as far as the fourth-floor mezzanine, and we got growled at. It was kind of like the *Poltergeist* movie. The other spirits tried to keep the girl protected."

Although the group prefers to investigate at night, they have found that some places are just as active in the daytime as they are at night. An example is Slavehaven Underground Railroad Museum in downtown Memphis. "We've gotten pictures in there in the daytime," Michael says. "One of the eyewitnesses was an employee who worked at the gift counter there. He watched the front door open, and then he heard a couple of doors slamming all over the building. It's like a shotgun-style house. You can see all the way from the front to the back. He ran out the door and never came back."

One of the group's most memorable investigations is the Tennessee Brewery, where Gold Crest beer was brewed until 1957 or 1958. Because Michael has made friends with the owner, the group can visit the brewery whenever they want. So far, the group has conducted fifteen investigations at the brewery. On several occasions, the group has made personal contact with the other side in the brewery. "When you're walking up a flight of stairs and you stop, you can hear footsteps continuing," Michael says. "We've had members who were touched, pushed, pinched. In the past, we've taken new members here to train them. I figure if they can make it there on an investigation, they can pretty much go anywhere we take them." The last time the group visited the brewery, Michael passed out while he was doing automatic writing: "They said I was talking in a very low voice. I got just a mental picture of who it was." Michael believes that the spirits in the brewery are upset because the owner is preparing to build condominiums on the site. He felt it was the group's responsibility to warn the spirits about the building's impending demolition. "We told them it would be a good time to leave now before the brewery is torn down. I don't know if they took my advice or not."

One prospective member's first investigation turned out to be memorable, too. At the time, the group was investigating the Hunt-Phellan Home, which is where the Underground Railroad started in Memphis. "He had a very high-power listening device," Michael said. "He heard a woman say, 'Get out!' He took the headphones off and looked at Ginger—she's my lead investigator—and said, 'Did you just tell me to get out?' Ginger said, 'No.'" Michael, who was standing outside, was shocked to see the young man dash out of the house at full speed: "He did not come back. That was his first investigation in a house, and his last. He said it was too much."

The Memphis Paranormal Investigations Team investigates private residences as well. Michael admits that the group has visited a few homes where they felt bad afterward. A good example is a house called Leisure residence. "The mother was a single mother," Michael said. "The children played with a Ouija board, and they got something nasty in their house. I got out a pad and did some automatic writing, and I figured out who he was." One particular room gave off a horrible smell like sulfur. "This was not some place you'd want your little grandchild staying," Michael said. During the investigation, the mother told the group that she had put a baby monitor up in the attic, and late at night, she could hear something walking around and knocking over boxes. Michael and the group went up to the attic to investigate: "We went up there to make sure there was not a living person up there. When we went back downstairs, we could hear him walking around in the attic. I think that's the only really bad place we've been to." Michael believes that the saving grace of the house was the fact that the woman's sister also died in the house: "Her sister's favorite thing was to sit in one of those little A-frame swings. Her sister used to rock herself in that, and we've got a picture of the chair rocking, and there's this huge, bright ectoplasmic form sitting in it. That was pretty neat." Michael suspects that the disturbances finally became more than the family could bear because the last time he drove past the house, he did not see any cars he recognized.

In situations like this, the group's primary goal is to identify the source of the disturbance, not to remove it. However, on rare occasions, the group has asked spirits to leave a residence: "I don't like to clean houses because it's really not my place," Michael says. "When I clean a house, I tell the spirits they are dead and need to cross over the other side." He never calls in the clergy because, in some cases, the presence of a minister or a priest has intensified the activity: "I've read too many cases where someone calls a Catholic priest, and he starts sprinkling Holy Water, and the chairs start floating in the air." Actually, Michael does not believe it is possible for a priest or anyone else to force a spirit to leave a house: "I'm always leery of groups that say they can come in and get rid of the ghosts in your house. We get good results because we ask. You can't say, 'In the name of Jesus, I order you out of here.' They'll leave when they're ready to leave."

Michael says his group has been to only two places where the members collected no evidence at all. In both cases, the houses were owned by lonely, elderly women. On one of these investigations, the members showed their compassionate side: "A lady called and said she had a ghost leaving hair all around," Michael said. "She had samples of his hair and all that. So I said, 'O.K. We'll check it out.' About two minutes after I'd been there, I told her, 'O.K. I'm going to step outside for a second.' I went over to the group, and I said, 'You know what this is, don't you?' They said, 'Yes.' The lady wasn't well." Michael was very proud of his group for pretending to do an investigation: "They didn't have to do that. They could have gotten in a car, called her a crazy old bat, and left, but they didn't. We allowed her to save face, and that was good."

Following an investigation, Michael always calls the clients to make sure that everything is O.K. He has found that most people feel much better after the group's visit: "Usually, we are able to make them feel more at ease. People are scared at first, but we tell them, 'Your grandmother is not going to hurt you because she does not know that she is dead.' I usually tell them to take control of the situation. 'You're the head of the household. You need to stand in the middle of the living room and tell them what year it is.' The clients need to tell the entity, 'You're no longer living. This is my house.' 'They'll be surprised what results they'll get.' "

The Memphis Paranormal Investigations Team has not had open criticism from the religious community, even though they have had several clients who were very religious: "They never see us break out a Ouija board," Michael says. "We have had clients who were very skeptical until we did an investigation in their house or building." One of these clients, who was interviewed by a local newspaper, said, "I saw what pictures they got and what evidence they got, so we went out the next day and bought cameras, and we got the same identical pictures in the same identical places."

Michael credits the group's large number of successful investigations to the respect the members show for the dead: "We never take a picture without asking permission. If we have the slightest inkling that someone doesn't want us there, we leave. The cemetery's their home. You never walk into someone's home without asking permission." At a couple of cemeteries where the group has conducted multiple investigations, some of the members have reported feeling like they are being hugged. "We have also built two memorial gardens, one at Slavehaven, and that helps, too," Michael says. "The memorial at Slavehaven cost us one thousand dollars out of our own pockets. At one graveyard, there is a section where they bury the infants, and we will take flowers there. We do this for the dead at the places we investigate. Any time, day or night, we can take pictures at these places, and we get beautiful,

beautiful orb shots. The spirits love it." Michael went on to say that some groups try to buy as much equipment as they can, but Memphis Paranormal Investigations prefers to spend their money showing their gratitude to spirits who cooperate: "We try to show them the respect they did not get when they were alive."

Needless to say, the Memphis Paranormal Investigations Team has no patience with those groups who conduct Halloween investigations dressed in costumes: "Do they know how disrespectful and tacky that is? That's the most disrespectful thing I can think of. It ranks with pissing on someone's grave. Of course, they never get any evidence, because they're making fun of the dead. Cemeteries are not a place to party. They are a place to be reverent and remember, and that's what we do, except we take videos and photographs." Prior to an investigation, Michael instructs his members to observe decorum when passing through the cemetery: "Don't walk over tombstones. If you pass one and you feel like you need to stop and bend down and put your hand on it [then] listen and be reverent. We're never disappointed. It's good for us to be in a place where you feel you're welcome."

The group's protective attitude toward cemeteries has limited their public relations and fund-raising opportunities: "We've had dozens of e-mails asking us if we did ghost tours of Memphis," Michael says. "We were kind of thinking of doing that, but one of our members said, 'If this gets out, they will start locking up the cemetery, or they will start defacing the tombstones.' That's the last thing we'd want to do is to bring anything bad into a cemetery." Michael also tells his members to leave if they feel uncomfortable in an area.

This is not to say, though, that the Memphis Paranormal Investigations Team is an invisible presence in Memphis. "People find out about us through the Web site," Michael says. "Every member has a set of car signs for their cars—magnetic signs. We pass out bumper stickers to our clients, and they've been nice enough to put them on their cars. It's usually word of mouth, but we're on the news a lot. We've been on the Travel Channel twice, and we just got through filming a television show for the BBC. It will air in Europe and Canada."

Like most directors, Michael Espanjer has a wish list of sites he and his group would like to visit someday. The places on Michael's list, however, are a little closer to home, such as Ernest P. Hazel's, a famous bar and grill in Memphis: "They're famous for their hamburgers. You can smell them all the way down the street. The janitor has worked in the daytime from six A.M. until noon cleaning the place. He has seen many, many apparitions walking up and down the staircase, but it doesn't seem to bother him. He has seen the ghosts of call girls. It was a brothel back in the mid-1800s." Michael has no desire, though, to visit the most famous private residence in Memphis, Graceland: "They don't allow investigators at Graceland. It's strictly a money trap. We very seriously doubt that Elvis is here. If he did return, this is the last place he would stay. Graceland was a tomb for him. He couldn't go out. It was like a prison. I think he'd be where his parents were, probably Tupelo."

Texas

Central Texas Ghost Search

CISCO, TEXAS

Sarah Zell, Founder and Director

Some might say that Sarah Zell was destined from childhood to become a ghost hunter: "My parents' house is haunted, so I kind of grew up in that environment. I was only scared once. . . . the ghost liked to hide things and move things around. Lights would come on, and I would walk over to unplug them, and they weren't plugged in. I'd hear people walking around when I was home alone, and it always seemed to happen when I was home alone. I'd hear people walking in the kitchen. Then it progressed to things flying out of the top cabinets in the kitchen. It'd tap you on the shoulder. You'd turn around, and there'd be nothing there. You'd try to sleep, and the lampshade would start shaking. It wasn't a poltergeist, though, because it wasn't dangerous." Whenever Sarah told her parents what was going on, they simply told her she had been watching too many scary movies. Her father began to take Sarah's stories more seriously when he heard moaning sounds: "It sounded like someone was in misery. The first time my dad heard it, it was at three in the morning. He got up, and I was pregnant at the time with my son, and he thought it was me. He couldn't figure out where it was coming from. It seemed to be in one room. Then it would move to another room. The moaning usually happened at three A.M." Her parents really became believers, though, after they remodeled the bathroom and "stirred up" whatever had taken up residence in their home. The weird noises continued every day for a week.

These days, though, the disturbances occur only once in a while: "Things wouldn't happen for a year. You'd forget about it, and it'd start up again. I brought in groceries one day. I was the only one here. I put one bag on the table and one on the counter. I went back out to the car, and when I back in, the one on the table was gone. I found it [in another room]. The ghost also knocked a glass off the counter." Sarah insists, though, that her interest in the paranormal did not really take root until she began reading about it. To date, she has not researched the history of her house.

One of the first investigations that Sarah's group conducted was at her parents' house: "We've gotten pictures of vortexes and orbs and mists. We have a formal investigation of the house. A friend of mine who's a member of the group came over, and we got some EVP's that we couldn't understand, and he set up a video camera and got some orbs." Sarah feels that the EVP's the group collected are more important than the orbs because orbs can be caused by dust and moisture. "EVP's are more reliable," Sarah says, "because they are produced through questions asked by an investigator."

Of all the evidence her group has collected, Sarah feels that the photographic evidence is the most compelling. One of her favorite photographs was taken at Cedar Hill in a cemetery: "It looks like an older gentleman with a beard. I've sent the picture to people without telling them about it, and they've said, 'We see an older guy standing by a tree.' That one was taken with a digital camera."

Sarah's group did not really get underway until she purchased Microsoft's Front Page and set up her Web site in December 2004. Prospective members can apply by filling out a form on the Web site. "We will accept almost anybody into the group, but I try to meet them before we take them out," Sarah says. "You kind of like to know who you're dealing with. Some people join just so they can say they're members, and you never see them again." All members wear special T-shirts out in public on investigations.

So far, Central Texas Ghost Search has conducted only four home investigations. She reports that all four families were glad that they had their house investigated. "One lady said, 'I'm so glad to be talking to somebody who doesn't think I'm crazy.' Of the four houses we investigated, one [was haunted] for sure, one maybe, and we got nothing at the other two. One lady had had things happening to her for about fifteen years. She had moved three times to get away from the spirit, and every time she moved, the spirit followed her. Every place she went, things started happening—knocking things out of cabinets, knocking pictures off bookshelves. The first time she contacted me, I toyed with the idea of setting a recorder out and asking questions so that she could get a name or something, and she called back the next day and said she had a conversation [with the entity]." Not only did the investigators record several EVP's at the house, but they also photographed vortexes, mists, and orbs streaking across the screen of the video camera. "It's hard to deny orbs if you see them moving across the camera," Sarah says.

The group has not conducted very many investigations of historical sites. In March 2005, several members conducted a somewhat clandestine investigation of the Driskill Hotel in Austin. Built in 1886 by a wealthy cattle baron, Colonel Jesse Lincoln

Driskill, the hotel is reputed to be haunted by three ghosts: the ghost of a little girl who fell off the grand staircase, the ghost of a Houston woman who shot herself in a bathtub after her fiancé called off their engagement; and the ghost of Driskill himself. Sarah did not tell management that her group was going to conduct an investigation because she had heard that the new owners were trying to play down the hotel's haunted reputation. After taking one of the local ghost tours, the investigators checked into Room 427, where the "Houston Bride" committed suicide: "That was really freaky. We got a really bright orb and some EVP's. We left the recorder running while we were out on the town investigating, a few glasses clinked together, and we also left the video camera recording. So we knew there was nobody in or out of the room. But then a couple of drinking glasses clinked together again on the table. Both the video camera and the EVP were turned off, and the video camera didn't record anybody turning them off, but [something] had turned the switches to the off position almost at the same time." After the investigation, Sarah was driving home when she received a frantic phone call from one of her members: "You've got to see it. It's awesome! It's the picture of a little girl." At the time of the interview, Sarah had not yet seen the photograph.

Occasionally, the Central Texas Ghost Search is asked to investigate local businesses. In 2004, they received a phone call from the manager of a movie store, which occupies the first floor of an old apartment complex in downtown Cisco. For several months, employees had complained about being watched while they were in the restroom. Also, voices have been heard upstairs when no one was up there. Prior to the investigation, Sarah gave the manager several forms absolving the owners of liability in the event that a member of the team was injured on site. She now regrets having taken that precaution: "The manager said, 'Oh, I didn't know that this was such a formal thing. Maybe I'd better call the owners and ask them.' He called me back later that night and said the owners didn't really want him to do that."

The group hopes to have better luck when they investigate the Hilton Hotel in Cisco. The old hotel has been converted into a theater, which is used by the Cisco Junior College for theatrical productions. It also houses the chamber of commerce and a museum upstairs. Sarah learned the importance of word-of-mouth publicity when she was contacted by the museum: "The museum had heard that we had already done an investigation and wanted us to come back and do an investigation of the museum part upstairs. It makes me feel good when somebody calls us and wants us to do something."

One of the Central Texas Ghost Search's most memorable investigations was actually a preliminary investigation of a local cemetery. She decided to check out the old graveyard one afternoon just prior to the formal investigation. At the time, her son and her two dogs were in the car: "I drove into the driveway, stopped the car, put it in park, and kind of looked around. My dog just went crazy. Her hair was standing up on end. She was scratching at the window. I looked around and didn't see any animals or anything. We were outside looking around, and I called people to see if they wanted to go with me on another investigation, and my son said, 'Are you going to talk to those people?' And I said, 'What people, Sweetie?' And he said, 'Those two ladies who were standing by the car. They were wearing long, blue dresses.' I said, 'What are you talking about? There's nobody by the car.' And he said, 'You didn't see them?' And he was just as serious as he could be. I asked him where he saw the ladies, and he pointed to [the direction] where the dogs were scratching. I went 'Wow!'" After taking her charges home, Sarah joined the group at the cemetery later that night. While Sarah was analyzing the photographs they had taken at the cemetery, she noticed that there were two vortex-lights in every photograph. All of the lights displayed a bluish tint. The EVP's they recorded there were even more surprising: "I got two EVP's that night that I could definitely tell clear as day. One of them said, 'I like the dog.' And the other one said, 'He saw us.' That's the really creepy one. My son's heard me tell the story, so now I'm afraid he's going to start doing it for attention. I try to not involve him."

Sarah Zell admits that her attitude toward ghost hunting has changed dramatically since her group first started out: "The first whole year that I had the Texas Ghost Search, I was just having fun. Well, not having fun, really—I was just trying to figure out what that stuff going on in my parents' house was. So I wasn't really looking to see if a place was haunted or wasn't haunted. It was just kind of for fun. Now we want to prove that ghosts exist." Her members are still disappointed when they find a rational explanation for the disturbances in private residences, but they usually go away feeling good about having helped somebody.

Lone Star Spirits

HUMBLE, TEXAS

Peter Haviland, Founder and Director

Peter Haviland's initiation into the world of the paranormal occurred when he was twelve years old: "I was watching television in my parents' house, and my dog was with me, and I felt the room start to get cold. I felt the hair on the back of my head stand up. My dog stood up and turned around and started walking up the stairs—my parents had a two-story house. I saw my grandfather walking down the stairs, and my grandfather had passed the year before. He walked down the stairs and into the closet. I was never afraid of my grandfather in life, so at that point in time, I never thought that he was dead or anything." Peter got up and opened the door, but his grandfather was not there. Peter then noticed a plaque that his grandfather had brought back from Italy. "It had a sort of angel on it," Peter said. "He had that in his houses. He built two houses in New York, and it hung in both of them. So I kind of thought he walked into the closet because the plaque was in there. I guess the plaque was an energy drawing point."

After this encounter with his dead grandfather, Peter began reading every book he could find on hauntings and paranormal phenomena. "At junior high school they used to call me 'the

289

Ghost Boy' because I carried ghost books wherever I went," Peter said. In high school, his fascination with the paranormal intensified. He and several of his like-minded friends began going out to haunted locations to see if they could document in photographs what they had been reading about. "Then we decided to try to help people," Peter said. "We had read stories about people being terrified, and we didn't want people to be scared in their own homes. Of course at that point in time, there was nothing we could really do to make someone feel better. We thought we were helping out by documenting it, and in reality, we were causing more of a panic. We were confirming what they were experiencing, but we didn't have any personnel to help them deal with it."

In college, Peter had an opportunity to develop his interest in otherworldly phenomena even further: "I had a professor who allowed me to write about parapsychology as long as it was in the context of what he wanted me to write about. That's what I did. I met some like-minded people there, and we branched off into more documentation. We had more of an idea of what we were doing now."

Peter started Lone Start Spirits in 1999. The idea for forming the group actually came from a friend of his, who told her husband she wanted to go to a haunted house for Halloween. Her husband told her, "There are plenty of haunted houses around here." She replied, "No, I want to go to a real one." Peter's friend posted a recruiting notice on the Internet for like-minded people, "and we kind of got together from there," Peter said. "I brought the experience that I had in the field as well as my personal experiences." Lone Star Spirits has twenty members with a core of eight active members. The membership includes a trained psychologist, an employee of NASA, and several parapsychologists.

The term *high tech* hardly begins to describe the group's equipment, which the members buy themselves: "We use a thermal energy camera, a four-camera surveillance system. It's a complete wireless set-up, so I can move the cameras around to get what we need. I've got video decks that record between twenty-four and thirty-six hours. We can also back it up to a standard recorder. We've got thermal gauges, which measure surface temperature in a room or on people. We've got EMF detectors, ion counters, digital cameras, analog cameras, 35 mm cameras. I've got one camera that has an infrared lens on it so that I can shoot in total darkness with the camera itself. I've gone all out for this. And my wife still talks to me! I thought I was going to get divorced when I bought that thermal energy camera. I bought it used. It's black and white. This one was five thousand dollars. It does what we want it to do. It takes temperatures and breaks them down into video signals. White is hot and black is cold. Then you've got your variance of gray. Color's great to have, but all that matters is that it shows the temperature. I guess I say that because I still want one, but my wife won't have it."

Most of the group's investigations are conducted at private residences. Peter describes his group's investigative approach as "walking the gray," which involves trying to marry the metaphysical evidence to the scientific evidence. "We tend to believe that there is a break there," Peter says. "My thought is that as long as you can get the equipment to verify the psychic, which can verify the history of what you're working on, and you have numerous amounts of things that weigh over on top of each other, as well as when your team goes through, and they can't explain things that are weighing over, that's good enough evidence for me." To ensure that the investigation will not be contaminated in any way,

Peter does not tell the medium or the equipment team where they are going. Only Peter and the camera team know the location because they have to know where to set up. "If I need to get a hold of somebody like a historian," Peter says, "I've got my cell phone with me, so I can say, 'I came up with the name Bob Smith. Can you find out something about him for me?'"

Rarely have the group's clients been disappointed, primarily because they are looking for answers, any answers. "They don't care if we find a logical explanation," Peter says. "If they are experiencing things, they want to know why, and if we can provide them with an answer, then they're happy." Peter usually brings along a medium for intervention in case a homeowner asks the group to remove a spirit. The group does not involve the clergy as a rule because most clients do not want their church to know that their home might be haunted.

Peter is very proud of the fact that one of his members has captured a couple of full-body apparitions on film: "They're not the best quality, but the photographer who took them cannot figure out why they're there. The apparitions look like people, like somebody took one shot and laid it over another one." He is certain that the photographs are not double-exposures because of the professionalism of the young woman who took the shot. Still, Peter spent the better portion of two hours trying to calm her down in the darkroom. The same photographer took a picture of one of the mirrors, and in the mirror right behind her, the image of a lady floating right above her is clearly visible. "That was pretty wild," Peter said.

Although the majority of the group's investigations have been conducted at private residences, the members have visited a few historic sites, such as the Presidio La Bahia in Goliad,

Texas. In fact, Lone Star Spirits was one of the first groups to be given permission to investigate at the old fort. During the Texas Revolution of 1836, Colonel James Walker Fannin Jr. and his 342 men surrendered to Mexican forces. They were imprisoned and subsequently massacred on General Santa Anna's orders on March 27, 1836, in violation of the honorable terms upon which they had laid down their arms. "We rented a room out there for the weekend and had the whole place to ourselves," Peter said. "You walk in there, and it's just awe-inspiring, the whole grounds. To walk out there at midnight is very humbling. Anytime you're dealing with a place that has a high emotional charge, it can be very depressing, but I can't tell you if I felt that way because of the history that I know about the place or if I was really feeling it." While the investigators were at the Presidio, they got a large number of EVP's and photographs of orbs. Peter considers these orbs to be more significant than the run-of-the-mill variety: "The orbs we got coincide with the mediums saying that they're speaking with somebody and the orb is there where they say they're seeing the person." Peter believes the orbs could represent the memory of the executions that occurred at Goliad so many years ago.

Peter's most memorable investigation was conducted at the historic Baker Hotel in Mineral Wells, Texas. For generations, people were attracted to the area because of the mineral springs, which were supposed to be good for the health. Hundreds of children suffering from mental illness were brought to the hotel to be cured. All the mirrors in the ballroom are tinted pink to make it appear as if the guests have a rosy glow.

Before arriving, one of the researchers on the team uncovered a host of "skeletons" in the old hotel's many closets. Years ago, a bellboy died after being pushed out of an elevator. A call girl who had died in one of the rooms was tied up and displayed in a window in the hope that someone passing by would claim the body. A woman took a swan dive out of a window and missed the pool. A man shooting craps in one of the rooms was shot to death. The son of the owner died of a heart attack in the hotel the day before he had planned to close it down.

Peter describes the activity there as "just incredible." One of the members of the group chased down phantom footsteps, only to find that no one was there. "I had a team member upstairs call me on the walkie-talkie and tell me that something had grabbed him by the leg. I brought psychics, who confirmed some of the deaths out there and even brought out some information that wasn't published." One of these mediums described the death of the bellboy, even though she had not been informed of the incident beforehand. She also channeled a mental patient who had been brought to the hotel to drink the water. Another medium was picked up and thrown against a wall. "I've got that on videotape," Peter says. "So I would say that was the most intense place to go."

Ghost hunting is an expensive hobby, and Lone Star Spirits has found ways to avoid financing their investigations totally from their own pockets. "We have to generate some kind of income, so we sell equipment on our site," Peter says. "I've just done a merchandise thing for shirts. Nothing really hokey. It just says 'Ghosthunters' on it. The other stuff is our logo on shirts and mugs and stuff like that." The group also asks clients for expenses, especially to offset the cost of hotel rooms and gas.

Even though the group sells T-shirts, the members don't wear them on investigations. "Most people don't like to call attention to the fact that their house is being investigated, so if you have a bunch of people running around with ghost shirts just because they want to show off, our clients wouldn't be very happy with that," Peter says. He believes that his group's low-key approach has also gained them access to places in Houston that are off-limits to other people. Many homeowners and caretakers prefer not to publicize an investigation.

The members of Lone Star Spirits keep a high profile in Houston. Peter offers ghost-hunting classes in the metaphysical shop where he works. He has also spoken at colleges and business luncheons, and his group has been featured on radio and television programs. "We do this because it generates interest and leads as well," Peter says. For a group this well known, negative publicity is a given, but Peter takes it all in stride: "I occasionally get e-mails from people who question what we do, and I tell them that I respect their opinions, and that's pretty much it. I don't do this because I'm trying to make someone a believer. It's more of a calling for me." Peter says he is much more concerned of the opinion his clients have of his group. Peter is sure his members will do a good job as long as they maintain their professionalism: "The team's the most important thing to us. As long as we all get along real well and we have a good relationship with each other, everything else will work out."

Metroplex Paranormal Investigations

CARROLLTON, TEXAS

Vicki Isaacks, Founder and Director

Vicki Isaacks traces the birth of her interest in the paranormal to an old horror movie: "I was six years old. I watched my first horror movie, *I Was a Teenage Werewolf,* [starring] Michael Landon. It was my birthday. I had gotten a new bike for my birthday, and I had left it out front of the house, and my dad made me walk through the back porch so nobody would get a hold of it. And as I walked up the steps of the porch, he flung the door open and scared me, and he continued to do stuff like that to me for as long as I can remember. I was into horror movies my whole life, and then for some reason, I began focusing on the ghost aspect of it." When Vicki moved to the Dallas area, she was delighted to find there were groups that actually went out and did paranormal investigations. She joined a couple of groups, but she did not like the way they were run, so she started her own group in 2001. She now has twenty members. "That's a little more than I like," Vicki says. "I capped it at twenty-five because I don't like to tell anybody they can't go on an investigation because there are too many people." Vicki's members are from all walks of life, including an emergency room nurse, a middle school assistant principal, and a nonactive member who is with Homeland Security. Vicki is the pharmacy department manager for Wal-Mart. Most of the members, though, are in blue-collar occupations.

Vicki has come upon a unique method of supplementing the group's equipment, most of which the members buy themselves: "We are trying to get registered as a nonprofit organization, so that any equipment they've bought or film they've used on an investigation, they can take off their income tax and donate it to the group, and then we all decide what to do with it. Once the equipment is bought, it remains with the group. It's the group's equipment, so that if somebody leaves the group, they can't say, 'I donated ten bucks. Give it back.'"

Vicki's group has been investigating a large number of private residences lately, possibly, she believes, because of all the exposure the paranormal is getting on television: "I think people are either more aware of stuff that's going on, or maybe they just get a kick out of ghost hunters coming to their house." Increased media exposure has also made Metroplex Paranormal Investigations a more visible presence in the community: "We've done a lot of print media," Vicki says. "We helped a guy with a book. We've done local television, so that helps." Vicki admittedly enjoys the attention she receives from her colleagues and customers at Wal-Mart after she appears in a magazine or on television: "The media publicity gets the word out. There's definitely a rise [in phone calls] after an article [appears] in a newspaper or magazine. I can talk, and that's fine, but I'm not real comfortable being on camera. I always joke with them: 'Shoot from the waist up.' I'm way too conscious of the camera." On Halloween, Vicki teaches an introductory ghost-hunting class for one of the recreation centers and takes them out on an investigation. "That helps get our name out, too," she says. Two years ago, though, one of the recreation centers received some phone calls complaining that a Satan worshiper was teaching a class at their facility. So two weeks before the next class started, Vicki added the following to the Web site: "We are not Satanists. We don't sacrifice farm animals."

The members of Vicki's group prefer to investigate at night. "Some of the members [believe] that if they are using their night-shot equipment with the infrared, they're more likely to pick up something," Vicki says. "I just prefer the ambiance. Things seem to be more active at night, but if they're active in the daytime as well. Most people are at work, or they're running around and don't notice these things going on, but they generally notice them at night."

Unlike some groups, Metroplex Paranormal Investigations does not remove spirits from a house. In fact, the members believe that blessing a house could actually make matters worse. The group prefers to document the activity using a more scientific method with their equipment. However, the group also brings along a psychic who is well known in the area. "Rita backs up whatever scientific equipment is tested," Vicki says. "We don't back up whatever her impressions are. If she says we need to take a picture, we take a picture. We've gotten orbs this way."

The mere presence of orbs, however, does not convince Metroplex Paranormal Investigations that a site is indeed haunted. "Nine times out of ten, when we do home investigations, we get orbs," Vicki says. "The homeowners get copies of the report and pictures, whatever we got. The last house we did, we did have orb activity, but we didn't have anything else to go with it. In the report we gave them, we told them we did have orb activity, but we couldn't rule that place haunted simply for orb activity. I said something like 'Possible paranormal activity' and recommended a follow-up visit."

She dismisses orbs as viable evidence because she believes orbs are dust or light refracted from the camera. "Even if it is a paranormal orb," Vicki says, "it's probably picked up things from the environment to give it mass and enable it to be photographed." The members put more stock in EVP's than in orbs, but they do not accept EVP's by themselves as proof of a haunting, either. She cites as an example an investigation conducted by T.A.P.S. on *Ghosthunters*. The group believed the voices they had recorded in a private home were genuine until they realized that they could hear voices coming from the registers all through the house. Because investigators usually cannot ask a family to leave while they conduct an investigation, sounds produced by normal activity make if very difficult to record EVP's at private residences.

Vicki readily admits that although investigating is serious business, the investigators are not serious all the time. She cites as an example an investigation they conducted at the Granberry Opera House in Granberry, Texas, when the group had just gotten started. After a couple of hours, the members photographed a large number of orbs; in addition, the lights came on by themselves. They were thrilled because, back then, orbs were good enough as evidence. Toward the end of the investigation, Vicki walked across the street to the actors' dorm and retrieved the key to the costume shop, where all of the costumes were made and stored. "Nobody knew that I had the key," Vicki said, "so I unlocked the Costume Shop and brought a bunch of people in and came out and there were two people waiting to get in. We let them go in, and I pulled out the key and locked them in. So we went around to the back door, which had been sealed up with sheet metal, and took our fingernails and scratched it, and we could hear them inside. 'Oh, my gosh! Did you hear that? Did you hear that?' And then we'd hear them running down the hallway, and they couldn't get out. And they said, 'Oh, my gosh! You've got to be kidding me!' I finally walked over and unlocked the door." She went on to say that after the serious part of an overnight investigation is completed, the members tend to play around. "We're a very social group," Vicki says. "Everybody, with the exception of two or three people, has been a member of the group for two or three years."

The only time Vicki has been really frightened occurred when she was the butt of a joke played on her by her friends: "We went to the Baker Hotel in Mineral Wells. We were filming a documentary, and the caretaker at the Baker had allowed someone to use a couple of the bottom floors for a spook house. The cameraman had decided to follow me and a couple of the other members around. We went into where the showers and stuff were. They had one of those old-timey saunas that you sit in and your head sticks out when the doors close. So it was dark, and I saw something in the sauna, and I said something that is unprintable. They got it all on video, and it turned out to be a bloody doll's head sitting in the sauna. So I was pretty scared until one of my group members walked over and picked up the head and said, 'What? Are you scared of this?'"

The group's inclusion in a book by Mitchell Whitington entitled *Ghosts of North Texas* has inspired Vicki and the other members to write their own book: "We've actually thought of getting together our exclusive investigations and doing a book simply because all the books that I've read show the outside of the place that's supposed to be haunted and mention what's supposed to be going on, but they never show what's going on. You'd think that even orb activity for a book would show something." If their book is published and is not too regional in its appeal, the group plans to use the money to upgrade their equipment. "We're not low tech," Vicki says. "We're medium tech right now. We don't have that Sci-Fi contract to buy all that equipment." Until the royalties start rolling in, Vicki will continue to improvise: "We have a laptop, but we don't have high-tech cameras. So what I did was, I bought a security system like a department store has. It uses a monitor, and it tapes directly to a VHS tape. And the cameras switch back and forth, and they have sixty feet of cable, so it's almost like [T.A.P.S.'s] laptop and their cameras."

Right now, Vicki is enjoying the thrill of investigating and the notoriety that is generated by it. In 2004, one of her members threw a big barbecue and invited all the leaders of all the other ghost groups we have in the area. Vicki was reluctant to go, but she went anyway. Now she is glad she did: "They were all so excited to meet me. I was thinking, 'What's your problem?' I went home and said to Amy, the cofounder, 'Did you know I was Miss Thing?' She said, "I always thought you were Miss Thing. We need to buy you a tiara.' They told me I was famous around this area for ghost hunting. I'm like, 'I didn't know that.'" Vicki's only regret at this point is that she has never had a psychic experience, even though several members of her group have. In fact, she says she would do almost anything to acquire psychic powers: "I think I'm going to get our psychic to hit me in the head with a baseball bat. She told me to clear my mind, and my mind's constantly going, and I can't do it."

Society for Paranormal Investigation

DALLAS, TEXAS

Joel-Anthony Gray, Founder and Director

J oel-Anthony Gray is one of many paranormal investigators who have been interested in it the supernatural their whole life: "It's a combination of being fascinated by the dark, the mystical, the forbidden. Since childhood, I've been reading ghost stories. When I got older, I went to the library, and I was always in the 'Weird Phenomena' section, where they talked about UFO's, the Bermuda Triangle, things like that." Joel-Anthony speculates that most people are interested in the paranormal because it's one of the final frontiers: "We've got to have something to push against to test our mettle and our resourcefulness. We've got to have something to chew on, and the paranormal is my chew toy. I think it's understanding and conquering different aspects of ourselves." From Joel-Anthony's point of view, the notion of investigating a haunted castle and coming up against some kind of antagonist is the stuff of *Scooby Doo* or Hollywood. The challenge of learning something new or finding answers to age-old questions is especially appealing now: "Studying the dead helps us to understand the reality we take for granted," he says.

Joel-Anthony is attending college to study advanced video effects and animation. He currently works as a consultant in software analysis for medical and defense communities. He is also involved in graphic and Web site design. His long-term goal, though, is to expand the range of the Society for Paranormal Investigation: "I've got multiple ventures, one of which is promoting SPI to the point where it becomes part of a larger project, be it a grant or TV show. I've studied a lot of Feng Shui as well, and I find that has a lot of bearing on places that are haunted."

Joel-Anthony founded the group in 2002. In 2004, the Society for Paranormal Investigation began expanding: "My assistant director was going back and forth to visit Washington, D.C., her home town. Then I began recruiting area reps, so we decided to expand so she could visit the places out there." The Society for Paranormal Investigation now has branches in four states, mostly in metro areas. "We talk to people all over the nation," says Joel-Anthony. "We call them units. There's a Seattle unit in Washington State. Of course, Dallas–Fort Worth here in Texas, New Orleans in Louisiana, and Washington, D.C., in Maryland. Our group is the home base in the sense that I'm the director and I administrate. But to be honest, I pay more attention to the other markets than I do to the Dallas market."

Finding money is a constant concern for the Society for Paranormal Investigation, as it is for most paranormal investigators. Unlike many groups, though, Joel-Anthony's does not sell equipment on its Web site: "We don't do any equipment sales because it's not a high enough profit margin. It's too competitive. I don't want to give any more competition to the people who are already in it. I have these people listed on my Web site." The group does accept donations, but Joel-Anthony finds that some clients do not always carry through with the promises they make on the telephone. Someday he would like to receive funding from an outside agency: "In my opinion, the only way to do it is to have a sponsor or grant or to become a parapsychologist, but it costs fifty thousand dollars to get a Ph.D. in parapsychology. We are looking into getting grants. I've had some people looking into it, but it's proving to be more of a challenge than I thought. I will probably end up writing a grant myself, probably a federal grant." Like most directors, Joel-Anthony would like to be compensated for all the time he spends updating the Web site, doing the research, interviewing, and researching the historical background of specific locations. "If you're not careful," he warns, "it can get out of control, and you're spending 24/7 on the subject. You've got to set limits and decide what's really important." Recently, Joel-Anthony has scaled back some of his administrative duties, especially those pertaining to the Dallas area, so that he can focus on the stronger markets.

In recent months, the Society for Paranormal Investigation has been visiting more private residences. "Those are the ones who approach us the most," Joel-Anthony says. "We also tend to get more activity at private residences. It tends to be fresher and something that nobody else knows about. You don't have to crowd against people like you do in a place that's been haunted for decades. The problem with reputation is that it gets embellished over time. Things get distorted out of proportion. Also, it's really pretty rare to have an experience in a public place. If there's a funny noise and there's thirty people there, it'd have to be a pretty odd and funny noise to stand out."

Joel Anthony has found that most homeowners who are experiencing activity fall into one of two groups: they are genuinely afraid, or they want validation. Many clients seem to enjoy having a group of professionals come out to their homes, show them their equipment, go through the paces, talk to them, and listen to them, not laugh at them. They want to be assured that this sort of thing has happened to other people in the past and continues to happen in the present. Joel Anthony admits that things can get a little bit "odd" when people have mental disorders or when there is a financial motive: "I had one person who had a really cool-looking house. It was owned by a magician. He was planning to fix it up like a bed and breakfast and turn it into the Myrtles. I was tempted to tell him, 'You want us to come out there and put our stamp of approval on it so you can say it's haunted and sell it to people.'" Conversely, a number of public places and businesses tend to downplay the spirits on the premises, especially if a belief in the paranormal goes against the religious convictions of the owner or manager. A good example is the Excelsior Hotel in Jefferson. "It is run by the Garden Club," Joel-Anthony says, "and they're Baptists, and they're against having their staff talk about the ghosts. If you're a guest there late at night and you're taking photographs or infrared readings and you're not bothering anybody, nobody's going to know or say anything. This is the only way you can do an investigation at a place like this." He goes on to say that the biggest mistake investigators can make in a location like the Excelsior Hotel is to draw attention to themselves by opening locked doors or walking around in plain view with EMF detectors and digital recorders.

Presenting a professional demeanor in private residences is so important to Joel-Anthony that he does not accept prospective members who appear to have a nervous temperament: "I get the feeling distinctly that we will take them out somewhere, and they will freak out. We're not a treatment center. I don't want them to use us to try to fix their fears. We are serious researchers. [If we are in a private home], it makes us look unprofessional. We have to be rock-steady in order to help our clients." Joel-Anthony also disapproves of people with psychic inclinations who claim to "sense a presence" when they hear the floors creak or the shutters blow.

Joel-Anthony insists also that the group members dress appropriately during investigations. He is particularly to the wearing of T-shirts: "I used to belong to a group that did wear T-shirts, and they were cute, but I don't think 'cute' is the image I really want to portray to the public. I don't think T-shirts are very professional. I think badges or armbands are O.K. Sometimes, we dress pretty nice. I wear a sports coat and slacks if we are going to a five-star hotel or we need to make a little better impression."

Besides identifying the cause of disturbances, the Society for Paranormal Investigation also drives out spirits. "I have had to do a cleansing ceremony, or participate in one," Joel-Anthony says. "It happened this weekend at a private residence in north Dallas. I did it with a friend of mine. She's familiar with the metaphysical. I was there mostly as an observer to see how she did things. She had Holy Water, sage, sea salt, incense, a gong—the whole nine yards." He disagrees with purists who believe that one must follow a set protocol when cleansing a house: "I don't think it matters to get too dogmatic about procedure. I think you need to be educated about it, but I don't think there is only one right way to cleanse a place."

Even though Joel-Anthony does incorporate a few metaphysical elements in his investigations, he does not have any psychics in his group. "I believe in it," he says, "but I haven't met anybody I felt was capable enough and low-maintenance enough to integrate with our group. I'm interested in having them come in. The problem is I'm going to have to have performance standards. Otherwise, I'll have all sorts of resumes coming in, and a lot of them won't be any good. I think [fewer] than 10 percent of them are as good as they claim." Several years ago, Joel-Anthony did invite a woman who he thought was a genuine psychic to join the group, but she turned him down. "I think the people who are really good at it don't really make a show of it," Joel-Anthony says. "If I found someone who met my requirements, we could justify it. But right now, we're looking for more empirical evidence."

One of the group's most memorable experiences happened at a private residence in Grand Prairie. "We were setting up the infra-red camera and had not put retro-illumination on it," Joel-Anthony said. "And I was setting something up in front of the camera—I wasn't even near it—and we asked the spirit to show us a sign, and the lamp on the camera flipped on by itself. It's a rotary switch, and you have to locate it through three positions, so there's no way it could have happened by itself."

Another memorable incident occurred at a historic site, the Shoenberg Theater. It was after midnight, and Joel-Anthony was sitting in front of the stage with his EMF meter: "Very loud steps were walking across the stage right in front of me, and the EMF meter spiked with each step. That was interesting confirmation, a correlation between an energy reading and a sound, which you don't get very often. I did record the sound, but not very well. I had a camera running, and the problem is that the built-in microphones that Sony has are not very good." Joel-Anthony says the sounds of the footsteps are audible, but one has to listen very closely to really hear them.

Although the Society for Paranormal Investigation has not met any opposition from religious groups, a Catholic friar in San Antonio distracted the group by giving them a tour of an abandoned mission in San Antonio. "It was a clever way of getting us not to do an investigation," Joel-Anthony says. "Dallas is just corporate enough to where people leave well enough alone. You have a different attitude toward the paranormal here than you do in a place like Seattle."

Joel-Anthony Gray believes that the Society for Paranormal Investigation is riding the crest of the public's rising interest in the paranormal. He credits three factors with turning paranormal investigations into a national pastime: "First, there are the TV shows that have been around for years, the Internet, and digital cameras. They have really caused it to explode. There's a proliferation of information on the subject through Web sites. With digital cameras, you don't have to spend any money for developing. You have instant gratification." Unfortunately, the increasing popularity of ghost hunting has its downside—the thrill-seeking ghost hunter: "About fifteen years ago, a parapsychologist or a ghost hunter was a very, very rare animal. There was just a handful of them all over the world. Now you've got hundreds of groups springing up all over the place. Some of these people want to do the right thing, but others try to be amateur psychologists and gurus and shamans and Tibetan monks rolled into one." In his opinion, the amateurish investigators are mostly orb chasers who believe that every luminous globe they photograph is a ghost. This obsession with orbs is not only detrimental to the ghost community, but it is ridiculous as well. "It's pathetic to think that when I die, I'll turn into a blob of light," Joel-Anthony says. He finds photographs of full-body apparitions to be much more convincing, but no one in his group has one on film yet. The prospect of photographing the human-like image of a ghost someday inspires the members of the Society for Paranormal Investigation to keep going.

Texas Paranormal Research Team

DAYTON, TEXAS

Matt Novotny, Founder and Director

M att became an enthusiast of the paranormal as the direct result of the purchase of a sixty-year-old house in 1997. He bought the seventy-five-thousand-dollar house when he was still in college. At first, he dismissed the strange events that began shortly after he moved in. As the number of unexplainable occurrences began to increase, so did his curiosity: "That's when I became interest in trying to seek out to see what it was. So I spent three years doing research and reading." Eventually, Matt reached the point where he could no longer keep the eerie side of his house all to myself, so he invited a paranormal group to come in and investigate. He was not impressed with their technique: "They had no organizing skills whatever. These people just came and took pictures and said, 'Oh, look at the orbs!' I looked at the pictures and realized that those weren't orbs. They were just dust particles." Matt suspected that not all paranormal investigators were thrill seekers, so he contacted other groups throughout the state and discovered that most of them employed more scientific methods in their investigations. Their examples inspired Matt to begin investigating on his own: "I realized that I could take the knowledge [obtained from my research] and integrate it into my ghost investigations."

Matt founded the Texas Paranormal Research Team in 2003 when he realized that he could not "do it all" by himself. Once his Web site was in place and applications for membership began pouring in, his group started posting their findings. Matt was surprised by the response from the general public: "You know, there are lots of people out there who are requesting this type of information. I didn't realize how many people contact you once you put something on-line. It's almost ridiculous all the people who call me. Some of the are nut-heads. I try to stick with the more educated people."

Most of Matt's members possess skills that have proven to be very useful on investigations. For example, one of his members is a forty-eight-year-old photographer and electrician who has been doing investigations for fifteen years. He first became interested in tracking down the paranormal when he began noticing that he was capturing images in his photographs that were not present when he took the pictures. Matt also has a sensitive in the group who scopes out places with high energy levels and points the rest of the investigators in the right direction. "She walks up to a place and tells us what she feels," Matt says. "A lot of times, we've been successful gathering evidence where she's felt energy fluctuations. We've taken pictures that have some pretty interesting details."

Matt's day job as an arson investigator has prevented him from spending as much time tending to his Web site as he would like. He believes that his degree in forensic science and his skills as an arson investigator have made him an effective ghost researcher: "Law enforcement personnel tend to make good ghost hunters. When I solved my first arson case, it was very rewarding. I didn't think I was capable of doing such a thing. I always doubted science even after school because I never got to use it in the real world where I could see results. But if I could prove who started the fire and what the point of origin was and what was the accellerant used and everything else and the fire spread by science, then you could prove anything by science." His innate skepticism comes in very handy when he receives a call from a homeowner: "Law enforcement personnel see things differently. We don't trust anybody. We don't even trust ourselves half the time. You can't just see something and say, 'Oh, it's a ghost!' My goal is to disprove that. Very rarely do we get positive results." Of the forty-five investigations the group has conducted so far, only two or three of them have yielded positive results. He also writes off the borderline cases as negative because he does not want to be plagued by lingering doubts afterward.

During the interview process that precedes the investigations, Matt listens closely to what the clients say to make sure that they are not "full of it." He does not want to repeat the mistakes the group has made in the past: "Some of the clients were almost minors in age, and they contacted us just because they thought it was cool to have someone to come into their house and find a ghost. Of course, we didn't stay there very long." Matt usually returns for a second interview and asks the clients to tell their story again without interruptions. "You can't ask them leading questions," Matt says. "You have to ask them open-ended questions. If you say, 'Was the orb red?' or 'Did it have a tail behind it?' they feel that the only answer that is right is one of those answers, so you have led them to say that. If you're a terrible interviewer, people will just give you statements that you want to hear, and you're going to say that's a positive investigation because that's what you want to see." Once the investigators are convinced that the clients' claims are genuine, they mark the location of telephone wires or telephone towers, appliances, electrical devices—anything that could produce electromagnetic fields in the house. Ideally, Matt would like to spend a month in a single location collecting and comparing data. Practical concerns, like the necessity of earning a living, make such a scenario highly unlikely for Matt and the rest of his team.

Private residences account for the majority of the Texas Paranormal Research Team's investigations so far. Matt feels very strongly about not charging his clients: "How can you possibly charge somebody for the service if you're doing it for your own benefit? If they're going to allow you in their house, you shouldn't charge them." While Matt will gladly offer his clients an explanation for the disturbances in their homes if there is one, he refuses to perform exorcisms: "Two days ago, I had somebody ask me to cleanse a house. I told them that I'm not a holy man. I'm not a preacher or a priest or anything like that. That's where a professional can become unprofessional. If you don't know what you're doing and you're not experienced in that type of field, you shouldn't be chasing spirits out of houses. Actually, I don't even believe that it can be done."

One of the most convincing pieces of evidence Matt has ever collected was from a private residence. After the occupants had left, the group captured an orb that transformed itself into an apparition. "It wasn't a full-body apparition," Matt said, "but more like a mist or a cloud. Then it dissipated in front of the camera. I had two video cameras set up pointing at each corner of the room, and both cameras caught it on film. One was a digital, and one was a regular VHS. It makes it more valid if more than one piece of equipment catches it on film."

One of the scariest experiences the group has ever had was in a subdivision. The exact location was a cemetery in the Newport subdivision in Crosby, Texas: "We saw a black, shadowy apparition," Matt said. "We don't know what it was. There was no form to it. It looked more like a rain cloud. It spooked all of us, and we ran. It was pitch-dark outside, so it was black on black." His only regret, aside from spraining his ankle as he and the others ran away, is that no one thought to take a picture of the entity.

Ironically, the most memorable place Matt has investigated is the house he purchased in 1997. When the activity started up, he researched the history of the house and discovered that it had been owned by a woman who had lived there her entire life. She died in the house when she was in her nineties. He also learned that she spent hours tending to her well-manicured lawn. Over the past eight years, Matt has accumulated over two hundred pages documenting the paranormal events in his own home: "I've had a large piece of furniture move a substantial distance while watching it in broad daylight. I've had witnesses to this. I've had pictures flying off the wall violently." At first, Matt theorized that a poltergeist was disrupting the peace and quiet of his home, but when the disturbances didn't meet the guidelines for a poltergeist case, he decided to contact the entity directly through EVP: "Most of the EVP's weren't answers to questions. They were recorded when nobody was home. One day, I got the voice of a female voice saying 'Hello.'" Later on, we got another EVP of the same female voice. It was real shaky. But after enhancing it about three times, it was very clear. It said something about, 'Oh, where is my hat? Where is my hat?' Well, it's funny because the first day I moved in, the only thing that was left in the house was the hat rack in the laundry room that consisted of the 1940s to 1950s hats that old ladies wore. Of course, my mother liked these hats, so I removed these hats from the hat rack and replaced them with my ball caps. I'd come home and find my ball caps on the ground, and after that, I'd find the whole hat rack on the ground." Later on, the lady's neighbors told Matt that she always picked out a different hat for every day of the week.

The recurring activity in Matt's house led him to research the history of the location before the house was built. He discovered that the house and the ones next to it had been constructed over the site of an old cemetery that had been moved to a spot a mile south of Matt's residence in the 1930s. He has found concrete proof verifying the old story: "In the back yard behind some bushes, there was a piece of tombstone that had some writing on it. I have found other pieces of tombstone in my neighbors' yard. There was a definitely a cemetery here, more like a private cemetery. There weren't a lot of people buried here, though."

Matt had hoped that he would eventually become less scared in his own house after doing the research, but this was certainly not the case: "My wife and I were lying in bed, and there was a big bang in the room. We didn't know where it came from. And then the mini-blinds were shaking, and a shadow covered the whole room. You know when it's sunny outside, and you're inside your home, and a cloud moves over your house and it's darkened almost instantly? That's what this was like. There was also a temperature drop, and then the pendulum on the mini-blinds stopped swinging. I turned to my wife and said, 'You know, it'd be freaky if that thing started swinging again,' and no sooner had I said that when it started to move again."

This incident was only one of many that occurred as long as Matt and his wife stayed in that particular bedroom: "The door would close after being wide open all night and wake me. I'd wake up, and all the lights would be on in the house, and every cabinet and drawer in the kitchen would be open asymmetrically to each other. Items have been moved to different places. There might be months with no occurrences, and then the disturbance would take place every day back to back for a week." An examination of the documented disturbances revealed that most of the activity had occurred in September and October. Not surprisingly, the previous owner of the house died in this bedroom in September. The couple is now sleeping in a different room.

Matt's wife has been more than understanding since moving into her husband's house: "I got married to her on October 20, 2004. When I first told her about these things, she kind of laughed. Then she started seeing things herself. One time when I was conducting an investigation here, I started getting some results, and she became truly frightened. But now she's getting better. She's starting to take an interest in it. She's a part of our team now. She's very good. She has an eye for things." Matt hopes that someday his wife, who is a writer, will write a bestseller about their home. "There's almost enough material now for a book," Matt says. "She might want to change the address, though."

Virginia

Center for Paranormal Research and Investigations

BLACKSTONE, VIRGINIA

Bobbie Atristain, Founder and Director

B obbie Atristain's two main interests—science and the paranormal—appear on the surface to be mutually exclusive. However, she seems to have successfully reconciled the two fields: "I am a programmer analyst for a local university. I also teach at a technical college on occasion. I have received no flak from colleagues about what I do. It's on my resume. I think it's a good resume builder. I just wrote my first article dealing with my research. My special interest is the effects of the paranormal on brain chemistry. I just had my first article on my preliminary research published in *Ghost Magazine*. We're really trying to get into the research aspect of the field, working with universities and publishing some of our findings and approaching it that way through academia."

She founded the Center for Paranormal Research and Investigations in May of 2000. The membership includes a number of professional people, including environmental scientists, an engineer from NASA, a scientist from the nuclear-chemical field, a teacher, an architect, a hydrologist, and a health-care worker. Bonnie has several members in law enforcement as well, including her husband, a former homicide investigator. He is also a former director of the Norfolk UFO Network (NUFON).

She believes that her group has attracted so many people from the sciences because of its logical and empirical approach to the paranormal: "I think people are impressed because we don't use psychics, although I'm leaning more toward wanting to research mediums or empaths. When I first started the group, the whole theory was that we should somehow capture some empirical evidence, and we'd do it in such a way that we would foster a scientific community that would actively pursue this and not view it as a pseudo-science. We are getting people of that caliber."

Recruiting for the Center for Paranormal Research and Investigations team seems to be self-defeating in that Bobbie tries to dissuade people from applying for membership: "We tell people right off that they have to be high caliber. Just starting this year, we're doing criminal background checks and asking people if we may ask their employer [for character references]. We want to know where you claim to have gone to school. We do all that to let people know we're really serious about it." Prospective members are required to e-mail their intention to join to the membership committee. The executive vice president then asks for the applicant's qualifications. If his or her applications are acceptable, the applicant is invited to the next meeting at Bobbie's house. After the meeting, the regional director and the membership committee conduct a formal interview with the applicant. If the applicant makes it through the interview, he or she is given probationary status and admitted into the group's training course. The applicant must attend at least one full-scale investigation and one preliminary investigation where available. If the applicant has been attending meetings regularly, he or she is voted in and given full membership.

Potential clients find out about the Center for Paranormal Research and Investigations through the Web site. Bobbie also does a lot of interviews with the local media, especially during Halloween: "We've been in the *Washington Post*, the *New York Times*, and the *Washington Times*. I've done interviews with a lot of Richmond newspapers. I also did [an interview with] *The Pilot*, which is a Virginia Beach newspaper. Plus when you type in 'Ghosts in Virginia,' we are the number-one site that comes up. I used to have a phone number on there, and I found I had a lot of out-of-state people contacting me. I also have a newsletter that I publish once a month. We have a mailing list of people who want to keep up-to-date. We might even have a TV show coming out with MTV. We're in negotiations now. It would give us huge national exposure."

The Center for Paranormal Research and Investigations always does a preliminary on-site investigation during the day so the members can check out the outside of a building and look for any thing that could be contributing to the phenomena, such as high-power tension lines or power plants. Bobbie administers a psychological test and an EMF sensitivity test to everyone who has experienced something in the house. Before the investigators can take EMF readings, they cut the power to the house and wait for any residual energy to dissipate. "Then we go through with a Tri-Field meter and look for any anomalous electrical energy," Bobbie says. "We go through again with the power on because people don't normally sit in their house [with the lights] blacked out. Then we get another reading. And based on that, we might do an all-night investigation." Because all of the members have day jobs, they start on a Friday or Saturday evening, just before dark. Generally, the investigators do not begin setting up their cameras until nine P.M. Then they stay all night because most people report more activity at night between ten P.M. and four A.M. If resources are available, Bonnie might start an investigation on a Saturday and pull out Sunday midday: "We try to expand our investigations over more than one day because this stuff is so random. Another thing we try to determine during an all-night investigation is what is the frequency of the all-night activity. If it appears that the activity is somewhat predictable or seems to happen frequently enough, then that's one of the main combinations that we're going to conduct. It's what we call a full-scale investigation. If the activity is sporadic, the chances of us encountering it between just ten P.M. and four A.M. is really rare." Bobbie says that when the members are doing an extended investigation, they try to be as unobtrusive as they can. On one investigation in Kentucky, the group had a camper, and they ran wires through the yard and placed cameras all around the house to monitor everything from the camper. That way, the family went about their normal activities without distraction from the investigators.

One private residence in particular turned out to be quite an "adrenaline rush." The PBS television station of Virginia was producing their *Things that Go Bump in the Night* program for Halloween, and the director invited Bobbie's group to come along. Bobbie was unable to go because she was about to undergo surgery. She served as a consultant instead. The station had selected as the focus of the show a house out in Chesapeake, which Bobbie believes is the most legitimately haunted house anywhere in the world: "The family are Mennonites. When the couple who owns the house were young and first got married about twenty or thirty years ago, there was a big old farm house there. It was pre-Civil War, a very old house. But I guess it needed work and was bigger than wanted. Being newlyweds, the couple didn't have the money to have the house actually removed from the property, so they built their new house on top of the old house." The older house was the scene of a host of tragic events. According to legend, the family who built the house was so poor that they could not afford to feed all of their children. Boys were considered to be more valuable because they could work on the farm, so the parents allowed their daughter to starve to death. A few years later, one of the sons fell into a vat of very hot water while his mother was doing laundry and lost one of his legs. Another son ran off and was never heard from again. It was also rumored that a Civil War soldier was murdered and buried on the original farm. The current owners of the house, the Shandlings, were featured on *Montel Williams*. When Montel was there, the camera crew's keys were locked in their car, and they couldn't get their equipment out. When the Shandlings finally got their equipment out, the cameramen actually filmed what looked like Predator in stealth mode. "He's clear, but you can see the outline of a figure," Bonnie said. The crew also filmed the outline of a human walking down the hallway.

Four of Bobbie's members went along on the PBS investigation of the house. Crystal, a quasi-member, and the producer were placed in the attic, where most of the aggressive spirits were supposed to be: "They sat in the dark up in the attic with two chairs," Bobbie said. "They had a night-vision camera trained on them. It was connected downstairs to a monitor and a VCR that was recording. So we had five people including the PBS camera that was filming. Some of the family members were there, my guy, and

323

the other PBS producer watching the monitor to see if anything was going to happen. All of a sudden, they all witnessed this kind of fog appear behind the ladies, and this fog became more focused, and two legs of a human began to form. The legs were walking in a robotic fashion toward the two ladies. The producer freaked out. She was wondering what this thing was going to do to these two women. They were chatting, and they had no clue this was going on behind them at all. She screamed bloody murder, ran to the steps leading to the attic, and yelled, 'Get down! Get down from there right now!' They didn't know what was going on." When the group reviewed the videotape afterward, the apparition was gone. It is unlikely that the cameraman, who had been conducting paranormal research for twenty years, would have made a mistake. "So the only thing we have for posterity is PBS's cameras showing everyone's reaction watching the monitor and the girls screaming and going to get them," Bobbie said.

Even though Virginia is rife with history, only 5 percent of the invitations the group receives for investigations are from historical sites. Approximately 30 percent of the group's historical investigations involve some aspect of the Civil War: "We actually have an ongoing investigation of a museum in Harrisburg, which is in extreme southwestern Virginia," Bobbie says. "It's the Andrew Johnson House. It's a museum. It was also a Civil War hospital. The curators actually contacted us. We had another Civil War hospital out in Charlottesville called the Exchange Hotel Museum. They called us, too. On our own, we do a lot of Civil War sites. We live in the Richmond area, so there are tons of Civil War stuff around here, so it's really easy to do those." A number of these historical cases have proven difficult to document, especially buildings that are reputed to have served as Confederate hospitals.

One of these Civil War—related sites is a subdivision that was built just off Cold Harbor battlefield, where thirteen thousand Union troops and perhaps five thousand southerners died between May 31 and June 3, 1864. The battlefield is almost in the backyard of some of the houses in the subdivision. Two of the homeowners reported seeing strange men who were standing in their yard one minute and gone the next. Another homeowner had a three-year-old daughter who said she kept seeing a man who had become her "imaginary friend." Her parents reported seeing flashes of light in the house, as if someone snapped a camera. Bonnie found this house difficult to investigate because the activity was very sporadic: "It wasn't something that happened a lot. It wasn't something that was predictable. So we went out there and did a preliminary investigation. The little girl's mother kept in touch through e-mail. We never conducted a full investigation there."

The group's most memorable investigation was conducted at Salubria, one of the oldest brick buildings in Culpepper County. There is also a groundskeeper's cottage that is maybe five hundred feet from the house. It is currently owned by the Germania Club, which is trying to raise money to restore it. The house was built by Detmus Foxworth, one of the earliest governors of Virginia. After he died, his widow married a minister, who built the house for her. One ghost story associated with the house is that one of the governor's widow's sons left home to fight in the Revolutionary War. He was killed in the war, and to this day, his mother's ghost can be seen pacing around waiting for him to come back. From a ghost hunter's viewpoint, the house is ideally suited for an investigation because there is no electricity or running water, reducing the possibility of EMF interference from artificial sources.

The Center for Paranormal Research and Investigations arrived at the old house at 6:00 P.M. on a rainy, cool day in April 2002. The members drove up in one of the member's mobile Big-Foot Lab, which enabled the group to have power outside of the house. It was also equipped with a night-vision camera and thermal imaging. The members anticipated that something was going to happen because a fellow investigator had done a preliminary visit there, and he reported that weird things had happened to him. After spending an uneventful evening in the old house, Bobbie was ready to call off the investigation: "It was midnight. It was raining, and we were cold and wet. One of our members was in this area with a hand-held radio. The other radio was at mission control. He said, 'I hear a baby crying.' Suddenly, I realized we had broken our cardinal rule: 'Don't go into a place alone. Your imagination can run away with you.' I went into the house and, as I figured, I didn't hear a baby crying. I didn't hear anything."

Suddenly, Bobbie heard a woman's moaning coming from upstairs. Her first instinct was to run out of the house. The young man with the radio said, "Come on! Let's go after this!" The two investigators ran upstairs but found no one there. Then the members inside the Big Foot Lab called back on the radio. They reported that no one had compromised the perimeter, so Bobbie asked a few of the investigators to come inside the house: "I had about five or six investigators come into the house. We placed a tape recorder upstairs in the proximity of the area where we heard the woman moaning. We just sat there, and we all started to hear someone walking across the floor upstairs. The problem was that the two entrances to the house were in the foyer area—the back and the front door—and it was a straight walk-through. We were in that area, and no one had come through and gone up the stairs.

We were right in front of the stairs. The footsteps started out softly and just got louder, and everyone was like, 'What is going on? We hear someone walking.' It was like someone was pacing the floor. So a couple of people went upstairs to check our tape recorder. It sounded like someone went up to the tape recorder and went 'Phew!' just blew into the mike. It was like seven or eight people all heard someone walking upstairs, and there was no one up there. There was nothing that could have created that noise. The upstairs was empty." Bobbie wishes that someone else besides her and the other investigator had heard the moaning, too. "This kind of stuff never happens," Bobbie said.

When analyzing evidence from investigations like the one conducted in the house in Culpepper County, Bobbie dismisses photographs of orbs entirely. In fact, she does not even deal with them anymore unless someone actually sees them. She cites as an example a lady in western Virginia who saw three orbs: "They were three different colors. I think one was blue, purple, and orange. And they maneuvered intelligently around her house and through her window. A few days later during the summer, she had just put a screen window up, and she noticed three circular burn patterns right where the orbs exited through the screen. She said she took the screen down and put it in the shed. Twenty years later, she moved into the main house and rented the trailer to a friend. They started having problems, so she contacted us and mentioned the screen in passing, so we took it to our radio-chemist who, at the time, was working at the Naval Lab in Norfolk. We wanted it analyzed to see what those burn marks were." Bobbie was shocked to learn that something changed the screen to Cobalt 60, which is the amount of radiation equal to or greater than a plutonium reactor. The woman's neighbors should have been vaporized or, at the very least, suffering from radiation sickness. The lady's doctor asked her if she had ever had cancer, and she said, "No. No one in my family has ever had cancer. Why do you ask?" He said, "Because your bone, including the replacement hip joint, has a lot of tiny holes, which is indicative of someone who has been treated with cobalt radiation." He asked her if she had been violently sick during that time, and she said she did remember being very sick in the early 1980s, but she couldn't remember if it had been before or after she had seen the orb. Bonnie says that what happened defies our understanding of nuclear energy: "We tested portions of the screen that were not discolored, and they were normal. It was an aluminum screen window. The military does have a weapon that comes out and looks like little balls. A couple of military guys were showing on marine TV a weapon that fired projectiles that would go through the top of a car seat. It made a perfect hole, and everything around it was not radiated. It burned a hole clear through the seat itself. It's highly unlikely, though, that the government fired this weapon through this lady's house."

The unreliability of orbs as evidence has not caused Bobbie to dismiss photography out of hand. One of the members took a fascinating photograph at a private residence in western Virginia. "It's not a person, but it almost looks like a string of pearls," Bonnie said. "A guy took it with a still camera. It was one of these disposable 35 mm cameras. It was developed by a representative of Kodak. He'd just installed a new processing machine. He said he'd been developing photos for over thirty years, and he'd never seen anything like that. This wasn't a processing error. We tried to replicate it, thinking it was a camera strap or a piece of hair, a finger. We couldn't do it." Bobbie also had the negative viewed by some professional photographers who said it was definitely not a processing mistake. Whatever the image was, it was in the negative.

Like most groups that emphasize science over the metaphysical, the Center for Paranormal Research and Investigations has a very low "success" rate. Bobbie estimates that only 5 percent of her group's investigations reveal genuine hauntings. She has found over the years that telling homeowners their house is "clean" is not always taken as good news because a lot of people wish they had ghosts. Some of these people have been overly influenced by television programs like the History Channel's *Haunted History* series. Then there are those clients who are misinterpreting logical phenomena. "A lot of people e-mail in or call in, and they say their TV is changing channels by itself," Bobbie says. "Quite a few of them live in subdivisions, and if their neighbor has a new TV—especially in the Richmond area—it's possible that their neighbor is changing the channel." The third category includes people who, in Bobbie's words, "flat-out lie." Bobbie's members are usually able to spot this small percentage of clients before they travel to the home.

Because the Center for Paranormal Research and Investigations is not very well known in the area, the members are increasing their promotion efforts. "We sell T-shirts and things. We do things at Halloween. We do things in the community. Last Halloween, we spoke at the historical society in Chesterfield, which is right outside of Richmond. A few times a year, I present a paranormal lecture at a historical house in Richmond called Wrexham Hall that dates back to the 1700s. It's open to the public. We did a presentation at a high school in Charlottesville. We do these things whenever we're asked." The group does not charge for presentations, except for an occasional small fee to cover the cost of the reception.

Bobbie is also aware that too much publicity can be counter-productive. She sympathizes with those groups who have been manipulated by the media, for example, The Atlantic Paranormal Society (T.A.P.S.): "I knew the *Ghosthunter* guys before they were Sci-fi stars. I interviewed Grant for an article in *Ghost Magazine*. The *Ghosthunters* are really nice guys, and they're victims of edit-ing. I talked to Jason not long ago, who told me they only spend three hours on any investigation. It doesn't appear that way, but they do. Then they have to analyze it and return the next week-end. I don't fault them too much because they're under a lot of pressure. They're getting paid a lot of money. I think they're under pressure to produce. No one would want to watch us on an investigation because we'd be watching an empty room with night-vision cameras for six hours [and] it's really boring. In this business, it's hours of boredom and seconds of panic."

The Center for Paranormal Research and Investigations occa-sionally gets opposition from religious groups. In fact, Bobbie believes that living in the Bible Belt might explain why she does not receive an overabundance of requests for investigations: "People tell us things like 'The only ghost is the Holy Ghost.' My whole thing is that just in the Old Testament alone there are many references to spirits. If there's life after death, what's the big deal in believing that there's communication from the other side?" However, personal experience has convinced Bobbie that being religious does not necessarily preclude a belief in ghosts: "One lady was a devout Lutheran church member. She looked me up in the phone book and called me up and said, 'Honey, I've got a ghost in my house.' And she was very matter-of-fact about it."

Some people are taken aback when Bobbie tells them that for her, investigating the paranormal has nothing to do with proving that there is life after death: "Our goal right now is to find out what's behind paranormal phenomena, be it something we don't understand yet or forces we do understand, like geometric fields. We have an open mind. Our official stand is that we don't know if ghosts exist or not. We investigate claims that people think are paranormal to find out what they really are."

Tidewater Paranormal Investigations

NORFOLK, VIRGINIA

Connie Picard, Founder and Director

Connie Picard is unique among directors of southern paranormal investigating groups in that she is a wildlife rehabilitator in the Hampton Roads section of Norfolk, Virginia: "Being a wildlife rehabilitator is a handful. A lot of these birds and animals are orphaned or injured. Spring and summer are our busy months during baby season, so we get a lot of orphans. We nurse them back to health and release them back into the wild." Although biology is her professional field, she has always been fascinated in the paranormal and occult studies. Curiosity about the local legends and history or her region inspired her to start up her nonprofit paranormal group: "I started the group in the middle of 2003 with just myself. We have six official members and a few who come out with us occasionally."

The membership of Tidewater Paranormal Investigations includes a registered nurse, a health-care manager, a couple of stay-at-home moms, and a science teacher. Connie also has a coworker in her group: "Her name is Sheila Carver. She and I work together to organize the group. Both of us have a long history as to metaphysical background." Connie has been studying metaphysics for fifteen years, and Sheila has been studying metaphysics for twenty years. Connie and Sheila are careful not to allow their psychic abilities to interfere with investigations: "While doing investigations, Sheila and I take notes, but we keep them to ourselves because we don't want to influence the other investigators. If we get a feeling that some presence is around, we will point the others to that spot—'Take some meter readings in this area.' Our abilities definitely help out when we are checking for energy fields."

When Connie first started the group, the members had planned to go out only a couple of times a month. However, they have found so many promising sites that they now go out every seven to ten days. "We do this on weekends and nights." Connie said. "With everyone working full-time jobs, the whole team can't go out on every investigation, so we have people who can go out on this date or that date and others that can't go at all."

Because Virginia is rich in history, Connie's group tends to focus investigations primarily on outdoor historic sites, especially Civil War battlefields, such as Cold Harbor and Petersburg Battlefield, places that supposedly have a lot of paranormal and Civil War history: "A lot of the areas that report paranormal activity—like Civil War sites—are open to the public. We do preliminary investigations in the daytime the first couple of times just to get a feel for the area and to find out if we can come out at night without violating any laws." Tidewater Paranormal

Investigations does respond to calls for private residences, but the group usually does not publicize these on their Web site or anywhere else.

One of the downsides to conducting outdoor investigations is the likelihood that the visual and audio evidence might have a natural origin. Connie is very critical of groups who are eager to classify every orb as evidence of spirit activity: "They should check the other facts first, like dust particles, insects, moisture. I have found that digital cameras produce a lot of orbs and anomalies, especially the digital cameras with a lower number of pixels. Less than 5.0 pixels, you see a lot of anomalies with digital cameras. We use digital and 35 mm. When we go out, we take a minimum of four cameras with us. We use video, too." So far, the group has recorded only one outdoor EVP. However, Connie has not ruled out the possibility that it, too, might have a natural origin. In fact, Connie includes always brings along skeptics on her investigations who encourage the other members to rule out any natural causes.

One unforgettable investigation the group conducted took place at the site of one of the bloodiest battles of the Civil War, Cold Harbor. Sheila and Connie visited the battlefield ahead of the rest of the group in order to do a preliminary investigation there. At first, the women did not capture anything on film or audiotape. However, when they began walking down one of the trails, their minds were bombarded with psychic images: "It was really phenomenal. At one of the rifle pits, I recall hearing the name of a young man. I kept getting the name 'Joshua' ringing through my head. When we left, we felt like someone was walking with us." Connie insists that she was not scared because she was expecting to encounter paranormal energy in some form.

Ironically, Sheila and Connie had a terrifying experience at a location without any known connection to the Civil War: "We did an investigation at a place called Elba Road in Virginia Beach on the Virginia Beach/Chesapeake border. We got out of the car and started taking pictures, and for some reason, both of us were scared to death. The energy at this place was so overwhelming and oppressive. She and I were hard-pressed to even finish our investigation." Not surprisingly, members captured some photographic images that they can't explain: "Our husbands looked at our pictures to try to eliminate things. My husband, who is a major skeptic, looked at the pictures and said, 'I have no idea what that is.' It was very odd, like a mist."

From Connie's point of view, an investigation is not necessarily a failure if no convincing photographic images are collected: "We also take into account that just because we don't always catch something on film, that doesn't mean it's not there." Connie would love to capture a full-body apparition, but she knows the difficulty in doing so. In fact, she is very skeptical of the photographs some groups have posted on their Web sites: "I've seen pictures of [full-body apparitions] on the Internet, but I take them with a grain of salt because of the things you can do with computers these days."

The Tidewater Paranormal Investigations team take research very seriously: "Most of all, we are after indisputable proof. If we find an alternate or scientific explanation for the phenomenon, we're not disappointed." Connie believes that if the members were not so dedicated to uncovering the truth, the percentage of investigations that reveal genuine hauntings would be much higher than 35 percent. In her point of view, not only will the group's professionalism help it grow, but it will also make them one of the preeminent groups in Virginia: "Certain other paranormal groups are very well known and respected, and we'd eventually like to fall into that category."

Virginia Science Research

LEESBURG, VIRGINIA

Joseph Holbert, Founder and Director

Joseph Holbert is a rarity in the field of the paranormal. He is a full-time investigator, with an assortment of part-time jobs: "I don't have a day job. This is what I do. I wrote a book, which helps. I give tours. I do a lot of public speaking, and I am an E-bayer, so I guess you could say that is my day job. I have a store on E-bay where I sell books and antiques. I've gotten some strange things on there, like a human skull." Not surprisingly, the tours he gives are ghost-related. He began giving tours in 1992 when he was on the board of directors of the local museum: "We needed a fund-raiser, so I thought we'd do a Halloween ghost tour. In the process of setting that I up, I began looking for ghost stories. I put an ad in the newspaper. People started calling me and telling me these ghost stories. A lot of these weren't ghost stories. They were eyewitness accounts. People talked about having ghosts in their houses, and these were members of the town council, heads of major corporations. They weren't kooks or anything like that. They were very nice people. It got my curiosity going, so in the process of doing the research for the tour, I had something happen in my house that I couldn't explain." Joseph wrote a book, *To Boo or Not to Boo*, which contains his personal recollections as a tour guide and paranormal researcher: "There are some ghost stories in there, but most of it is ghost-related stuff, like some of the weird people I've met and strange things I've seen."

Thanks to Joseph's efforts to promote himself and the group, Virginia Science Research has a high-profile presence in the Leesburg area: "I promote myself through the Web site. I've got the ghost tour, and I get written up a lot in the local papers. If you mention the word 'ghosts' in this area, my name comes up. My license plate is 'GHOSTGUY.'" He believes getting publicity is healthy for a group. However, the members ended up losing money when they tried to promote the group through T-shirt sales on their Web site in 2004, so Joseph hands out fliers instead.

Unfortunately, there is also a downside to the group's high visibility in Leesburg. Not only has Joseph been criticized by religious groups, but he has even received death threats: "I had two of them, both by mail, which isn't real bright. They had no return address, but we know one of them came from Maryland, and the other one came from California. They were both Christian right groups. I had some members of the Christian right on one of my tours. After the tour got underway, they started with their baloney. I tried to be nice to them and asked them to leave." Joseph says that usually, the crowd takes care of troublemakers, and that is exactly what happened on a different tour: "I had to call the police one night because a couple of guys around forty years old were going to beat this one guy to death. They hated him. One of these guys asked this preacher or whatever he was, 'Why are you doing this?' And he said, 'I'm doing it to save the souls of girls like that there.' The guy looked at the girls and said, 'Those are my daughters, and I'm tired of your Bible-thumping B.S.' And that's when the fight started." Joseph says his members are more afraid of Christians than they are of the paranormal.

Virginia Science Research has been operating since the early 1990s. It currently has six members. The group's general manager is a woman who was a medic in the U.S. Navy and who is now running a hospice program. She also interviews witnesses. Carol, one of Joseph's researchers, works for a deed and title search company. "She finds out the background of the houses we visit," Joseph says. "She's twenty-three and very attractive and intelligent and comes off very well on TV." Randi, another researcher, has a degree in psychology from Radford. One of the members, Kate, is working on a degree in forensic psychology at East Carolina State University, and she's working on her degree in psychology. She will eventually get into forensic psychology. Mike, who handles the cameras for the group, is a professional photographer. "He does fine art and still-lifes," Joe says. "He's about to get his first book published and has a major show going on."

Virginia Science Research investigates both historic sites and private residences. Joseph has found battlefields to be easy places to collect paranormal evidence: "We get a lot of activity there. You are almost guaranteed to get stuff there, if you know what you're looking for, of course. The park rangers take reports from people who have experienced things on the battlefields. They will talk to you, but it's always off the record." The members are not allowed to discuss some of the high-profile historical sites that have contacted them because of privacy issues. Joseph usually investigates private residences all by himself: "I just take a Tri-Field meter with me and no one else because 95 percent of these cases are going to deal with residual fields, which aren't really that interesting. Primarily I do it because people ask me to. And I do it to alleviate their fears. I let them know that there's nothing in their home that's going to hurt them. I find that the scientific explanation usually appeases them. Sometimes, they are disappointed that grandma's ghost isn't haunting their house, but when I explain to them how it works, they say, 'Oh, that makes sense' because what they were looking at didn't make any sense to them."

Some of the new members of the group are surprised to find that paranormal research is not at all like it is on TV. Joseph removes the "scary" aspect of investigations in his training sessions: "None of my members have been frightened on an investigation. We aren't afraid of these things. I train them. Kate and Camille both went a year with me in training. I took them right up close and personal to what people call ghosts about a foot from it. I've had them touch it. I've even had them walk right into them." New members also discover very quickly that investigating is not nearly as exciting as it has been depicted on television programs and in the movies: "We spend a lot of time doing nothing, waiting for something to happen," Joseph says. "Ghosts don't do things on command. And for the most part, we're not talking about intelligence anyway." Most of the time, the members just walk around taking readings with their Tri-Field meters.

In fact, the members of Virginia Science Research put more faith in their Tri-Field meters than in any other piece of equipment. The members do use 35 mm cameras, but only to document where they are setting up their equipment. However, Joseph is experimenting with ways to photograph light as it is refracted through an electromagnetic field: "If an electromagnetic field moves toward a doorway, I'll have Mike, our photographer, set our camera up on a tripod. He sets his shutter speed at seven or eight shots per second, trying to see if we can pick up any differential on film." The members do not even try to photograph ghosts because as far as Joseph is concerned, it has never been done, and it never will be done. For this reason, orbs are totally unreliable: "The best place to get orbs is outside in the fall and spring because you get mist in the air. You can also get orbs when you have a very deep depth of field. If you focus on infinity, you will get water droplets that are right in front of the lens. The flash will light them up. You get dust, water droplets, and bugs. Orbs are also caused by the flash of your camera."

He also believes that EVP's can be unreliable because of the way most groups record them: "The way they do it, they are guaranteed to get sounds on there. A lot of them use white noise as background. Electronically speaking, you're going to get what's called wave collision. Some of those waves are going to collide and bounce back in a different frequency than they went out in. That by itself won't do much. It will just get garbled sound. But then they run it through a program that digitalizes the sound and then cleans it up. It takes out the original background sound, which leaves just the collision sounds. Then the program adds to that to make it sound like words. So what you get eventually is words where there are no words."

As the group's title suggests, the members of Virginia Science Research take a scientific approach to investigating. "Anything we use, any theory has to conform to scientific principles," Joseph says. "There's no psychic energy. That doesn't exist. If energy is expended, I can detect it. There's nothing paranormal, really. Our mission is to find out what's real. What are these people seeing? How do they see something? Does it override your brain patterns?

Does it make you see? It's a matter of perception. Override is a kind of interference caused to your brain's synapses. The interference resembles a normal brain pattern that you would get when you see something, only it's not the thing that's there. It's something else you're seeing." Not surprisingly, Joseph discourages his members from using the word *ghost* in their investigations. He does not use the word *ghost* on his tours, either: "I prefer the terms *anomaly* or *electromagnetic anomaly*, some kind of scientific description. Many of the 'haunted' buildings I have investigated have electric fields that should not be where they are and should not act the way they do. On the tour, I start off by telling people we don't use that term, and then I tell them why." He has found that children on his tours do not, as a rule, find Joseph's scientific approach to phenomena to be scary enough to be interesting. Nevertheless, Joseph's tour has had good press, having been written up in the *Washington Post*. The tour was also chosen by one travel magazine as the best tour on the East Coast.

In 2004, Virginia Science Research filmed an episode of the Sci-Fi Channel television show *Proof Positive* at Moundsville Penitentiary, which opened in 1876. In 1929, a project to double the size of the penitentiary began. It was not completed until 1959 due to the steel shortage in WWII. A total of ninety-four men were executed there between 1899 and 1959. From 1899 to 1949, eighty-five men were hanged. In 1951, the state began using the electric chair. Nine men were electrocuted at Moundsville until the state banned the death penalty in 1959. In 1986, the West Virginia Supreme Court ruled that the penitentiary's tiny cells constituted cruel and unusual punishment. Moundsville Penitentiary closed its doors in 1995. The old penitentiary is owned by the state, and it is open for tours year round.

Virginia Science Research had visited Moundsville Penitentiary several times before filming the *Proof Positive* episode. "At least twice a year, we take the public with us, and we spend all night in the prison," Joseph said. "That's the most haunted place I've ever seen. It's a good place for us to test the equipment. It's not so much a matter of 'Will we have something happen to us tonight?' as 'How many times will something happen to us tonight?' Between eleven hundred and twelve hundred were just murdered there in prisoner violence. They had a large riot, and several prisoners were killed in that. Generally, the place is not a nice prison." On *Proof Positive*, his goal was to establish the existence of a moving, self-contained field, a notion that violates at least two laws of physics: "What I was hoping to do was get a good enough reading, and then we would probably try to get into a place where we would get a scientific paper published. I've had several physicists who have seen what we are doing, and they believe I'm on the right track. If I can figure out how to put it so they can see it and the world can see it and we can document it, they are willing to peer-review me for a paper." The group wired three Tri-Field meters into an analog converter board. The converter board runs through a computer program and can pick up something moving through a room. "If there's a field that's moving, we can pick it up," Joseph said. The producers of *Proof Positive* required that someone who did not belong to the group check his work. He selected a person who was past-president of the local Skeptics Society in Washington, D.C.

The Virginia Science Research's segment was, however, proved negative on *Proof Positive*. Joseph was neither surprised nor disappointed: "Proving that the field was there was our secondary objective. Our first objective was to showcase the group. We were working with a large crew. We had a total of fifteen people on the shoot crew, which means that we had all these electrical fields walking all over the place. And [some unauthorized people] could not understand the words, 'Do not enter this area.' I'd look up, and there was a cameraman or a sound man or a lighting man standing in the area we were supposed to be monitoring. At one point, a crew member said, 'We're ready to make this happen.' And I said, 'You don't understand. We are not controlling this. It doesn't work like that.' We were dead before we started. I knew that. But I wanted to showcase the group, and it did work for that." After the *Proof Positive* episode aired on December 15, 2005, the group received a large number of hits on the Web site. Although the group had been interviewed by local television stations and newspapers in the past, this was the first time they had received national exposure.

Virginia Science Research has also been featured on Penn and Teller's *Bull*—television show on Showtime. "They love us," Joseph says. At the time of this interview, Joseph was planning to take Penn and Teller to four places where people have witnessed real activity. The segment was to be part of a show they were planning to do on ghost hunters. [Penn and Teller] called him and said, "We want to bring in a psychic, and we want to compare her results with your results." Joseph replied, "She will have a horrible day." And they said, "Yeah, we know."

Joseph was on the board of T.A.P.S., another nationally televised group, for a while. He resigned after a disagreement over the use of demonologists on investigations. "In the first show, they're telling this girl that she didn't have a ghost; she had a demon in her house," Joseph said. "The psychological impact of that is horrible. I slammed them publicly on that one, and the result is that they don't like me and I don't like them." He also believes that producing a weekly television show about genuine investigations would not be very entertaining: "You'd fall asleep. It's not that interesting." He does believe, though, that *Ghost Hunters* could generate interest in the field of the paranormal.

Although Joseph is glad that the paranormal is receiving so much media exposure these days, he is concerned about the way "hauntings" are portrayed. The most harmful effect of these misleading shows, Joseph says, is the expectations they create in the minds of clients: "People tell you what they think you want to hear. They want to please you when they tell you a story like this, so they exaggerate, and they take things out of movies because they think that's the way it's supposed to be." Joseph has watched hundreds of horror movies over the years because people ask him what is good and what is not. He believes that *The Others* (2001) is one of the most realistic ghost movies he has ever seen. His favorite, though, is *The Haunting* (1963): "It's excellent. It's all psychology. You never see anything. That movie's what we see hauntings as looking like, except for the cold spot in the house. We don't use digital thermometers because there's not such thing as cold spots. Actually, the hair follicles on your body react to the electrical field. This is why you get goose bumps, and you think you're cold."

In 2004, Joseph spoke before the National Capitol Area Skeptic Society for their fall convention. He spoke for two and a half hours in front of 150 skeptics. Most of the questions people asked dealt with why people think there are ghosts, how the EMF fields affect people, and why these fields make them think there are ghosts. "They asked me why do 48 percent of the American populace believe there are ghosts and 20 percent believe they've seen one. They liked what I said, but one member of the audience had a little trouble with my Tri-Field meter. I told him I just bought it. It's an off-the-shelf device. 'Here, you look at it.' He did, and he said, 'This is pretty neat.' And I said, 'Yes, it is.'" Joseph has found that even his most skeptical critics find the science of investigation irresistible.

Joseph says that right now he is having the time of his life. In an average week, he gets three lunches paid for by someone wanting to talk: "I'll be sitting in a restaurant, and somebody will go, 'Aren't you the ghost guy?' And I'll say, 'Yeah.' They'll sit down and talk to me, and the next thing you know, they're picking up the bill. I always bring books with me, too, so I get a free lunch, and I sell books. I have a great life. I'm having a ball."

CONCLUSION

The interviews I conducted with forty-three directors of groups from the South revealed more similarities than differences. All of the directors were proud of the diverse composition of their groups. Ghost research crosses all kinds of professional boundaries. It is not at all uncommon for physicians, housewives, law enforcement personnel, and lawyers to go out onto an investigation together. The ages of the members vary as well; however, because of the physical demands of investigating, most of the individuals in the core groups were under the age of fifty. Twenty-seven of the forty-three directors were male, but the composition of most of the groups was roughly half male and half female.

The missions of the groups are essentially the same. Most of them are trying to prove the existence of an afterlife. A majority of the directors ascribed altruistic motives to their investigations of private residences. They see themselves as performing a public service by alleviating the mental anguish of homeowners who are convinced that they are being tormented by supernatural forces. At the same time these groups are explaining the causes of the domestic disturbances, they are also working toward their goal of collecting evidence of the existence of the paranormal.

Funding was a problem for almost every one of the groups. Only two of the groups in this book charged for investigations, although several of them accepted donations for travel expenses. Some of the directors expressed loathing for those groups that try to profit from their investigations. Almost all of the members purchased their own equipment. In a few cases, the directors themselves bought the most expensive equipment. Approximately a third of the groups tried to raise money through T-shirt sales. All of the directors, with the exception of several who were retired, had day jobs. Consequently, different work schedules forced many groups to conduct investigations at night or on the weekends. All of the directors wished that they could conduct investigations full-time, but the need to earn a living has relegated their ghost hunting to an interesting hobby.

Most of the groups used the same types of audio and visual equipment. The basics seem to include digital cameras, 35 mm cameras, digital cameras, analog tape recorders, digital voice recorders, digital thermal thermometers, and electromagnetic field detectors. Most of the members bring along their own photographic equipment. A majority of the groups use both digital cameras and 35 mm cameras. Digital cameras are appealing because of the low cost of producing photographs; 35 mm cameras provide the researcher with a negative, which enhances the credibility of the photographic evidence.

All of the groups promote themselves. Almost all of them used their Web sites to get the word out. Most of them take advantage of any media opportunities that come their way, especially at Halloween, when local newspapers and televisions are looking for ghost-related stories. Two of the groups, in fact, have appeared on such nationally broadcast television shows as *Proof Positive* and *Ghosthunters*.

All of the groups have experienced negative comments from the community. Most of the criticism seems to take the form of playful mockery from their friends, relatives, and their colleagues as work. Surprisingly, very few of the groups have received opposition from religious groups, despite the fact that most of them are operating in the Bible Belt. Several attributed this silence to two factors: their efforts to completely divorce themselves from anything associated with the demonic (e.g., Ouija boards) and the large number of Christians in their groups. Still, in highly religious locales, Leesburg, for example, some residents become very upset about the activities of ghost hunters.

The single point on which the groups agree the most is their attitudes toward the Sci-Fi television show *Ghosthunters*. Almost all of the groups disliked the show intensely, primarily because of the director's abusive comments and because of rumors that the show fabricates evidence. Several directors admitted to being jealous of the expensive equipment used by The Atlantic Paranormal Society (T.A.P.S.), which, according to the rumors, has been purchased by the Sci-Fi Channel. The only groups that found the show fascinating were the new, inexperienced groups and the groups that were part of the T.A.P.S. network.

The groups differ in just a few areas. The choice of locations is largely dependent on several factors. Relatively new groups that have not established a reputation for themselves usually confine their investigations to public places, such as cemeteries and battlefields. The more established groups, especially those who have had media exposure, have no trouble receiving invitations from private residences and historic sites. The prohibitive cost of staying at historic sites that required payment for security guards restricted the number of museums and forts that these groups were able to visit. Most of the groups do not choose outdoor sites for their investigations because of the possibility of interference from such environmental factors as insects, mist, and ambient noise.

The directors were evenly divided in their views toward orbs, the circles or spheres that frequently appear on photographs taken at haunted locations. Some directors dismissed orbs entirely as proof of the paranormal because of the possibility that they may be nothing more than insects, dust particles, or droplets of moisture. Others claim that orbs that possess tails or that are not perfectly round are quite possible visible manifestations of spiritual energy. Moving orbs captured on video are generally considered to be more reliable as evidence. One director said he is so fascinated with orbs that all of his investigations are devoted to catching them on film.

The most important difference between the groups lies in their approaches to investigations. Over half of the groups employ both metaphysical and scientific methodology. They routinely use psychics or dowsing rods to show the other members where to direct their cameras, voice recorders, or EMF detectors. Other groups, however, disparage the use of anything that does not render data that is empirically sound. These are the groups that put all of their faith in their equipment, most of which is high tech. Several of the directors wistfully longed for the day when all ghost investigating groups will reconcile their differences and agree on a single approach to the collecting of evidence.

Despite the efforts of paranormal investigators in the South and elsewhere to legitimize their field through the use of high-tech equipment, their efforts are viewed by many scientists to be nothing more than folly. In 1963, Dr. Jule Eisenbud, a psychiatrist at the University of Colorado Medical School, published an article in which she presented the keystone argument against the existence of the paranormal. If paranormal phenomena are genuine, the scientists should be able to replicate them in strict laboratory conditions. Therefore, the findings of paranormal investigators cannot be accepted as valid proof without undermining the very foundations of the scientific method (Baker 1999, 180). Other scientists contend that paranormal investigating is an imprecise science because it relies too heavily on personal observation and anecdotal evidence (Guiley 2000, 155). However, Alan Baker, author of *Ghosts and Spirits*, refers to one of the most fundamental laws of nature to support the existence of the paranormal: "If we accept the assertion of physics that energy can neither be created nor destroyed—only transferred from one form to another—then we are left with the question of what happens to the energy fields of which consciousness seems to be composed when a human being dies (Baker 1999, 266).

One explanation for the long tradition of ghost sightings down through the ages could reside within the human brain itself. The psychologists Sheryl Wilson and Theodore Barber developed the theory that a very small percentage of the adult population are "fantasy prone" people who "experience fantasies of a vividness and frequency unknown to the rest of us" (Dash 2000, 355). Hilary Evans observed that many witnesses of paranormal events are undergoing a traumatic event in their own lives, such as adolescence (Evans and Huyghe 2000, 268). The neurologist Michael Persinger proposes that a large number of people claim to have seen ghosts because electromagnetic fields have interfered with their brain activity (Atristain 2005, 26). Persinger, professor of psychology and head of the Neuroscience Research Group at Laurentian University, Ontario, Canada, believes that the mind generates a "sensed presence" when the right hemisphere of the brain—the seat of the emotions—is stimulated, forcing the left hemisphere—the seat of language—to make sense of the nonexistent entity (Atristain 2005, 26). Writer Bobbie Atristain suggests that a dysfunctional family unit, bipolar personality disorders, and childhood trauma and sexual abuse might also cause people to see ghosts. Studies conducted with ESP experiments led Gertrude Schmeidler to conclude that believers scored higher than nonbelievers. Loyd Auerbach speculates that believers might also be much better receivers of signals from spectral forces than non-believers (Auerbach 2004, 11).

This seemingly irreconcilable rift between parapsychologists and scientists has produced an array of fascinating explanations for the anomalies collected by paranormal investigators. The term *ghost*, for example, means something entirely different for believers in the paranormal and scientists. Rosemary Guiley, author of *The Encyclopedia of Ghosts and Spirits*, says that according to followers of spiritualism, "ghosts are souls of the dead trapped on earth, either because they are confused, or because they don't yet realize they are dead. Mediums believe they can communicate with ghosts and help them move on" (Guiley 2000, 150). The parapsychologist Loyd Auerbach says that when most people use the term *ghost*, "they are referring to anything truly unusual—an image, sound, smell, feeling, emotional state, or movement of objects—and they usually mean some sort of force left over from death" (Baker and Nickell 1992, 117–18). These metaphysical explanations for ghosts stand in stark contrast to the more scientific theorists. Hans Holzer believes that ghosts are electromagnetic fields encased in the physical body. When the physical body dies, the electromagnetic field is free to move backward and forward in time and space (Baker and Nickell 1992, 119). The psychologist Robert Baker and the author Joe Nickell state that the belief in ghosts "grow out of and in response to some basic and universal human need," a theory that accounts for the fact that every culture has superstitions concerning ghosts (Baker and Nickell 1992, 114). Baker and Nickell go on to say that the inability of a spirit or phantom or soul to find its way to the Elysian Fields, Valhalla, the Happy Hunting Grounds, or Heaven led to the idea of wandering ghosts (Baker and Nickell 1992, 115). Some of the strongest critics of paranormal sightings are, ironically, the investigators themselves. Most psychical researchers have discovered that the overwhelming majority of ghost reports they have investigated have a natural or rational explanation (Guiley 2000, 151).

For years, parapsychologists have claimed that orbs, the most common type of ghost photographs, are the visual manifestation of ghostly energy. Orbs are accepted by many investigators as proof of the paranormal, but only if those orbs meet certain criteria. Rosemary Ellen Guiley says that false orbs are often pale white, blue, and transparent (Guiley 2000, 270). Troy Taylor, author of *The Ghost Hunter's Guidebook*, says that genuine orbs are brighter and denser than false orbs (Taylor 2000, 147). Joshua Warren, author of *How to Hunt Ghosts*, says that the most compelling orbs are the ones that are partially hidden behind objects in the photograph, showing that they are far away from the camera lens, unlike specks of dust or moisture. Warren also claims that the most spectacular orbs he has ever seen were captured on video or with infrared technology, such as digital cameras (Warren 2003, 156). The most scientifically based investigators agree with the critics that most orbs are probably created by stray light sources, insects, or dust particles (Guiley 2000, 269).

Another common photographic anomaly is mists. Troy Taylor finds these foggy streaks that sometimes appear on photographs to be much more interesting than orbs because they cannot be as easily explained away (Warren 2003, 371). Joshua Warren speculates that mists could be either a physical byproduct of a ghost's appearance or a phantom undergoing a state of transition (Warren 2003, 158). The scientific explanations for the source of most of these nebulous masses are cigarettes, fog, moisture on the lens, or condensation from the investigator's breath. Both Warren and Taylor admit that many overly enthusiastic investigators have succumbed to the temptation so see faces or shapes in mists because "the human imagination wants to find an explanation for what it can't explain" (Taylor 2001, 149).

Even more tantalizing than orbs and mists, from an investigator's viewpoint, are electronic voice phenomena. One of the first men to attempt to communicate with the dead scientifically was Thomas Edison. According to a friend of Edison's, Joseph Dunninger, Edison was working on a prototype of a machine to communicate with the dead until his death in October 1931 (Taylor 2001, 136). The first recording of a spirit voice was achieved by the Reverend Drayton Thomas, who, in the 1940s, claimed to have taped his dead father at a séance (Williams 2005, 36). In the early 1950s, the psychic Attila von Szalay and Raymond Bayless began recording EVP's with a device that Bayless had invented. Bayless's recording machine consisted of a box with an interior microphone that was connected by a cord to an exterior tape recorder. Around 1959, a retired Swedish opera singer, film producer, and birdwatcher named Friederich Jurgenson was recording bird songs in the woods near his home. When he played back the tape, he heard what sounded like snippets of human speech. Jurgenson immediately recognized his mother's voice (Taylor 2001, 136). In 1968, a student of Jurgenson's named Dr. Konstantin Raudive published a sampling of the thousands of EVP's he had recorded in a book entitled *Breakthrough*. In 1972, R. K. Sheargold, chairman of the Society for Psychical Research's Survival Joint Research Committee (SJRC), assured his colleagues that the phenomenon was genuine after capturing several voices himself.

Most modern paranormal researchers use a conventional tape recorder with an external microphone placed at least three feet away. Troy Taylor advocates the use of brand-new tape that comes directly from the factory in a sealed package. Most investigators either leave the recorder running in a room, or they hold the recorder in their hand and ask questions, such as, "Will you give us a sign of your presence?" (Taylor 2001, 137).

Although many paranormal researchers rate EVP's above orbs as evidence of the paranormal, the phenomenon has come under serious attack in recent years. The primary problem with EVPs is that the voices are so faint that rarely do two people interpret any given communication the same way. Critics also point to the brevity and nonsensical quality of the utterances (Dash 2000, 379). Between 1970 and 1972, D. J. Ellis, who was asked to investigate EVP's for the Society for Psychical Research, reported that the phenomena were probably random noises that were being mistaken for voices (Baker 1999, 187). John Spencer and Tony Wells argue that electronic equipment of any kind can pick up radio signals, which could be the source of most EVP's (Baker 1999, 188). Spencer and Wells also brought up the difficulty of interpreting EVP's correctly because most messages are drowned out by the surrounding static.

In recent years, paranormal researchers have enlisted the aid of science to verify the existence of ghosts. The parapsychologist Loyd Auerbach has observed correlations between the appearance electromagnetic fields and the locations where ghostly activity has been reported (Auerbach 2004, 99). These moving electromagnetic fields range in size from that of a baseball to that of a basketball. Researchers have also noted that a primary component of these electrical fields is a DC field, similar to that emitted by mammals (Evans and Huyghe 2000, 13).

Paranormal researchers have discovered that the existence of cold spots might also be proven through scientific techniques. Portable infrared thermometers have registered drops in ambient temperatures by as much as twenty or thirty degrees in spots where ghosts are said to have appeared. However, William Roll, a parapsychologist at the State University of West Georgia, has used Geiger counters to detect traces of radioactivity in the presence of ghosts, prompting some researchers to posit the existence of hot spots (Evans and Huyghe 2000, 13).

Is the disparity between the metaphysical and scientific approaches to ghost hunting proof that the study of paranormal phenomena is nothing more that pseudo-science? The general consensus among many ghost hunters is that their field will gain more acceptance by the scientific community following more technological advances. The interest shown by physicists in the Virginia investigator Joe Holbert's ground-breaking study of moving electromagnetic fields indicates that some ghost hunters are already getting the respect they yearn for. Most of the directors claimed that they value acceptance more than anything else. One wonders if the mocking glances and sneering remarks that follow many ghost investigators around will someday turn into admiration and words of praise.

GLOSSARY

Anointing oil — olive oil mixed with frankincense and myrrh and blessed by the clergy. Anointing oil is rubbed over doorways to ward off evil

Anomaly — something unusual, irregular, or abnormal

Apparition — the visual appearance of a spiritual being

Astral body — a spiritual life force capable of separating from and returning to the physical body

Automatic writing — a technique employed by a medium using a pencil and pad to deliver messages from the dead, usually while the medium is in a trance

Cassadaga — Founded in 1895 in Florida by George Colby, the town of Cassadaga sprang up around the Spiritualist Church. The town is now composed largely of mediums who tell fortunes and contact the dead

Cayce, Edgar (1877–1945) — Known as "the sleeping prophet" and America's greatest psychic, Edgar Cayce is best remembered for his predictions, such as the destruction of New York City, Los Angeles, and San Francisco in some sort of cataclysm and the reemergence of Atlantis

Channeling — the temporary possession of a medium by a spirit during a séance

Clairsentient — a form of ESP that allows a person to perceive distant objects, persons, or events, including "seeing" through opaque objects and the detection of types of energy not normally perceptible to human beings (e.g., radio waves)

Clairvoyance — a form of extrasensory perception involving the powers of telepathy and precognition

Cold spot — isolated areas characterized by sudden drops of temperature in a haunted site

Demon — a tormenting, evil force, usually identified as a minion of the devil

Dowsing — interpreting the movement of rods, sticks, coat hangers, and other such instruments to obtain information

Ectoplasm — a spirit substance created by or accompanying a spirit's materialization, oftentimes during a séance

Electromagnetic energy — a combination of electrical charges and magnetic fields that bind nature

Electronic voice phenomenon (EVP) — inaudible ghost voices recorded on tape

Empath — a person who can feel the emotions of other living entities, such as human beings, plants, or animals

Entity — a conscious, interactive ghost

Exorcism — the expulsion of a spirit from a haunted site through the practice of religious rites

Extrasensory perception — obtaining information by means other than the five senses; the three types of ESP include telepathy, precognition, and clairvoyance

Ghost — a spirit of the dead

Haunting — the incidence of strange phenomena attributed to ghosts or spirits in a specific location

Incubus — a demon, masquerading as a man, that molests women

Legend — a traditional narrative, usually based on historical fact, that is believed to be true by the narrator

Materialization — the process through which a spirit makes a visual representation of itself

Medium — a person who can communicate with the spirit world on behalf of someone else

Near-death experience (NDE) — undergone by someone who is clinically dead or very close to death; the person often experiences visions of the afterlife

Orb — an unexplainable circle or ball of light that often appears in photographs

Ouija board — a device with numbers, letters, and words used for obtaining answers to questions and communicating with spirits

Paranormal — something outside of the scope of human experience or scientific explanation

Paranormal investigation — a controlled, scientific inquiry into a location reputed to be haunted

Parapsychologist — someone who studies the evidence for such psychological phenomena as psychokinesis, telepathy, and clairvoyance

Pendulum — an object suspended from a fixed support, usually a string or cord, used to communicate with spirits

Phenomenon — an unusual occurrence that can be perceived by the senses

Poltergeist — an interactive entity or energy that manifests itself through noises and, occasionally, destructive behavior

Portal haunting — the arrival of spirits through a "doorway" to another dimension

Precognition — the ability to foretell the future

Psychic — a person who is responsive to phenomena that are not explainable by natural laws

Psychokinesis — the ability to move objects through the power of the mind

Residual Haunting — the replaying of psychic impressions—
sights, sounds, and smells—in a place where a traumatic
event has occurred

Retrocognition — the ability to see into the past

Revenant — the visible spirit of a dead person returned from
the grave

Séance — a gathering of individuals, usually presided over by
a medium, organized for the purpose of communicating
with the dead

Sensitive — a person who can detect paranormal events
beyond the range of his or her five basic senses

Spectral — ghostly

Spirit — a supernatural being, such as a ghost

Spiritualism — a nineteenth-century social and religious
movement based on communication with the dead

Succubus — a demon, masquerading as a voluptuous woman,
that molests men

Supernatural — an occurrence or order of existence outside
of the natural world

Telepathy — the ability to communicate (nonverbally,
inaudibly) using the power of the mind

Traditional haunting — the presence of interactive spirits
consisting of the energy and personality of a person who has
remained behind

Vortex — an opening or doorway between the living world
and the spirit world

Wicca — a religion whose followers believe in a God and
a Goddess and in the existence of magic. Wiccans also yearn
to connect with nature

FILMOGRAPHY

The Amityville Horror (1979). **Directed by Stuart Rosenberg. Starring James Brolin, Murray Hamilton, Margot Kidder, John Larch, Helen Shaver, Rod Steiger, and Don Stroud.**
In this sensationalistic film treatment of Jay Anson's "nonfiction" book, a Catholic family moves into a house in which a teenage boy murdered his family. Although best known for the campy command "Get out!," its eerie lullabye-like theme song, and Rod Steiger's hammy performance as a priest, the movie is more concerned with real-life scares (e.g., losing money) than with the fear of the paranormal. Oddly enough, the cliché-ridden film's saving grace is the complete absence of flashy visual special effects. The sound effects, though, are unsettling.

The Amityville Horror (2005). **Directed by Andrew Douglas. Starring Melissa George and Ryan Reynolds.**
This violent remake of the 1979 film focuses on George Lutz's descent into madness but substitutes contrived scenes for the original's re-creation of supposedly true incidents in Jay Anson's book (e.g., a daughter nearly plummets to her death from the roof). Still, many viewers found the new version to be much scarier than the original.

Below (2002). Directed by David Twohy. Starring Scott Foley, Bruce Greenwood, and Olivia Williams.

This suspense-thriller set in a submarine during World War II is an old-fashioned ghost story/mystery tale whose characters attempt to learn the identity of their ghost and its reason for return. Like all good horror movies, *Below* never allows the special effects to distract the viewer from the story line. The movie demands that the viewer pay attention, but the resolution makes it worth the effort.

***The Blair Witch Project* (1999). Directed by Daniel Myrick and Eduardo Sánchez. Starring Heather Donahue, Joshua Leonard, and Michael C. Williams.**

This classic independent film, reportedly made for under $100,000, both thrilled and disappointed viewers. Based on an invented local legend, the young leads attempt to uncover the factual basis for the strange occurrences that have terrorized residents of a small New England town for over a century. While the film's premise is intriguing, the director's attempts to achieve verisimilitude (e.g., constant profanity and the wobbling camera) are very distracting. However, this reviewer believes that the ending redeems the entire film.

***Carnival of Souls* (1962). Directed by Herk Harvey. Starring Sidney Berger, Candace Hilligoss, and Stan Levitt.**

A young woman who has just survived an auto accident walks into a small town, where she has been hired as a church organist. She begins to suspect that something is wrong when nobody seems to be able to see her. This cult film benefits immensely from its low budget, which lends *Carnival of Souls* a *Twilight-Zone*-like atmosphere. A crumbling amusement park was used as the setting for the movie's creepy climax.

The Changeling (1979). **Directed by Peter Medak. Starring John Colicos, Melvyn Douglas, Jean Marsh, George C. Scott, Madeleine Thornton-Sherwood, and Trish Van Devere.**

A recently widowed musician moves into an antique Washington mansion. He soon realizes that he is sharing his home with the ghost of a child. The best haunted-house movie since *The Haunting*, *The Changeling* substitutes creepy set-pieces (e.g., a ball bouncing down a darkened stairway) for gory thrills.

The Devil's Backbone (2001). **Directed by Guillermo del Toro. Federico Luppi, Eduardo Noriega, and Marisa Paredes.**

A young boy is left abandoned at a completely isolated orphanage during the Spanish Civil War. The movie invites the audience to view the evils of the adult world through the eyes of the children, most of whom have been placed in the orphanage for protection. Although promoted as a horror film, *The Devil's Backbone* is actually a drama populated with ghosts. This beautifully photographed film is much more frightening than most of the horror-thrillers produced by Hollywood every year.

Dragonfly (2002). **Directed by Tom Shadyac. Starring Kathy Bates, Kevin Costner, Linda Hunt, Joe Morton, and Ron Rifkin.**

Dragonfly is the story of a Chicago medical doctor who receives messages from his dead wife and an assortment of young patients who have had near-death experiences. Panned at its release as a re-hash of *The Sixth Sense*, *Dragonfly* is a moving account of one man's spiritual journey. The startling revelation in the end will haunt the viewer for sometime afterward.

Dark Water (2002). **Directed by Nakata Hideo. Starring Hitomi Kuroki, Rio Kanno, Shigemitsu Ogi, Mirei Oguchi, Yuu Tokui, and Isao Yatsu.**
Newly divorced mother Matsubara Yoshimi moves into a cheap apartment in a Tokyo suburb to prove that she can provide a solid, secure life for her five-year-old daughter. Often compared to another atmospheric Japanese horror film, *Ringu*, *Dark Water* excels at revealing the potential horror in places where most people feel secure (e.g., a bedroom, a hall corridor, a child's kindergarten). Tension mounts as the heroine battles problems both human and supernatural.

Dark Water (2005). **Directed by Walter Salles. Starring Jennifer Connelly, Ariel Gade, Perla Haney-Jardine, Camryn Manheim, Debra Monk, Pete Postlethwaite, John C. Reilly, and Tim Roth.**
A single mother moves into a strange apartment with her young daughter. The American version of the Japanese original eschews horror and flashy special effects for drama and psychological intrigue. This movie, which was promoted as a horror flick, is actually a film about real people with real problems.

The Entity (1983). **Directed by Sidney J. Furie. Starring Margaret Blye, Jacqueline Brookes, Barbara Hershey, and Ron Silver.**
A woman is beaten and raped in her own home by an invisible being. Based on the real-life experiences of Carlotta Moran from Culver City, California, *The Entity* is of interest to ghost enthusiasts primarily because of the efforts of parapsychologists to drive out the phantom. Although the movie is exploitative and

sensationalistic at times, it is also a riveting account of a woman's encounter with malicious spirits.

The Fog **(1980). Directed by John Carpenter. Starring Adrienne Barbeau, Jamie Lee Curtis, Hal Holbrook, John Houseman, and Janet Leigh.**
On its one hundredth anniversary, a small Californian coastal town, Antonio Bay, is besieged by the fog-shrouded specters of a murdered leper colony. Modeled after the moody horror films of the 1940s, *The Fog* is well directed but obvious. Still, the film does include a few memorable scenes (e.g., the first sighting of the ghost ship by fishermen).

Ghostbusters **(1984). Directed by Ivan Reitman. Starring Dan Aykroyd, William Atherton, Ernie Hudson, Rick Moranis, Bill Murray, Annie Potts, Harold Ramis, and Sigourney Weaver.**
Three paranormal investigators discover that driving out ghosts in New York City can be a thriving business. This blockbuster comedy benefits greatly from Richard Edlund's first-rate special effects and hilarious performances. On a more serious note, *Ghostbusters* can be credited with making terms like *paranormal research* and *ectoplasm* household words.

Ghost Ship **(2002). Directed by Steve Beck. Starring Gabriel Byrne, Ron Eldard, Desmond Harrington, Julianna Margulies, and Isaiah Washington.**
A salvage crew encounters a long-lost ocean liner and decides to investigate. This formulaic horror-thriller is noteworthy primarily for a few very gruesome set-pieces.

The Haunting (1963). Directed by Robert Wise. Starring Claire Bloom, Julie Harris, Richard Johnson, Lois Maxwell, and Russ Tamblyn.

A college professor, assisted by a couple of psychics and a young heir, conduct an extended investigation of a ninety-year-old haunted house in New England. Considered by many to be the greatest haunted-house movie ever made, *The Haunting* creates an unremitting sense of horror, not through excessive gore or splashy special effects, but through restraint. Through the use of weird camera angles and eerie sound effects, as well as excellent performances by the cast, Wise has turned Shirley Jackson's novel into an unforgettable exercise in cinematic terror.

The Haunting (1999). Directed by Jan De Bont. Starring Bruce Dern, Catherine Zeta-Jones, Virginia Madsen, Liam Neeson, Lili Taylor, and Owen Wilson.

This film is a dull, special-effects-laden remake of the 1963 classic. This plodding film lacks faith in the viewer's ability to create a feeling of horror through the imagination. The movie's only redeeming feature is Lili Taylor's sympathetic performance as a lonely woman who feels drawn to the house.

House (1986). Directed by Steve Miner. Starring Susan French, William Katt, Kay Lenz, Richard Moll, and George Wendt.

A Vietnam veteran and horror novelist who is suffering from his disintegrated marriage and the disappearance of his son moves into the Victorian house where his aunt hanged herself. Fanciful special effects and a light-hearted touch make this an entertaining, but not very frightening, horror movie.

***House on Haunted Hill* (1959). Directed by William Castle. Starring Elisha Cook, Carolyn Craig, Richard Long, Alan Marshall, Carol Ohmart, and Vincent Price.**

A bored millionaire offers his guests $10,000 apiece if they can spend the night in his mansion, where a series of gruesome murders was committed years before. Any film that opens with the host handing out guns as party favors is bound to be no run-of-the-mill thriller. *The House on Haunted Hill* is more of a campfest than a genuine horror movie, although it does have a few macabre touches (e.g., the acid-filled vat). The verbal sparring between Vincent Price and Carol Ohmart are fun to watch.

***House on Haunted Hill* (1999). Directed by William Malone. Starring Famke Janssen, Chris Kattan, and Geoffrey Rush.**

A wealthy amusement park manufacturer offers five people a million dollars if they will spend the night in a former insane asylum where the patients murdered the sadistic staff members. However, the five guests who show up are not the ones who were invited by the host. The chills generated by the gory opening scene are sustained until the conclusion, where the computer-generated effects take over. Geoffrey Rush's imitation of Vincent Price is very amusing.

***The Innocents* (1961). Directed by Jack Clayton. Starring Pamela Franklin, Megs Jenkins, Deborah Kerr, Michael Redgrave, and Peter Wyngarde.**

Based on Henry James's *Turn of the Screw*, this is the tale of a sexually repressed governess who is trying to protect her young charges from the corrupting influences of the former governess and her lover. The screenplay by William Archibald, photography by Freddie Francis, and the superb performances combine to make this one of the most intellectually stimulating haunted-house movies ever filmed.

The Legend of Hell House (1973). **Directed by John Hough. Starring Roland Culver, Pamela Franklin, Gayle Hunnicutt, Roddy McDowell, and Clive Revill.**
Based on the novel by Richard Matheson, who also wrote the screenplay, *The Legend of Hell House* is the story of four paranormal researchers who are paid to prove that evil spirits haunt the Belasco Mansion. Like the best haunted-house movies, this film achieves its chills without showing very much blood or gore. Even though *The Legend of Hell House* does incorporate a number of clichés, it still remains one of the better films of the genre.

The Old Dark House (1932). **Directed by James Whale. Starring Melvyn Douglas, Boris Karloff, Charles Laughton, Raymond Massey, Gloria Stuart, and Ernest Thesiger.**
Stranded passengers take refuge in a crumbling mansion during a howling storm. The director of this tongue-in-cheek haunted-house comedy creates a menacing atmosphere through his use of high shadows and sardonic dialogue. Even though Boris Karloff received top-billing as the mute butler Morgan, this film is actually an ensemble piece.

The Old Dark House (1963). **Directed be William Castle. Starring Mervyn Johns, Robert Morley, Tom Poston, and Janette Scott.**
This remake of the 1932 classic bears hardly any resemblance to the original. It is an uneven blend of comedy and horror, with the emphasis on broad comedy.

The Others (2001). **Directed by Alejandro Amenábar. Starring Christopher Eccleston and Nicole Kidman.**
In 1945, a mother and her two children await the return of her soldier-husband in a fog-enshrouded island off the British coast. This chilling film is a welcome return to the great haunted-house films of the past, most of which rely heavily on sound, atmosphere, and suggestion. Although the first hour is devoted mainly to exposition, the second half will tantalize the viewer with its clues, which lead to the inevitable—and unforgettable—denouement.

Poltergeist (1982). **Directed by Tobe Hooper. Starring Dominique Dunne, Craig T. Nelson, Oliver Robins, Heather O'Rourke, Beatrice Straight, Zelda Rubinstein, and JoBeth Williams.**
A family moves into a newly developed subdivision and finds their home inhabited by unfriendly spirits who attempt to kidnap their five-year-old daughter. Although the pre-CGI (computer-generated imagery) effects are very impressive (e.g., the ghosts descending the stairway). director Tobe Hooper's ability to imbue everyday objects (e.g., chairs, food processors, television sets) is the true source of the unrelenting terror in this classic horror film. This is also one of the first major films to portray a modern scientific investigation of a haunted house.

The Ring (2002). **Directed by Gore Verbinski. Starring Martin Henderson and Naomi Watts.**
In this American adaptation of the 1998 Japanese horror film, a Seattle reporter investigates the death of her niece, who reportedly died seven days after viewing a mysterious videotape. The horror produced by this deceptively simple plot stems more from psychological tension and eerie visuals than from grotesque

imagery, which is used sparingly. This is definitely a film that one should not watch on television alone in a darkened room.

Ringu (1998). Directed by Hideo Nakata. Starring Yutaka Matsushige, Nanako Matsushima, Katsumi Muramatsu, Miki Nakatani, Yoichi Numata, Rikiya Otaka, Hiroyuki Sanada, Hitomi Sato, and Yuko Takeuchi.
A female reporter investigates a video that causes anyone who watches it to die. Based on an urban legend, the film depends heavily on atmosphere. The psychological horror in this film is much more intense than the terror generated by the American version, which depends more heavily on visual effects.

Rose Red (2002). Directed by Craig R. Baxley. Starring Kimberly J. Brown, Julia Campbell, Emily Deschanel, David Dukes, Laura Kenny, Judith Ivey, Tsidii Leloka, Yvonne Sciò, and Kevin Tighe.
A college professor takes a group of assorted psychics on an overnight investigation of the haunted Rimbauer Mansion. This very derivative film, whose very premise is borrowed from *The Haunting*, is long on CGI effects and short of genuine scares. Even the haunted house is modeled after the Winchester Mansion in San Diego, California. Most of the characters are very broadly drawn and two-dimensional. The screenplay was written by Stephen King.

The Shining (1980). Directed by Stanley Kubrick. Starring Scatman Crothers, Shelley Duvall, Anne Jackson, Danny Lloyd, Barry Nelson, Jack Nicholson, and Joe Turkel.
An alcoholic novelist takes a job as an off-season caretaker at the Overlook, an isolated resort hotel. Although the film has been criticized for speeding up the writer's descent into madness, this atmospheric thriller still packs a punch with its editing and

startling tracking shots. Director Stanley Kubrick mixes graphic scenes (e.g., the decomposing woman in the bath-tub) with revelatory images (e.g., the typewritten sentence "All work and no play make Jack a dull boy") for maximum effect. Jack Nicholson's near-hysterical performance ("Here's Johnnie!") is one of the most memorable of his career.

The Sixth Sense (1999). Directed by M. Night Shyamalan. Starring Toni Collette, Glenn Fitzgerald, Haley Joel Osment, Donnie Wahlberg, and Bruce Willis.
A child psychologist attempts to help a nine-year-old boy who claims he "sees dead people." Despite the film's reputation as a "ghost story," it is actually a psychological drama with supernatural overtones. The shocking twist ending will not deter viewers from watching the film again in order to spot the clues foreshadowing the story's resolution. This is truly a movie that transcends the genre.

The Skeleton Key (2005). Directed by Iain Softley. Starring Maxine Barnett, Joy Bryant, Kate Hudson, John Hurt, and Gena Rowlands.
A guilt-ridden young hospice worker takes a job as a live-in care-giver for the aging owners of an isolated plantation house with a sordid past. The supernatural undertones are presented in a real-istic way, resulting in a shocking—but not totally unexpected—conclusion. Folklore enthusiasts will find the plot elements relating to voodoo and hoodoo to be particularly interesting.

Stir of Echoes (1999). Directed by David Koepp. Starring Kevin Bacon, Illeana Douglas, and Kathryn Erbe.
A blue-collar worker who has recently moved to a decaying urban neighborhood begins having disturbing visions and nightmares

after being hypnotized. Largely overlooked because it was released around the same time as *The Sixth Sense, Stir of Echoes* is essentially the story of a man teetering on the brink of madness as he convinces himself that he is really seeing a ghost. Based on a novel by Richard Matheson, this film is both psychological thriller and murder mystery.

The Uninvited (1944). Directed by Lewis Allen. Starring Donald Crisp, Ruth Hussey, Ray Milland, Alan Napier, Gail Russell, and Cornelia Otis Skinner.
A brother and sister buy a haunted mansion on the Cornish coast of England. This is one of the first serious ghost stories ever filmed, and it remains one of the best. Some of the film's scariest scenes involve a séance and a midnight walk through the darkened house by candlelight. Even though the special visual effects are somewhat crude by today's standards, the sound effects (e.g., a woman's crying late at night) are spine chilling.

Thirteen Ghosts (1960). Directed by William Castle. Starring Rosemary DeCamp, Margaret Hamilton, Charles Herbert, Martin Milner, and Jo Morrow.
An all-American family inherits a haunted house. The movie was originally filmed in "Illusion-O," a 3-D hybrid that required special red and blue filters. This is an appropriate haunted-house movie for children, or adults, who are too sensitive for today's gory supernatural thrillers.

Thirteen Ghosts (2001). Directed by Steve Beck. Starring F. Murray Abraham, Embeth Davidtz, Shannon Elizabeth, Matthew Lillard, and Tony Shalhoub.
A widower and his two children are trapped in a maze-like house and encounter twelve spirits. This "in-name-only" remake of

the 1960 classic is devoid of genuine thrills, due largely to the ultramodern structure that passes for a haunted house.

What Lies Beneath (2000). Directed by Robert Zemeckis. Starring Harrison Ford, Joe Morton, Michelle Pfeiffer, James Remar, and Amber Valletta.
A seemingly happily married woman senses the presence of a ghost in her beautiful Vermont home, and she suspects that her husband might be involved somehow. This old-fashioned horror movie has some scares, but it adds nothing new to a formulaic plot. In addition, a twist toward the end renders the conclusion illogical.

White Noise (2005). Directed by Geoffrey Sax. Starring Harvey Gold, Deborah Kara Unger, Michael Keaton, and Ian McNeice.
A recently widowed man discovers that his deceased wife is trying to communicate with him through the "white noise" found on radio and television. The first major motion picture to deal with electronic voice phenomena, *White Noise* begins as a serious exploration of the paranormal but ends as a typical horror-thriller with its emphasis on evil spirits.

TELEVISION SHOWS

Fear (MTV)

Teams of young contestants, armed with video cameras and walkie-talkies, investigate a series of locations to determine if they are actually haunted. Each contestant is required to perform a dare at the site. The haunted places include a West Virginia state penitentiary, the Duggan Brothers cement factory, and the Hopkins Military Academy. Similar in concept to *Scariest Places*, *Fear* appears to be much more realistic.

Ghosthunters (The Sci-Fi Channel)

Full-time plumbers Jason Hawes and Grant Wilson lead a small group of researchers on investigations of historically haunted buildings and private residences at night. This controversial reality show has both enthralled and frustrated serious ghost hunters. While the show does a fine job showcasing standard ghost-hunting techniques and state-of-the-art equipment, it also focuses on the sometimes contentious interaction between the investigators themselves. Because of time and budget restrictions, the group only spends a few hours at each site, often resulting in investigations that are incomplete. Still, the show does reveal haunted sites that other groups might be interested in visiting.

Haunted History (The History Channel)

Using dramatic re-creations on the actual historic sites, each episode of this series presented a sampling of four or five ghost stories from some of the nation's most haunted cities, such as Baltimore, Charleston, Chicago, Gettysburg, Hollywood, Key West, New Orleans, San Antonio, and New York. The episodes also include interviews with local historians and eyewitnesses. This intriguing series would be especially appealing to those ghost enthusiasts who prefer a heavy dose of historical background with their ghost stories. Selected episodes from the series are also available on DVD.

Most Haunted (Travel Channel)

Host Yvette Fielding and a ghost-hunting team use night-vision cameras, thermal-imaging cameras, psychics, and séances to determine if a number of European locations are actually haunted. Team members include medium Derek Acorah as well as prominent experts from the paranormal field. The combination of scientific and metaphysical techniques often produces very convincing conclusions.

One Step Beyond (ABC)

This early television series from 1959 to 1961 is one of the first anthologies of "true" ghost stories. Narrated by John Newland, the series includes such historically verifiable tales as George Washington at Valley Forge, Abraham Lincoln's dreams, and the sinking of the *Hood*. The music, photography, and acting combine to create a truly scary series. Selected episodes are available on VHS.

374

Real Ghost Stories (The SciFi Channel)

Host Patrick MacNee took viewers to some of the world's most documented haunted places (e.g., the Black Hope Horror, the tower of London). Not only does the show provide historical background, but it also features interviews with eyewitnesses and paranormal investigators. Viewers with a serious interest in paranormal research might enjoy this series. Selected episodes are available on DVD.

Scariest Places on Earth (The Family Channel)

Hosted by Linda Blair, each episode of this reality series takes a family or group of friends to a historically haunted site to "solve the mystery." All of the participants are given paranor-mal investigative gear to assist in their investigations. The extensive use of night-vision cameras heightens the atmosphere. Although the sites themselves are fascinating (e.g., Leap Castle, Waverly Hills Tuberculosis Sanitarium, the University Campus of Ohio, Bunnyman Bridge), the show has been criticized for staging special effects. Selected episodes are available on VHS.

Unsolved Mysteries: Ghosts (NBC)

Narrated by Robert Stack, the ghost-themed episodes from the 1980s series used re-creations to dramatize "true" ghost stories, which range from the familiar (e.g., Black Hope Curse, the *Mary Celeste*, Myrtles Plantation, Resurrection Mary) to the obscure (e.g., the Lake Wells Hunting, Moss Beach Ghost, Matchmaker Ghosts, Voice from the Grave). On-site filming and interviews with eyewitnesses are definite assets. Selected episodes are available on DVD.

DOCUMENTARIES

America's Haunted Houses (2001) (A & E; 1 hour)

This documentary employs interviews with tour guides and eye-witnesses as it relates the hauntings of some of the nation's most famous haunted sites (e.g., Alacatraz, the John Bell farm, the Octagon House, the Winchester House, the White House) and lesser-known sites as well (e.g., the Brookdale Lodge, Maxwell's Jazz Club and Southern Nights Bed and Breakfast in New Orleans, the Ghost Cat at the Capitol). A segment on psychic experiments conducted by the Rhine Institute at Durham, North Carolina, is very interesting. The documentary also features investigations of several sites in New Orleans by the parapsychologist Larry Montz and the International Society for Paranormal Research. The documentary balances the fantastic stories (e.g., the *Amityville Horror*) with interviews with such objective experts as Joe Nichols from the Center for Inquiry.

Ghost Detectives (Discovery Channel; 1 hour)

Parapsychologist Andrew Nickels, pyschic Gerry Rogers, and technical specialists Jack Roth and Scott Blay investigate three historically haunted sites in St. Augustine, Florida: the Castillo de San Marcos, the St. Francis Inn, and the St. Augustine Lighthouse. This documentary is noteworthy because of the group's reliance on scientific and metaphysical principles. The scene in which Gerry Rogers tries to communicate with the spirits of the St. Francis Inn through her dreams is very interesting.

Ghosts of Gettysburg, Vols. 1 and 2 (1995–1996) (History Channel; 2 hours)

Hosted by author Mark Nesbitt, this documentary features legends collected by Nesbitt when he was a park ranger stationed at the battlefield. The stories include a couple of women's ghostly experiment in the basement of Gettysburg College, the appearance of a spectral nun at Spangler's Spring, and the ghostly sounds at the Codori Farm. The dramatic re-creations that illustrate the eyewitness interviews are very effective.

Hauntings (2001) (TLC; 1 hour)

A sampling of America's most haunted sites is featured in this chilling documentary, including Marilyn Monroe's grave, George Reeves's former house, Jay Sebring's house, the Winchester House, the Los Luceros Hacienda, the Olathe Naval Air Station, the Myrtles Plantation, the USS *Constellation*, and Waverly Plantation. Of particular interest is parapsychologist Barry Taft's account of his experiences in the Hollymont House in Hollywood and a private residence in San Pedro, California. The film is enhanced by interviews with authors Daniel Cohen, Laurie Jacobson, and Arthur Meyers.

A Haunting in Connecticut (TLC; 1 hour)

Ed and Karen Parker, whose sickly son requires constant medical attention, unwittingly rent an old house that had been used as a mortuary. The couple place their son in a mental institution because he claims he can see apparitions and hear voices. When the disturbances continue, the Parkers contact Edward and Lorraine Warren for help. This well-scripted true story unfolds like a Hollywood movie.

A Haunting in Georgia (TLC; 1 hour)

Dr. William Roll, an Oxford-educated parapsychologist, investigates Andy and Lisa Wyrick's claim that two of their four-year-old daughter's playmates, an elderly man who pushes her on a swing and a younger man covered in blood, are ghosts. This true story's incomplete resolution is particularly unsettling.

More Haunted Houses (1995) (A & E; 2 hours)
This lengthy film includes in-depth stories of five haunted places. One of them is the tale of Jim and Johanna Donnelly, Irish immigrants who moved to Lucan, Ontario, and were murdered, along with a son and a niece, by vigilantes in their home in 1880. Also included are the stories of the octaroon mistress of a rich young aristocrat who died on the roof of the Bottom-of-the-Teacup townhouse in New Orleans, the devil baby of Hull House in Chicago, the Mary Surratt House in Clinton, Maryland, and the Winchester House in San Jose. The documentary contains interviews with psychics, authors, family descendants, playwrights, and local historians.

BIBLIOGRAPHY

Atristain, Bobbie. "Your Brain and the Paranormal." *Ghost! Magazine.* Winter 2005: 25–27.

Auerbach, Loyd. *Ghost Hunting: How to Investigate the Paranormal.* Berkeley, CA: Ronin Publishing, 2004.

—————. *Hauntings and Poltergeists: A Ghost Hunter's Guide.* Berkeley, CA: Ronin Publishing, 2004.

Baker, Alan. *Ghosts and Spirits.* New York: TV Books, 1999.

Baker, Robert, and Joe Nickell. *Missing Pieces: How to Investigate Ghosts, UFOs, Psychics, and Other Mysteries.* New York: Prometheus Books, 1992.

Batista, Vivian. "Ghost Team Visits Old Haunts." *Miami Herald*, October 30, 2003.

Bartlett, Beverly. "Tuberculosis Hospital Was Heart of an Isolated Community, Inspiring Loyalty in Patients, Staff." *Courier-Journal*, 1986.

Brown, Alan. *Haunted Places in the American South.* Jackson: University Press of Mississippi, 2002.

—————. *Stories from the Haunted South.* Jackson: University Press of Mississippi, 2004.

Brunvand, Jan Harold. *The Vanishing Hitchhiker: American Urban Legends and Their Meanings.* New York: W. W. Norton & Company, 1981.

Cave, Janet, Scarlet Cheng, Laura Foreman, and Jim Hicks, eds. *Hauntings.* New York: Barnes & Noble, 1997.

Dash, Mike. *Borderlands: The Ultimate Exploration of the Surrounding Unknown.* New York: Dell, 2000.

DeBolt, Margaret Wayt. *Savannah Spectres and Other Strange Tales.* Norfolk, VA: Donning Company, 1984.

Evans, Hilary. *Gods, Spirits, Cosmic Guardians.* Wellingborough, New York: HarperCollins, 1988.

Evans, Hillary, and Patrick Huyghe. *The Field Guide to Ghosts and Other Apparitions.* New York: Quill, 2000.

Bibliography

Ewing, James. *It Happened in Tennessee*. Nashville, TN: Rutledge Hill Press, 1986.

Frye, Georgia E. "Local Ghost Detectives Seek Evidence of Activity." *Meridian Star*, May 26, 2005: A4.

Guide to Haunted Places of the Civil War. Columbus, OH: Blue & Gray Enterprises, 1996.

Guiley, Rosemary Ellen. *The Encyclopedia of Ghosts and Spirits*. New York: Checkmark Books, 2000.

Hauck, Dennis William. *Haunted Places: The National Directory*. New York: Penguin Books, 1996.

Hauntings. New York: Time-Life Books, 1989.

Hensley, Douglas. *Hell's Gate: Terror at Bobby Mackey's Music World*. Jacksonville, FL: Audio Books Plus, 1993.

Kennedy, Frances H. *The Civil War Battlefield Guide*. Boston: Houghton Mifflin, 1990.

Montell, William Lynwood. *Ghosts along the Cumberland: Deathlore in the Kentucky Foothills*. Knoxville: University of Tennessee Press, 1975.

Ogden, Tom. *The Complete Idiot's Guide to Ghosts and Hauntings*. Indianapolis, IN: Alpha Books, 1999.

Scott, Amber. "Contact: Patti Starr." *Southsider Magazine*, October 2003: 25–31.

Taylor, Troy. *The Ghost Hunter's Guidebook: The Essential Guide to Investigating Reports of Ghosts and Hauntings*. Alton, IL: Whitechapel Productions Press, 2001.

———. *Haunted Alton: History and Hauntings of the Riverbend Region*. Alton, IL: Whitechapel Productions Press, 1999.

Wallman, Brittany. "In Search of Spirits." *South Florida Sun Sentinel*, May 13, 2003.

Warren, Joshua P. *How to Hunt Ghosts: A Practical Guide*. New York: Simon and Schuster, 2003.

Williams, Vincent. "EVP—Technically Speaking." *Ghost! Magazine*. Winter 2005: 36–37.

Wilson, Vince. *Ghost Tech*. Alton, IL: Whitechapel Productions Press, 2005.

INDEX